Blue-Eyed Boy

ALSO BY ROBERT TIMBERG

State of Grace: A Memoir of Twilight Time

John McCain: An American Odyssey

The Nightingale's Song

To Peter Tasi —
   A new friend.

Hope you enjoy this
book.
   Bob Timberg
   8/14/2014

Blue-Eyed Boy

A Memoir

———

ROBERT TIMBERG

THE PENGUIN PRESS

New York

2014

THE PENGUIN PRESS
Published by the Penguin Group
Penguin Group (USA) LLC
375 Hudson Street
New York, New York 10014

USA • Canada • UK • Ireland • Australia
New Zealand • India • South Africa • China

penguin.com
A Penguin Random House Company

First published by The Penguin Press, a member of Penguin Group (USA) LLC, 2014

Grateful acknowledgment is made for permission
to reprint excerpts from the following copyrighted works:
"Buffalo Bill's" from *Complete Poems: 1904–1962* by E. E. Cummings, edited by
George J. Firmage. Copyright 1923, 1951, © 1991 by the Trustees for the
E. E. Cummings Trust. Used by permission of Liveright Publishing Corporation.

A Country Such as This by James Webb (Doubleday, 1983). Used by permission of the author.

"Wichita Lineman," words and music by Jimmy Webb. Copyright © 1968 Universal–
Polygram International Publishing, Inc. Copyright renewed. All rights reserved. Used by
permission. Reprinted by permission of Hal Leonard Corporation.

Library of Congress Cataloging-in-Publication Data

Timberg, Robert.
Blue-eyed boy : a memoir / Robert Timberg.
p.   cm.
Includes index.
ISBN 978-1-59420-566-8 (hardback)
1. Timberg, Robert.   2. Journalists—United States—Biography.   3. Marines—United States—
Biography.   4. Burns and scalds—Patients—United States—Biography.   5. Burns and scalds—
Patients—Rehabilitation.   6. Vietnam War, 1961–1975—Veterans—United States—
Biography.   7. United States Naval Academy—Alumni and alumnae—Biography.
8. Iran-Contra Affair, 1985–1990—Biography.   9. Vietnam War, 1961–1975—Social aspects—
United States.   10. Vietnam War, 1961–1975—United States—Psychological aspects.   I. Title.
CT275.T6416A3   2014   2014005398
070.92—dc23
[B]

Printed in the United States of America
1   3   5   7   9   10   8   6   4   2

DESIGNED BY AMANDA DEWEY

Penguin is committed to publishing works of quality and integrity.
In that spirit, we are proud to offer this book to our readers; however,
the story, the experiences, and the words are the author's alone.

To Janie, Kelley, Charity, and Dr. Lynn Ketchum—
my heroes

And to my precious grandchildren—
Cecilia, Andrew, Natalie, and Ian

Buffalo Bill's
defunct
            who used to
            ride a watersmooth-silver
                              stallion
and break onetwothreefourfive pigeonsjustlikethat
                                                  Jesus
he was a handsome man
                        and what i want to know is
how do you like your blueeyed boy
Mister Death

                              —e. e. cummings

Sixteen KEEPING FAITH   *124*

Seventeen A FISH STORY   *131*

Eighteen SCARSDALE GALAHAD   *135*

Nineteen KANSAS CITY HERE I COME   *140*

Twenty RICHARD   *148*

Twenty-one PUNCH-DRUNK   *152*

Twenty-two THE OCCASION OF SIN   *157*

Twenty-three ON MY OWN   *161*

Twenty-four THE PINK BATHROBE YEAR   *165*

Twenty-five BLOWING MY CHANCE   *168*

Twenty-six QUESTION, ANSWER, *SQUISH*   *173*

Twenty-seven THE NIEMAN EFFECT   *181*

Twenty-eight OLLIE, BUD, AND JOHN   *188*

Twenty-nine THE BANALITY OF EVIL   *194*

Thirty THE PRIVATE WAR OF OLLIE AND JIM   *199*

Thirty-one THE NIGHTINGALE'S SONG   *207*

Thirty-two IDENTITY CRISIS   *212*

Thirty-three THE CROWN PRINCE   *217*

Thirty-four HOOSIERS   *225*

Thirty-five "LINDA IS COOL"   *233*

Thirty-six BUD   *239*

Thirty-seven CALL OLLIE   *246*

Thirty-eight "DIBS ON THE BOOTS"   *254*

MIRROR, MIRROR ON THE WALL

Falling asleep is never a problem for me. Waking up always is. My first night in South Vietnam I was sitting on a hill, relieving myself in a jerry-built four-holer ingeniously fashioned of plywood and wire mesh to keep out flying insects that once inside quickly became shit-besotted dive-bombers. Down the hill, maybe three or four clicks distant, a firefight was raging. As I watched the crisscrossing tracers, I murmured, "This is one scary fucking place." Then I headed for the tent that was my home until I could be transported to the outskirts of Chu Lai, where my battalion had already dug in. I lay down on a cot, fully dressed, the pop-pop-pop of small-arms fire buffeting my ears, the memory of intersecting tracers still claiming my mind's eye. Scary, yes, but I was asleep in less than a minute.

Waking up is a different story, as it was on the day, four decades later, that gave rise to this book. Sometimes I don't hear the alarm. Other times I hear it but hit the snooze bar and fall back to sleep for another half hour or so. But even with the extra rest, I often get up groggy and worried that I'll arrive at the office uncomfortably late.

So I hasten into the bathroom for my morning routine—shower, shave, and the other things that most men do on automatic pilot. By then I'm both groggy and moving quickly. I glance occasionally at the mirror as I shave, though not often because I only need to shave my neck and a tiny tuft of hair—I think of it as a survivor—on the left side of my chin. I sometimes focus briefly on my face, but I usually can ignore it. I'm used to it.

At least I thought I was until that recent day when, for no apparent reason, I stopped and stared at the face looking back at me from the mirror. And I lost it.

"Enough already!" I shouted. "I've been this way since 1967, forty fucking years, and it's time for this shit to end! The joke's over. It's not funny anymore."

It was, I told myself, time to return to normal, for my face to heal, for the scar tissue to become the soft, unlined skin it used to be. I had been wounded at twenty-six; I wanted to look like I would if I had just aged naturally. My guess was I would look pretty good. I had been a reasonably good-looking guy when I rolled over that goddamned land mine. And probably I would look younger than my years, slightly gray but limber, and reasonably attractive, at least to women within a decade or two of my age. I had four terrific kids with two great wives, though I had managed to screw up both marriages. And I was tired of being alone, as I had been for the past twelve years.

I am not being unduly hard on myself in saying that my actions wrecked both marriages. It's the truth. Along the way, though, I also did some good things. I had a hand—I guess I was a junior partner—in raising four kids I couldn't be more proud of. I was a newspaper editor and reporter for more than thirty years, mostly in Washington. I wrote three well-received books. I was editor-in-chief of a prestigious military journal. My most significant achievement, though, came much earlier, when as a young man I somehow reclaimed my future after a life-altering event that threatened to lay waste to the rest of my days.

"Reclaimed my future" has a bullshit, self-help-book sound that I hate. Don't worry, I won't resort to it again, at least I don't think I will. But I know there is something true here, something real and fragile

Thirty-nine THE KICK-ASS TROUBADOUR   257

Forty LOST   266

Forty-one FULL CIRCLE   270

Forty-two HIGHS AND LOWS   279

Epilogue THE FOOTLOCKER   285

Author's Note   291

Acknowledgments   295

Index   299

that now, as I edge into my seventies, I need to take time to look at. Properly. Slowly. Without screaming. Without fear of being late. I suspect there's something essentially human about what I fought my way through. Somewhere buried in my memory, hidden beneath this terrible mask of scar tissue. I want to remember how I decided not to die. To not let my future die.

— — — —

I am, of course, just one of many to confront such a decision. Another is John McCain. I am McCain's biographer, having written about him at length in two books. He is a man of extraordinary courage who was routinely beaten and tortured during five and a half years in North Vietnamese prisons. My interest in him arose because of his ability, rare among veterans of that long-ago war, to put Vietnam behind him, or off to the side, or in some forgotten corner of the attic where he keeps the rest of his war-related junk.

Doing so made it possible for him to fashion a productive life, without being immobilized by the past. I have a ready answer when asked how he was able to do so after the brutality he endured in prison: "I've always believed that when John McCain was released from captivity, he said to himself, 'Whatever life has in store for me, good or bad, I'm going to achieve it, prison or no prison.'"

At some point I realized that, facing different challenges, I had done the same thing. Like McCain's, my path was rarely smooth, and not always admirable. He caused great pain to some who loved and helped him. I did, too. And at times we both acted in ways that the code of conduct we carried from our mutual alma mater, the United States Naval Academy, would deem dishonorable. But we never kidded ourselves. Though we didn't advertise it, we always knew when we had crossed the line.

For years friends have urged me to write a book about how I regained my footing after the trauma of my wounding in Vietnam. Not that any of them knew the story, since I rarely, if ever, talked about it.

I always thanked them but said I'd never write that book. My friends thought it was because I didn't feel I could handle the pain of reliving those days. That was just a small part of it.

Mostly I felt that the world did not need another book about a heroic recovery and the courage it took to achieve it, least of all from me. Yes, I had displayed courage, or something akin to it, but I also had displayed less admirable qualities. No way, I realized, could I honestly tell the story without acknowledging my missteps along the way. And I had no desire to do that.

Until that morning in my bathroom when I was caught off guard by a visage in the mirror that I didn't want to be mine but most assuredly was. After my anger died down, and I accepted that no magic wand would be forthcoming to heal me, I thought about my life during the decades since that random land mine left me disfigured.

I was no more John McCain than I was Chesty Puller during my time in the Marine Corps. But I more than survived. I lived through thirty-five operations under general anesthesia, several more under local, and one with no anesthesia at all—possibly the most painful half hour of my life. For many years I endured shocked stares, and not just from children, until I figured out how to cope with them.

Over the course of some forty years, though, I had lived a full life, one perhaps close to the fate that had awaited me, land mine or no land mine. And after nearly the same number of years as a journalist, I knew it was a good story.

The question was, who would care? Maybe no one. But the time had come to tell it, especially those first, crucial few years after I was wounded, which dictated all that followed, good and bad.

One

SHORT-TIMER

Da Nang TAOR, January 18, 1967

The previous evening, just before turning in, I wandered off by myself, stared into the distance, and murmured, "There's no reason why I shouldn't die tonight."

I knew it was melodramatic, but I did it every night, without fail. In a way it was a message to a God in which I had long since stopped believing. Almost. If there was a God, I had concluded years earlier, He was at best an indifferent God, one just as likely to kill me during the night as He was to let me live through it. Depended on His mood. Did He have a good day or a bad day? Maybe it was an unprayer, a way of not praying to the God I didn't believe in, so He wouldn't notice me and decide to squash me for the hell of it.

I rolled off my cot that morning, pulled on my boots, and stumbled over to the contraption we used for shaving: a fence post driven into the ground, with a metal mirror nailed to it above a wooden ledge to hold a helmet filled with water. Marines, officers and enlisted, shaved in the morning when they could. Personal appearance counted, even in the field. It was a matter of discipline, and in a combat zone few things are more important.

"Almost ready, Lieutenant?" the Mighty Mite driver asked.

"Be there in a minute," I replied, ducking back into my tent. I pulled on my utility blouse. (We slept in our trousers. The company Command Post was mortared regularly. No one fancied running for the bunkers in their skivvies.) Then I slipped on my flak jacket, grabbed my web belt, on which hung a .45 caliber pistol and my sheathed Ka-Bar, and snapped it around my waist.

"Thought you were going on R&R today, Sir," said the Mighty Mite driver as we pulled out of the CP and onto the dirt road that led to Battalion Headquarters.

"Change of plans, Lance Corporal," I replied.

"You're one of the short guys, aren't you, Lieutenant?" asked the driver.

"Can't get much shorter, Lance Corporal."

A brief ride to Battalion HQ. The vehicles that would form our small convoy were waiting, their engines running. I passed the bulky canvas bag I had just been given to a Marine already on top of one of the two Amtracs and climbed up to join him. Moments later the convoy began to rumble down the hill and onto the road where my future awaited me.

———

I had not expected to be sitting on top of an Amtrac that morning. For the past couple of months, and until about 2100 the previous evening, I planned to be in Okinawa, looking for a string of pearls for my wife and scouting out stereo equipment for our small apartment atop a two-car garage in the breezy California community of Laguna Beach. That's what young Marine officers did as their Rotation Tour Date neared; take a few days of R&R in Tokyo or on Okinawa and load up on cut-rate, high-quality jewelry and electronic gear for the trip home. Tax-free and duty-free, too. My RTD, 1 February, was getting close. In thirteen days I would have been overseas for thirteen months, a standard tour for Marines and one month longer than the Army kept its troops in-country. The extra month never made sense to me, by the way, except as an exercise in one-upmanship on the part of the Corps, always paranoid, though not without reason, that it would be disbanded and its men and women scattered among the other services.

But there would be no shopping spree for me today, though at the moment I had almost enough money with me to buy out Mikimoto Pearls. Sadly, the money was legal tender only in South Vietnam. The dollar-bill-size notes, known as military payment certificates, came in various denominations and each carried, in the place of honor normally accorded to George Washington, Old Hickory, or Honest Abe, a woman who reminded me of Jackie Kennedy.

None of the money, which was stashed in the brown canvas bag I had clamped between my knees, was mine. It belonged to the five officers and eighty enlisted men of Bravo Company, First Antitank Battalion, First Marine Division (Rein), FMF, and thanks to me, and to the Leatherneck tradition that said Marines get paid every two weeks as long as they were not under hostile fire, they were about to enjoy another on-time payday. It didn't matter that you could only spend MPCs at a PX or some other service facility like an enlisted men's club, or that Bravo Company, especially its Second Platoon—a unit deep in the boonies and whose CP was the first stop on my paymaster rounds—was not likely to even smell a place like that anytime soon.

Bravo's five officers were the company commander, the executive officer—that was me—and three platoon leaders. All of us except the skipper took turns serving as pay officer. The honor was mine today even though it wasn't my turn. I had been dragooned into it because the platoon leader whose turn it was found himself otherwise occupied. This was, of course, a war. So the duty fell to me, and instead of R&R and methodically working my way through the PX at Futenma, trying to decide between a TEAC or a Sony tuner, then relaxing at the O Club with the popular gin-and-champagne concoction known as a French 75, I was scanning the sun-bleached terrain from atop an Amtrac as it bounced westward along a rutted, dusty trail toward the base camp of Bravo Company's presumably cash-strapped Second Platoon.

A word about the vehicle on which I was riding, since it was anything but an innocent bystander in this tale. The LVTP-5A1 Amphibian Tractor, the Amtrac's official designation, was designed to transport Marines from ship to shore as they assaulted enemy beaches, a primary mission of the Corps in World War II and, to a much lesser extent, during the Korean War (think Inchon, MacArthur's masterstroke). Since there were no opposed landings in Vietnam up to that time (or later for that matter), Amtracs were deprived of their primary mission. Instead, the Marine Corps used them as substitutes for armored personnel carriers. The Corps had no APCs of its own.

The Army's APCs resembled Amtracs; both were rectangular in shape and ran on tracks, like tanks. But there was one design feature that separated the Amtrac from the APC, and it would make all the difference in the world to me. Twelve fuel cells containing a total of 456 gallons of gasoline, with an octane rating of 80, lay between the hull and the deck plates of the Amtrac. This was not much of a problem when the vehicle was employed as intended, for churning through water on the way to a beach or crunching over a barrier reef; on land, though, should an Amtrac encounter a mine, it became a death trap, anyone inside instantly fricasseed. By this point in America's great Southeast Asian adventure, no one rode inside an Amtrac; you sat on top or clung to the side. The fuel cells were where they always had been, though, and an Amtrac was still an Amtrac, and not an APC.

— — — —

With thirteen days to go, I had long since qualified as a full-fledged short-timer. I had my handmade short-timer's calendar: a drawing of my wife sitting on the edge of a bed, in a T-shirt hiked up to midthigh. At first I was going to draw her naked, then I decided there was too great a chance that one of my fellow Marines might stumble upon it. But I played with the drawing enough that with a little imagination it began to look like the cover of one of the pulp novels I obsessed over as a kid. Then I superimposed one hundred squares on the drawing. I had been filling in a box a day since October

10, one hundred days from my RTD. The one-hundredth box was where you'd expect it to be. There was nothing subtle about anyone's short-timer's calendar, certainly not mine.

There were more serious concerns as my days in-country grew short. Notably, what next? I was a Naval Academy graduate and a Marine first lieutenant about to be promoted to captain. In less than a year and a half, I could resign my commission and begin a civilian career. Did I want to stay in the Corps or see what else might be out there for me?

I already had my orders home. I was going to the Fifth Marine Division, a newly mobilized unit based at Camp Pendleton, on the California coast between Los Angeles and San Diego. That meant my wife and I could remain in Laguna Beach, where we had lived before my battalion mounted out and which we loved. But scuttlebutt already had drifted across the Pacific that the new 5th MarDiv would be deployed to Vietnam within six months, no doubt bringing me back with it.

Then there was the war. Since I was in it, I didn't feel I could trust my judgment about whether it was a good war or a bad one. It didn't matter, not then. All I knew was that I was ready to go home, the sooner the better. In truth, I had not had a horrible war.

The First Antitank Battalion was a curious unit, with an even more curious weapon, a lightly armored, tracked vehicle called the Ontos (officially the Rifle, Multiple 106 mm, Self-propelled, M50A1). Its main armament consisted of six 106 mm recoilless rifles. *Ontos* means "thing" in Greek. It looked like a roach squirting here and there with six gleaming cannons protruding from its carapace. It was originally built for the Army, but the Army decided it didn't want it, so the Marines took it. Or so the story goes.

I was, as it happened, an infantry officer. To my mind, that designation made me a fish out of water in an antitank unit. But that, which I asked for and received upon graduating from Marine officers Basic School in Quantico, Virginia, did not guarantee me assignment to an infantry battalion, as I thought it would. I arrived at First Marine

Division Headquarters at Camp Pendleton in December 1965 only to learn that I had been assigned to the First Antitank Battalion.

I couldn't believe it. I hadn't set records at the Basic School, but I wasn't a fuckup, either; what the hell happened? I hurried to the headquarters of First Antitanks and reported to the battalion commander, a lieutenant colonel.

"Sir," I told him, "there's been a big mistake. I don't belong in this battalion."

"And why is that, Lieutenant?" he asked.

"I'm an infantry officer, Colonel, not an Ontos guy. I'm supposed to be a rifle platoon leader."

The colonel proceeded to explain to me, in a reasonably kind tone, that Ontos platoon leader, the position he had in mind for me, was an infantry officer's billet, though he himself was a tank officer.

I begged, pleaded, importuned, beseeched, entreated. "Sir," I cried, "please transfer me to an infantry battalion."

"Lieutenant," the colonel said, "the Marine Corps in its wisdom assigned you to this battalion for a reason. Not that I know what the hell it is. But you're here and you're gonna stay here."

By then his voice had taken on an edge.

"Sir," I said, "I'm from New York. I don't know squat about vehicles. I didn't learn to drive until I was twenty-three. I don't know how to change the oil in my car. I don't even know how to check the oil."

"Lieutenant," said the colonel, "the First Sergeant is sitting at a desk outside my office. I want you to go to him right now and get checked in. Welcome aboard."

— — — —

I don't know if we Americans were doing anything worthwhile in Vietnam. Seems like when I first got there I saw this old peasant ankle deep in a rice paddy, walking behind a plow pulled by a water buffalo. And I kept seeing him every couple of months, never in the same place, him and his water buffalo just plowing a rice paddy—a pair from central casting. He always had his back to me, so I never saw his face. In between sightings, though, my battalion engaged in search-and-destroy operations, convoy duty, resupply missions. And we'd get intelligence briefings that said the Vietcong were on the run, or lying in wait for us behind the next ridgeline.

Then I'd see the old guy again, him and his water buffalo, never giving any indication that a bunch of Marines armed to the teeth were half a football field away, or that anything we had done since I last saw him had had any impact on his life. I would have felt better if once, just once, he had taken off his wide-brimmed peasant hat and waved to us—or spit at us or given us the finger—but he never did. It was as if we weren't even there.

But Vietnam would not be my problem much longer. When my plane took off for the States in thirteen days, the war would be behind me. More important, all the demons that had tormented me since childhood would be left to fend for themselves. My parents were good people, and talented ones. My mother was a magazine cover girl before she even reached her teens, then a featured dancer in Broadway musicals mounted by the legendary showman Florenz Ziegfeld. My father was a composer who wrote much of the background music for Fleischer Studios cartoons such as *Popeye*, *Betty Boop*, and *Superman*. His older brother, Herman, a comic, was the family headliner. He also wrote the Marx Brothers' first vaudeville act. His sister, Hattie, managed their act. Dad led the band when Herman performed and was often pressed into service as Herman's straight man. When Herman and the Marx Brothers worked together, Dad often roomed with the brothers on the road and they delighted in playing tricks on him.

Both my parents were in vaudeville, which is where they met. She was Irish Catholic; he was Jewish. That should have been a problem back then. It wasn't, not for them—that is, if you don't count my deeply religious maternal grandmother routinely feigning suicide by putting her head in the oven when she heard her daughter, the oldest of her seven kids, coming home from work or a date with my father.

But there were other issues, which led to divorce, and for my two younger sisters and me, a seemingly endless diaspora. We lived with people all over the city of New York, sometimes together, sometimes apart. By the time I reached high school I had attended a dozen schools, three in the same year twice.

By high school all three of us kids were living with my mother. By then, though, she was an alcoholic and life was often hellacious. My father was a timid man whose fears undermined his enormous talent and may have contributed to my mother's alcoholism. I inherited his fearfulness; at least I believed I did.

I fought against it by constantly testing myself, doing things I never could imagine him doing. I boxed in the Police Athletic League, played football in high school and on the sandlots for a few years after that. I was a better baseball player, but I never even went out for my high school team. I didn't want to be distracted from football by what I thought of as a pussy sport, at least when compared to the action on the gridiron. After high school, I went to the Naval Academy instead of a normal college, selected the Marine Corps over the Navy because it was tougher, then became an infantry officer because I couldn't imagine anything tougher than that.

I was proud to be a Marine. Unlike many of my fellow Leather-necks, though, I wasn't thrilled that a war had materialized to allow me to put my training to use. But as my tour in Vietnam drew to a close, I felt I had done my time in Hell and, to my mind, I was finished testing myself. I was ready for a life devoid of madness. Time to drop my pack and just be happy.

I was going home to a lot. I had met Janie when I was a plebe at Annapolis, and for the next three years had courted her with varying degrees of success. For much of that time, she was cool to me but never fully dismissive. And I wouldn't take no for an answer. By the time I graduated in June 1964 we had caught fire. We were married under crossed swords at the Academy Chapel a year later, a few weeks after she graduated from Lake Erie College in Ohio.

We had six months together. I was stationed at Camp Pendleton and living in San Clemente, just north of the base. Janie fell in love with another seaside town a little farther north, Laguna Beach, a place wonderfully at odds with the stereotype of the Southern California coast.

Laguna was quirky, artsy, and unpredictable. It was studded with boutiques and galleries. Each summer the town mounted a festival in which costumed locals posed in tableaus of art masterpieces. The Laguna Beach Greeter was the town's signature feature, a wild-eyed old coot with a cane and long white beard, who stood in the middle of Pacific Coast Highway and waved to the tourists as they drove into town. Timothy Leary, the LSD guru, was kicking around Laguna during this time, too.

Janie found the apartment above the two-car garage, which was perfect for us, and a job teaching what were then called trainable retarded children, a term that has now gone out of favor, though the kids still face the same challenges. The beach was three short blocks away, and we could see the ocean from our kitchen window and tiny porch. The beach at the bottom of Thalia Street was our place. You couldn't swim there, but you could walk and sit on the rocks, poke the sea urchins, and let the eddies hypnotize you so for a little while you didn't think about the war that was beckoning and that made any discussion of a future not just premature but, if you were superstitious, an exercise in tempting fate.

Now, though, with my RTD just around the corner, I could think about it.

I could, of course, stay in the Marine Corps. I'd still have a year and a half of obligated duty left when I got home, time to decide if I wanted to make the service a career. And whenever I thought about the civilian world, I saw lots of jobs I thought I could do, but none that I had any passion for.

In one recurring dream, I saw myself before a large status board with a big Texaco star perched on top. I stood in front of the board, a pointer in my hand, telling a roomful of tanker-truck drivers where to haul their gasoline. The only explanation I've ever come up with for this curious image is that Texaco sent me my first credit card, when I was a senior at Annapolis. To this day, I still know my ten-digit account number by heart, even though I haven't had the card for years, stripped of it by Shell when it swallowed Texaco.

Truly, as my days in Vietnam wound down, I did not know if I would be a Marine or a civilian five years down the line. But I knew where I wanted to be—with Janie. Also, somewhere else, a place I sensed was awaiting me but that I only recognized years later when an Academy friend and fellow Marine, Ron Benigo, and I spoke about the call that had summoned us to the Naval Academy.

"I believe," Ron said, "we had visions of being someday at that critical moment when what we did would change the course of history."

Delusions of grandeur? Egomania? Maybe. All I knew for sure was that I wanted to do something that mattered, that gave my life meaning. And there I was, just thirteen days away from starting down a path toward whatever life had in store for me.

Two

WAR STORIES

I thought of my battalion, the First Antitank Battalion, as the real-world equivalent of the USS *Reluctant*, the bedraggled cargo ship that plied the backwaters of the Pacific in Thomas Heggen's iconic novel of World War II, *Mister Roberts*. The book told the tale of a young naval officer stuck in the rear despite his persistent efforts to get into the action. *Reluctant*, we're told, sailed "from apathy to tedium with occasional side trips to monotony and ennui."

It wasn't quite like that in First ATs. Our Ontos were bristling with cannons and looking for trouble. No vehicle in the world, no matter how thick its armor, could withstand an Ontos barrage, which should have made our battalion the scourge of the enemy's tanks. But this enemy had no tanks or any other armored vehicles, for that matter, which made it impossible for us to carry out our primary mission, antitank warfare. The absence of enemy armor made even our name seem fraudulent. We could have easily been the First Antidragon Battalion for all our name reflected what we did.

With no tanks for us to challenge, we were assigned other roles—direct-fire support of infantry operations, static defense, and convoy protection. Mostly we did convoy duty, escorting trucks of various sizes on resupply missions from base camps to the outskirts of Indian Country where the infantry was operating.

It was dangerous duty since convoys were vulnerable to mines, ambushes, and rocket-propelled grenades, but nothing compared to what the grunts faced every day. To my mind, escorting motorized convoys was the equivalent of *Reluctant* shuttling supplies to the combat vessels that were really fighting the war in the Pacific.

And I was no Mr. Roberts. All I did was piss off the battalion commander when I tried to transfer to the infantry. At that point, I said fuck it. Mr. Roberts never did, never stopped trying to get off *Reluctant.* (He finally made it to another ship and got killed.) So aside from the singular event that lies at the heart of this book, my war fell well short of the heroic dimensions that Ron Benigo had foretold for us. (Ron's didn't. He commanded a rifle platoon and an infantry company and was awarded a Bronze Star and a Purple Heart.)

And after all that happened, it's hard to believe that most of what I remember are the funny things.

— — — —

We were usually mortared once or twice a week, the first rounds triggering a mad scramble for the heavily sandbagged bunkers on the perimeter of our base camp. We usually hung out there until the shelling ended, either because our counterbattery fire had neutralized the Vietcong mortar teams or they had called it a night.

One evening, though, the manner of attack changed as we were awakened by the rat-a-tat-tat of machine-gun fire. At first glance—and second glance, too—it seemed evident that the tank company guarding the perimeter to our left front was taking heavy automatic-weapons fire. Like the firefight I watched from the shitter on my first night in-country, tracers were flying in from the perimeter and out from the guns of the tanks.

On third glance, though, nothing made sense. Instead of intersecting tracer rounds of distinctly different colors—red for us, green for them—all the rounds, incoming and outgoing, were red. And they seemed to be coming not from the trees well beyond the fence line where the VC normally dug in, but from the fence line itself. If so, that meant Charlie had closed on us more than ever before, in fact was almost on top of us. Either that or—was it possible?—we were shooting at ourselves.

That's what we were doing. Well, not us, not my company. The culprits were our neighbors to the left, the tank outfit, at least that's the story that went around in the wake of the attack that wasn't. It seems a tanker on guard duty thought he heard something threatening outside the fence line, which Vietnamese civilians were advised to give a wide berth after dark. The tanker reacted with a burst of automatic-weapons fire, which was almost immediately returned.

With that, all hell broke loose, as the other tankers on duty all along the perimeter opened fire with their heavy-duty machine guns. We, of course, were in our bunkers within seconds and could see the tracers flying back and forth, a scene "like Coney Island on the Fourth of July," a line I've cribbed from one of the many World War II movies I grew up with.

What had happened was that some of the tanker rounds were hitting the iron fence posts and bouncing back at the good guys, making it seem as though they were under fire. In a way, of course, they were, but not from the VC. As for the bad guys, presumably they were off causing trouble somewhere else. Or sitting in the trees laughing their asses off.

I tell this story reluctantly because I owe that tank company a lot. It may have saved me from a court-martial.

Our battalion was kept busy. Our squat but deadly Ontos provided security for numerous resupply convoys. We must have done the job well because we rarely came under attack. We also went on a number of search-and-destroy missions with the infantry. In the planning stages, these missions promised ferocious firefights.

At the briefings that preceded each operation, a series of battle maps mounted on easels set the stage. First there was a topographic map of the area in which the operation was to occur; then a sheet of clear, heavy-duty acetate was flipped over onto it. The positions of the enemy units we would be engaging were plotted in red. One North

Vietnamese regiment here, another one over there. A second sheet of acetate was then flipped over onto the first. This one showed units in blue.

We were the blue and, judging from the map, we would be virtually on top of the VC or North Vietnamese Army troops we were preparing to seek out and destroy. A helluva battle awaited us.

Except those battles hardly ever materialized. Either our intelligence was bad or the enemy had been tipped off. Most of us were convinced it was piss-poor security. Too many Vietnamese, both civilian and military, wandering around headquarters where the battle plans were hatched. So we would spend days out on operations in which not a round was fired at a known enemy target.

We had a lot of downtime, at least compared to the grunts, for whom the shit never ceased. One of the most difficult tasks was keeping the troops alert and ready for action when we were between convoys or search-and-destroy operations. As company XO, this job fell to me. My first achievement, a minor one, was procuring horseshoes for the troops in the company headquarters group.

Horseshoes were fun for a while, but it was sort of an old man's game and the troops were mostly in their late teens and early twenties. We needed something more physical, not just to allay boredom but to keep them in shape.

What we needed, I decided, was a basketball court.

We were operating out of a base camp in the vicinity of Da Nang, having moved up from Chu Lai with the tank company and several other units. The terrain was flat, with little vegetation. Perfect for basketball if we'd had (1) a basketball, (2) a basketball pole, (3) a backboard, and (4) a hoop, preferably with a net attached. Actually, we needed two of everything except the basketball since I envisioned full-court games. I figured we could get Special Services to supply the basketball. Maybe we could get the other things from them, too. That's what Special Services did, minister to the morale and recreational needs of Marines.

We found a patch of ground well within the wire that was just about the size of the basketball courts you find in school yards. Not regulation NBA size but plenty big enough for a fast-paced game. The problem was that the ground was all chewed up by tire tracks, littered with rocks, and pockmarked with holes of varying sizes, the handiwork of mortars and artillery shells.

We figured with a lot of hard work we could smooth out the ground and make it nominally playable. That would work, but it just seemed, well, cheesy. I realize this was a bizarre value judgment since we were talking about fashioning a basketball court in an unfriendly venue where the sound of mortars would be standing in for crowd noise.

I don't know who came up with the idea. Probably the First Sergeant or maybe Gunny Walker; it may even have been me. The idea? Get the Seabees, the Navy's construction force, a heavy-equipment outfit, into the game. Their base camp was just a few miles down the road.

In the minds of Marines, the Seabees had anything you wanted and could do anything you needed done, sometimes under orders, other times out of the goodness of their hearts, still other times in response to bribes. They built bases, roads, airstrips, bridges, medical facilities, and a lot more, including schools in villages as part of Marine civic-action programs.

We were looking to them for something far less ambitious. We just wanted them to build us a basketball court. And somehow, thanks to the negotiating skills of the Gunny and the First Sergeant, they agreed to do so.

Our negotiators were not without bargaining chips. Several of us, officers and NCOs, had smuggled a variety of adult beverages in-country, either when we first landed or on returning from R&R, and squirreled them away for times when it might be safe to enjoy them. So far, months into our deployment, the time never seemed right, so it wasn't all that painful to donate the booze to seal the deal with the Seabees.

It took two days to get the court built. The company commander was away, so I was in charge. The first day went smoothly. A grader arrived early in the morning, and before noon we had a smooth playing surface. Then some troops who knew about construction framed the putative court with long boards, two-by-sixes, I think, all the material and the tools compliments of the Seabees, who seemed to be getting into this cockamamy project.

That night there was a torrential storm, which turned much of the ground to mud, but the Seabees' cement mixer showed up as scheduled the following afternoon. Before long, concrete was pouring down the chute from the truck's rotating drum, slowly but steadily filling the space defined by the wooden frame. It took a few hours, but by mid-afternoon the concrete had been poured and smoothed. We had done it. We had built an outdoor basketball court in the none-too-friendly confines of a country at war. The poles, backboards attached, had even been set in place, implanted in the concrete at each end of the court.

The Gunny, the First Sergeant, and I were congratulating one another on our unlikely achievement when we heard some buzzing and loud cursing. We looked in the direction of the commotion.

The cement mixer, on its way out of our base camp, had sunk its two back tires in the mud. The driver was rocking the vehicle in an effort to extricate the monstrous piece of equipment from the quagmire, but it just seemed to be sinking deeper. Then the tires started spinning. Not only was the cement mixer stuck; it was now a sitting duck for enemy mortars and artillery.

We were in trouble. More precisely, I was in trouble. The CO had signed off on the idea of a basketball court but left it to me to make it happen. I knew the ground was soft and muddy, and there was no reason not to delay the cement mixer's work for a day or two until the ground dried. But I wanted to get it done while we all were excited about it, so impatience trumped common sense. The result? I had sunk a cement mixer in mud that was providing a dead-on imitation of quicksand.

"Any ideas, First Sergeant?"

"Yes, Sir," he replied. "Let's see if we can get Tanks to help out. Why don't you call them, Lieutenant? Or . . . um, maybe I should."

I have no idea what the First Sergeant said to his tanker buddies.

I'm not sure I wanted to know. All I know for sure is that I saw him talking into our sound-powered phone in a businesslike manner, as if he was cutting another deal, and a few minutes later two tanks came rumbling down from the hill on our left flank. I watched, bedazzled, then humbled and eternally grateful for the breathtaking ingenuity of enlisted Marines. The next thing I knew, chains were being run from the tanks to the cement mixer. The rumbling became even louder as the chains grew taut. Slowly the tires of the cement mixer gained traction and rolled out of the mud it had been trapped in, a sitting duck no more.

Special Services, as I knew they would, came through with a couple of basketballs, and a few days later, when we were sure the cement had dried, we were playing hoops, three-on-three, marvelous games.

Special Services, in addition to supplying the balls, the poles, and the backboards, made other contributions to the troops, including efforts to engage our intellect. What it did was send us several boxes of paperback books.

Until then our reading material had consisted of whatever we'd brought with us and Hong Kong fuck books, which just seemed to somehow materialize. The latter were the products of an enterprising publisher in the British Crown colony who fed the male desire to get to the salacious parts of any narrative by skipping everything in between. Many of these books—replete with misspellings, capitalization, and exclamation points—tilted toward hijinks between priests and nuns, which seemed to me an acquired taste, but there was more than enough standard porn to satisfy less ecclesiastical appetites.

Marines like to tell jokes regarding their literacy. This is one: "Yesterday I couldn't even spell 'Marine.' Now I are one."

In truth, Marines are smart and read a lot more than you may think, so we were excited to learn that boxes of books had just arrived at the company CP. Our excitement quickly cooled, though, when we discovered that the boxes Special Services had delivered all contained the same book: *Stacy Tower*, by Robert H. K. Walter, described on the cover as a "Raw, Powerful Novel of Life at a Big University." The cover also trumpeted excerpts from a *New York Times* review: "Student

Rioting . . . Dirty Politics . . . Sexual Episodes . . . Suspense and Drama . . . An Uncouth Giant of a Book."

At first I was pissed. Who the hell, I wondered, had the publisher paid off to get the Marine Corps to buy for troops in combat scores, maybe hundreds, maybe even thousands, of books about long-haired college kids, most no doubt draft dodgers, and the sexual shenanigans of their no doubt antiwar professors?

Actually, I didn't much care about long hair, draft evading, or professors preaching against the war. I did care about the Marine Corps letting itself be used by a publisher at the expense of the troops. When I cooled down, though, I decided it was laughable. *Stacy Tower* was harmless. Pretty well written, too. And if Bravo Company had a reunion in thirty years, men who hadn't seen or spoken to one another in decades would have something to chat about besides a war everyone wanted to forget. Perhaps they might enjoy sharing their feelings about Chet Nordstrom, the professor who lives in fear of World War III, and whether his timid nature is what drove his hot-blooded wife, Leah, into the bed of his closest friend. Or they might recall with a knowing wink the cheerleader, Binkie Landrum, whose wild, half-naked dance triggers a riot.

Of course, it wasn't all fun and games.

———— ———— ———— ————

I wasn't happy, as I rode along on that Amtrac, that I'd had to scrap my R&R. In fact I was feeling mildly fucked. Everyone in the company who had mounted out from Pendleton with First ATs had gone on two five-day R&Rs except me. And the reason I wasn't going a second time was because the platoon leader who was supposed to be pay officer had an inspection or some other kind of Marine green bullshit.

Not that I was fixating on it. Focusing on a personal grievance while moving through hostile territory, which meant every piece of land except the one you were standing on, was a luxury only an immortal could afford. From the top of the Amtrac my eyes constantly scanned the terrain, the desolate open area to the right, the tree line to the left, the uncomfortably well-worn trail our tracks were rolling over.

The ground was pitted with craters large and small, evidence of exploded mortars and artillery rounds and mines. But for weeks the trail had been used to resupply troops in the bush without incident. So we were cautious and alert, but we did not anticipate trouble.

Moments later, I felt myself lifted from the top of the Amtrac, as if in the eye of a hurricane, except in place of wind and rain I was being carried aloft by flames.

Three

SLEEPLESS DAYS, SLEEPLESS NIGHTS

On 18 January, a detail enroute to the second platoon position for administrative purposes received four WIA when the Amtrac upon which they were riding hit a mine at coord 939581.

—COMMAND DIARY, COMPANY B,

FIRST ANTITANK BATTALION

When I regained my senses, I was splayed out on the ground, a corpsman shaking me.

"Lieutenant, c'mon, Lieutenant, wake up!"

I knew immediately what had happened. Our Amtrac had rolled over a land mine, possibly a pressure-activated mine but more likely one detonated by VC crouching in the tree line to our left.

That meant whoever had set off the blast was probably preparing to take us under fire. Basic small-unit tactics decreed that you cover an obstacle by fire. In other words, when you've got your enemy dazed and flustered, as we were, you try to finish him off before he can clear his head and get reorganized.

A sergeant who had been on the same Amtrac as me raced over, looked down.

"You okay, Lieutenant?"

I knew I was wounded, badly, but oddly enough I wasn't in a lot of pain.

"Sergeant, we need to set out a perimeter defense," I said. "The VC are probably in those trees, but they could be anywhere."

"Already done, Lieutenant," the sergeant said.

"I called for a medevac, Lieutenant. The choppers should be here in a few minutes," said the corpsman. "Are you hurting?"

"Yeah, but not all that much."

"I can't give you morphine, Lieutenant, not with a head wound."

"Anybody else hurt?" I asked.

"Three other guys, but you got the worst of it. They'll be okay."

In those few minutes, as the pain gradually intensified, I checked myself out. My face and arms had been scorched and my throat felt raw, but incredibly I could see perfectly. I also could hear and speak. And the rest of my body seemed like it was intact. This felt serious, but was it?

Suddenly I was on a stretcher held by Marines front and back, being rushed to a helicopter that had just set down about fifty yards away, its rotors slowly slapping the air. Plop-plop plop-plop. Then I was aboard the chopper, the rotors whirred, and we lifted off.

My face was tingling and I was having trouble breathing by the time we landed, about thirty minutes later, amid an array of Quonset huts. I gathered we were at a military medical facility; it turned out to be the station hospital near Da Nang, at the base of Marble Mountain. Once again stretcher bearers were hurrying me somewhere, this time toward one of the larger Quonset huts. Before we got inside, a small contingent of doctors, maybe three or four, stopped us and huddled around me.

"Is it hard to breathe, Lieutenant?" one of the doctors asked.

"Yes," I said, my voice now raspy.

"He needs a trake," a doctor said. The others nodded.

"Lieutenant," the same doctor said, "your throat is closing up. You must have inhaled some of the hot fumes. We're going to have to give you an airway."

I gave the doctors a puzzled look.

"We need to cut a small hole in your throat and insert a tube so you can breathe. It's called a tracheotomy. We're going to give you a local, but it still may hurt a bit. We need to move fast on this."

A needle entered my throat just below my Adam's apple. Less than a minute later I felt a blade slice through the same area. I passed out.

— — — —

The next thing I remember I was in a bed, in a large hospital bay with lots of other beds. A male nurse or corpsman dressed in white came by.

"I'm gonna have to suction you out, Lieutenant," he said.

I tried to answer, to ask him what he meant, but no words came out even though my lips moved.

"You have to put your finger over the hole in your throat if you want to talk, Lieutenant," the corpsman said.

I did. "What are you going to do?" I asked.

"I need to suction you out. I'm going to run this tube through your airway and down your throat and suction out the fluid that's collecting in your lungs. Otherwise you'll choke on it."

He inserted the tube. I heard a gurgling sound from deep in my chest.

When he finished, he said, "You need to call us whenever you feel your throat filling up, so we can suction you out."

"How often is that gonna be?" I asked, my finger on the hole.

"Can't tell yet, Lieutenant, but the docs think you have pneumonia so it could be pretty often."

It turned out to be every fifteen minutes for the next two weeks. I barely slept the entire time.

— — — —

That gave me plenty of time to think. But I didn't think of much during those two weeks because phlegm, or whatever the hell that fluid was, would start draining back into my throat almost as soon as I had been suctioned out. Each time I had to wave down a nurse or corpsman.

In a split second my life had changed. The question was how much. My face and arms were wrapped in bandages, but I asked for a mirror during an early dressing change and was relieved to see that my features, though red and raw, were unaffected.

The doctors, without going into detail, were encouraging. As I recall, there was some discussion of second-degree burns and third-degree burns and skin grafts, but not much; all that would come later. And my mood, if not sunny, was not morose, either. Yes, the homecoming I had envisioned would probably be delayed, but I was hopeful in those early days that little else would be affected.

It wasn't long before my need for sleep became overwhelming, as much a necessity, it seemed, as air or water. But the need to suction me out every fifteen minutes meant that if I slept at all it was in snatches of five minutes or less. Any longer and I started to choke.

One day a heavyset Marine and another officer came to my bedside. "Lieutenant Timberg, I'm General Walt. This is Commander Glenn Ford. How are you doing?"

Lewis Walt was the commanding general of all Marines in South Vietnam. Ford, a Marine at one time, now a Naval Reserve officer, was a well-known movie star who I knew from such films as *Gilda* and, more recently, *Blackboard Jungle*.

"How are you, Lieutenant?" Ford asked.

My response was upbeat. Finger over the hole, I told Ford and the general that I was doing well and had been assured by the doctors that my condition was improving. I said I was looking forward to going home soon.

Looking back, my reaction was typical of a seriously injured soldier in the immediate aftermath of being wounded. In those early days, there is relief at having defied death and a kind of macho attitude that reflects the attention one is receiving and the camaraderie of fellow soldiers in similar circumstances.

It is a type of behavior that I have both observed and read about: the seriously injured serviceman who talks about how he's not going to let his wounds beat him and how he just wants to get back into the fight.

Those are honest emotions, but they are situational. The day ultimately comes when the attention diminishes, the good fellowship is no more because he is mostly alone, and he is faced with the chilling prospect of a lifetime of coping with what war has turned him into.

Some manage to maintain a hopeful outlook on life. Others think it a victory if they manage to get through one more day without giving in to an impulse toward suicide.

Four

JANIE

If Jane Carol Benson had been born five years later she probably would have been a hippie or a campus radical. As it was, born in 1943 she was a child neither of the 1950s nor the 1960s, but her personality displayed strains of both. She was responsible and, in many ways, conventional, but she was also fiery, independent, rebellious, and adventuresome. I sensed those latter qualities the first time I saw her and was immediately attracted to her. It didn't hurt that in her big sunglasses, in fact even without them, she could have been Audrey Hepburn's body double in *Breakfast at Tiffany's*.

Janie grew up in Homeland, a leafy community of rambling older homes bordering Charles Street, the main thoroughfare of the upscale northern section of Baltimore. I met her in 1961, late in my Plebe Year at Annapolis, at one of those closely chaperoned Saturday afternoon dances that the Academy—for reasons I've still not divined—calls tea fights. She was standing across the room, smoking a cigarette and chatting with two other girls. Her demeanor—posture and facial expressions—sent a message, as if she were saying, "How the hell did I ever get talked into coming to this dumb thing?"

I was having similar thoughts, though in my case I knew the answer. We plebes had been denied virtually any contact with females since the previous July, and by spring we were, in a word, a sanitized word, desperate. The Academy sanctioned three or four tea fights a year to enhance or, in some cases, introduce social skills. No stones were left unturned in making the dances as sexless as possible.

Refreshments consisted of nonalcoholic punch and little triangular sandwiches from which the crust had been removed. The small combo played nothing more earthy than Perry Como ballads and, occasionally going to hell with itself, the Four Lads. The young ladies, all invitees from elite private high schools and women's colleges in the area, were of an age and pedigree the authorities felt confident would ensure no touching of parts that mattered. It was as if Academy officials had scripted a Hollywood musical called *Holiday for Eunuchs*.

After a bit I tired of exchanging snarky remarks with my fellow midshipmen about the youth and uneven attractiveness of the girls and decided to see if the one who seemed as disgruntled as me had anything else going for her. I walked across the dance floor, uninhabited except for a few benighted couples, and introduced myself to my future wife.

"Hi," I said, "I'm Bob Timberg. You wanna dance?"

She didn't beam at me. At best she gave me a lame smile. But she did agree to dance. We pretty much spent the rest of the afternoon together, though that was more my doing than hers. I mean, I kept saying, "Hey, do you want to dance with someone else?" or "I feel like I'm monopolizing your time," and she never said "Yes, I do," or "Yes, you are," but I think that was just breeding. She gave me her address when the dance ended, but I sensed, correctly as it turned out, that she was underwhelmed by me.

That day set in motion a relationship that over the next three years never seemed to achieve equilibrium. My feelings toward Janie never changed; hers toward me were erratic, warm one moment, cool the next.

That had a lot to do with our differing circumstances. Even as an upperclassman at Annapolis, my movements and actions were sharply circumscribed: There was to be no consumption of alcoholic beverages within seven miles of the Chapel dome; no riding in cars (thus no reasonable way to get beyond the seven-mile limit and back in time for curfew); Saturday night liberty expired about midnight; no evening liberty the rest of the week. Worst of all, we almost never were permitted to leave Annapolis on weekends, even by soapbox, skateboard, or dogsled.

Janie, on the other hand, headed off that fall to Lake Erie College, a small women's school in Painesville, Ohio. She was not crazy wild, but she was not sedate, either. I received reports—from her, which should have told me something—of drinking and otherwise carrying on with similarly unfettered students from nearby Kenyon College or with a traveling crew of well-heeled frat boys from one major-league party school or another. In many ways, she seemed like a typical college girl, but she was more than that. She became involved in causes, at least once getting arrested and thrown in a police van at a civil rights demonstration

Meanwhile, I wrote her letter after letter professing my affection. She responded by saying I was too serious, that she wanted to enjoy college, and, in case I had missed the point, she had no desire to be a naval officer's wife.

I didn't give up easily. During one of my summer leaves, I hitchhiked with my friend Ron Benigo from my home in New York City to New Hampshire to a camp on a lake where Janie and Ron's girlfriend of the moment were working as counselors. Another summer I returned from a midshipman training cruise in the Mediterranean and hitched by car and military aircraft to Yellowstone National Park, where Janie had a job at Old Faithful Lodge, and where I met and enjoyed a brief friendship with Mike Reagan, the future president's son. The summer after I graduated, while at the Basic School in Quantico, my friend and fellow Marine Dave Wilshin and I got weekend jobs at a rowdy nightclub in Dewey Beach, Delaware, called the Bottle & Cork.

Janie and the woman Dave was dating—as it happened the same

one Ron had been dating a couple of years earlier—were working there as waitresses. Dave was a bartender; I checked IDs since I proved incapable of drawing a draft. All I got was foam.

We slept in a ramshackle cottage in the more sedate town of Rehoboth Beach, a few miles up the coast, behind a Chinese restaurant named Bob Ching's, and made politically incorrect wisecracks about the three-legged cat hobbling around the property.

By then, despite a few bumps still in our path, Janie had succumbed to my charm and persistence, probably in reverse order. The following July, we were married at the Academy, then honeymooned for a week in Banff and Lake Louise in the Canadian Rockies. Our activities, other than the usual stuff, included horseback riding on narrow mountain trails. I somehow found time to read *The Spy Who Came in from the Cold*, the beginning of a lifelong addiction to the novels of John le Carré. We returned to the apartment I was renting in San Clemente to learn my outfit was mounting out in a matter of weeks. But the weeks turned into months, which gave us through the Christmas holidays to live as newlyweds.

But we also were a Marine Corps family, and there was a war on. Less than four months earlier, the first American combat units, two reinforced Marine infantry battalions, had waded ashore in South Vietnam.

More had followed and others were on the way, including, without question, the First Antitank Battalion. Dave Wilshin, my Academy and Quantico roommate (and fellow retainer at the Bottle & Cork), was already there. So was Ron Benigo.

For Marines, the question was not if we were going but when. It was unlikely to be a classic mount-out of the "drop your cocks, grab your socks" variety. Our move would be orderly, though not leisurely, and, if not totally without warning, there wouldn't be much advance notice.

Opposition to the war already was stirring, but the civil rights struggle spearheaded by Martin Luther King Jr. claimed center stage for the better part of the year 1965. March marked more than the Marine landing at Da Nang; it also was the month in which black demonstrators and Alabama State Troopers clashed in Selma and Dr. King led a march of twenty-five thousand from Selma to the state capital in Montgomery.

President Lyndon Johnson signed the Voting Rights Act in August, guaranteeing black people the right to vote. It was landmark legislation, the force of which would be felt for generations to come, but it had little immediate impact on the intensifying anger of black Americans. Five days later, the Watts section of Los Angeles erupted in flames and racial violence, followed by similar disturbances in many of the nation's other large cities.

Meanwhile, the war was gathering momentum, as was the fledgling antiwar movement. More troops poured into South Vietnam and Air Force B-52s began pounding the North. And in late November, fifteen thousand Americans of all ages demonstrated against the war in the nation's capital.

Janie and I, without question, were living in increasingly turbulent times, as well as under a cloud of imminent separation. Neither of us was convinced the war made sense, but we didn't have a strong feeling that it was as muddleheaded and potentially divisive as it proved to be. In truth, ours had been a long-distance relationship for the better part of five years, a romance carried on in large measure through the U.S. mail. We spent the six months we had together making up for lost time. Our apartment came with a single twin bed. It never was a problem. We fit together in all ways that mattered.

— — — —

San Clemente was comfortable, but it was sleepy and something of a Marine town, though not nearly as much as Oceanside, just outside the south gate of Camp Pendleton. So Janie scouted around and discovered somewhat more diverse Laguna, about ten miles to the north.

That fall Janie got a job teaching learning-disabled children at a private school even though she had been an English lit major in college and had taken no education courses. She was a natural teacher, her warm, nurturing personality precisely what her needy kids required.

And we were happy. Sure, sometimes I'd get home late from a field exercise or a forced march in Pendleton's rugged mountains and I'd gross her out by ripping blisters from my heels and spraying them with a product called Tuf-Skin, which burned like fire on the raw tissue (of course I would manfully ignore the pain as sweat rolled down my forehead). And a lot of our conversations took place at a newspaper-covered kitchen table as I spit shined my boots and dress shoes each night or fieldstripped and cleaned my .45. There also were brief episodes of foreshadowing, as when we spent the better part of a Saturday dyeing my T-shirts green so that I would blend more easily into the foliage I expected to soon be tramping through.

But the war did not consume us, perhaps because we did not do a lot of socializing with other Marines beyond the formalities required by military etiquette. We made house calls on my commanding officer and his wife, dutifully leaving our calling cards on the silver platter near the door as we took our leave after staying the prescribed twenty minutes. You may think of Marines with camouflage paint on their faces and bayonets in their teeth, but failing to adhere to the social niceties can torpedo the career of even the most zealous Leatherneck, at least according to *The Marine Officer's Guide*, the behavioral bible of the Corps. Here's my favorite line from the book:

"You can make few social mistakes as avoidable, as conspicuous, or as lasting as selecting the wrong kind of personal cards."

Here's one of the helpful hints for avoiding calling-card-related social disasters:

"Name and rank are engraved no larger than 9/64" for the capital letters, with lowercase letters of appropriate size in keeping with the size of the capital letters across the center, where the name is printed."

I found this, and similar dictums, silly but harmless. Janie tried to disregard such rules. What did she call them? Oh yeah, her word for them was "bullshit." She felt threatened both by them and the legion of other strictures laid out in a companion volume, *The Marine Corps*

Wife, which she thumbed through somewhere, probably the library or a bookstore. I never had the guts to give her a copy. She also ignored invitations to join the Marine wives club or participate in any social event short of a command performance. She was not, she made clear, a Marine wife but a fully independent and liberated woman who happened to be married to a Marine.

None of this caused serious problems for us. We had our little apartment, our two Siamese cats, Franny and Zooey, and each other. We really didn't need anyone else. And we even got away a few times - to San Francisco, San Diego, Lake Tahoe—but the moment in each trip we cherished most was driving from the inland freeway toward the coast on Laguna Canyon Road, with its rocks, hills, twists, and turns, then suddenly mounting a rise and seeing lovely little Laguna and the sparkling Pacific spread out before us. It never failed to take our breath away.

We knew our time together wouldn't last forever, and it didn't. By January the First Antitank Battalion was aboard ship, on the way to Okinawa en route to South Vietnam. I last saw Janie from the deck of the USS *Talladega* (APA-208), a World War II vintage attack transport, waving to me from the pier of the naval base at Long Beach, as we steamed toward a place where, as we both knew, there be dragons.

—— — — ——

Many service wives, especially those of junior officers like me, returned to their hometowns or their parents' abode when their husbands deployed. Janie stayed in Laguna. She thought of it as her home and had no desire to relinquish her hard-won independence by moving back to Baltimore.

The decision had a downside. Because she and I had pretty much lived in our own little world during the five months we were together in Laguna, Janie did not have many friends outside a relatively small circle. And because she was wary of falling into the role of dutiful military wife, she steered clear of the spouses of my Marine friends. Mostly she taught and, at night, wrote long letters to me.

Janie threw away the tranquilizers and returned to her classroom. That evening there was a telegram waiting for her when she got home, from General Wallace M. Greene Jr., Commandant of the Marine Corps. It read:

THIS IS TO INFORM YOU THAT YOUR HUSBAND FIRST LIEUTENANT ROBERT R. TIMBERG USMC WAS INJURED 18 JANUARY 1967 IN THE VICINITY OF DANANG, REPUBLIC OF VIETNAM. HE SUSTAINED SECOND DEGREE BURNS TO THE FACE, HANDS AND ARMS WHEN AN AMPHIBIAN TRACTOR HE WAS RIDING ON DETONATED HOSTILE MINE WHILE ON PATROL. HE IS PRESENTLY RECEIVING TREATMENT AT THE STATION HOSPITAL DANANG. HIS CONDITION AND PROGNOSIS WERE FAIR. YOUR ANXI-ETY IS REALIZED AND YOU ARE ASSURED THAT HE IS RECEIVING THE BEST OF CARE. YOU WILL BE KEPT IN-FORMED OF ALL SIGNIFICANT CHANGES IN HIS CONDI-TION. HIS MOTHER AND FATHER HAVE BEEN NOTIFIED.

That was the last Janie heard from the Marine Corps, or anyone else who might have shed light on where I was and what was happening to me, for the next two weeks.

— — — —

Janie continued to teach as she waited for word on my condition and whereabouts. She prided herself on her ability to deal with a crisis. Now she knew beyond the shadow of a doubt that the last thing she needed was to take time off when there was nothing she could do to help me. Better to remain in the classroom with kids who needed her and for whom she felt affection akin to love.

This is not to say she didn't move heaven and earth to find out what was going on with me. She frequently ran into military officious-ness, which is more courteous but no less maddening than officious-ness at the motor vehicle administration or the doctor's office.

Even worse were instances of terrifying ignorance. At one point the Marines told her I had been missing for two weeks and they were trying to find me. About then she received a letter from me. My head, arms, and hands completely wrapped in bandages, finger over the hole in my throat, I had dictated it to an Air Force nurse at Clark Air Base in the Philippines, which proved to be a way station from Da Nang to somewhere else, though I didn't know that when I sent the letter.

On learning I was at Clark, Janie placed a person to-person call to "the doctor treating Lieutenant Robert Timberg." She was told that I was no longer there but had been evacuated to the naval hospital in Yokosuka, Japan.

Here's where my father played a small but crucial role. His response to difficult or threatening situations was to neutralize the danger by befriending those embodying the peril. A New York Jew who became a Christian Scientist, he refused, for example, to go to doctors but made friends with members of the medical fraternity, regularly taking two or three of them to dinner and giving them presents at Christmas.

This was a variation on that theme. Because I was in the Corps and in South Vietnam, he befriended the NCOs at the Marine recruiting station in Scranton, Pennsylvania, where he lived with his second wife. Nearly every day he'd stop in, say hello, sometimes take the guys to lunch. This was, I'm sure, his way of ensuring my safety.

This strategy having fallen thirteen days short of complete success, he was on the phone constantly with Janie, each trying to bolster the other's spirits. On the day she heard I was in Yokosuka, they were joyous; at least I had finally landed somewhere. That was true, except it wasn't Yokosuka, as Janie learned when she made a person-to-person call to the unknown doctor treating me at the naval hospital there. She was told I wasn't there; unlike Clark, though, they didn't tell her I had been shipped somewhere I hadn't. They just told her they had no idea who I was or where I was.

On learning this, my father went to his Marine buddies. Please, he begged them, find my son. The recruiting sergeant came up with the answer in a day.

Yokohama. Not Yokosuka. I was at the 106th Army General Hospital, widely known as Kishine (pronounced *ki-sheenie*) Barracks, the military burn center for the Pacific theater.

This time when Janie put in her person-to-person call to a doctor or doctors unknown, she was put through to Ronald Giralamo,* who identified himself as the physician treating me at Kishine Barracks. He came across as open, unhurried, thoughtful, most of all reassuring. He told her that my burns were third degree, not second degree as she had previously been informed, and that they involved my face, neck, arms, and hands. The good news, he said, was that neither my eyesight nor my hearing had been affected. At the time Janie did not know the difference between second- and third-degree burns, only that the latter were more serious.

"He'll be home in three weeks," the doctor said.

"Well, I'm coming over," said Janie.

The doctor replied that she shouldn't travel to Japan, that there was nothing she could do for me while I was in the hospital. She resisted. He pressed her to back off on the idea.

"He'll be home in three weeks," he said, more firmly than before.

Janie hung up and began searching for her passport. By then she didn't trust anybody.

— — — —

While Janie struggled to obtain information about my condition and whereabouts, my parents and sisters—Pat, twenty-two, and Rosemarie, seventeen—knew even less about how seriously I had been wounded.

All they had to go on was a telegram almost identical to the one Janie had received. "Second degree burns," "condition and prognosis

---

* Not his real name. I could not reach the doctor who treated me at Kishine and I felt I should not use his name without him knowing about it.

fair," "receiving the best of care"—an alarming missive, but not a chilling one. Pat would later tell me the news "didn't sound all that serious."

That changed on a Sunday a few weeks later. Pat and my mother were attending Mass at Queen of Peace church, our neighborhood parish. A priest, not one of the regulars, said in his sermon that he had just returned from Japan, where he had been visiting hospitals and conversing with wounded troops.

"I saw a young man from this parish," he said. The priest proceeded to graphically describe the "young man," whom he did not name, as having suffered very serious burns to his face, eyes, and ears.

Pat knew the priest was almost definitely talking about me. And for the first time, she realized I was in far worse shape than she had imagined.

The priest frightened Pat, but he also infuriated her. My mother was hysterical beside her. When Mass concluded, Pat stormed into the area behind the altar where the priest was changing out of his vestments. She was taking no prisoners.

"My brother is from this parish, and he's been burned," she said. "Were you talking about my brother?"

The priest said he didn't know.

"Well, is he okay?"

"I don't know," the priest replied.

"Is he going to be okay?"

"I don't know."

"How could you come in here and talk like this knowing his family may be sitting out there?" Pat demanded.

The priest sputtered something that sounded to Pat like an apology. Knowing Pat, I'm sure it was not good enough. At her best, or worst, she is a force of nature. She described the priest to me as having graying black hair. I'm sure when she finished with him his hair was completely gray.

Five

WHERE'S THE BURN?

My upper torso immobilized, I couldn't see much besides the clock on the wall as I peered through the two small eyeholes in the bulky dressing that covered my head and face. It was the same no-nonsense, government-issue clock I had seen at dozens of U.S. military bases on three different continents. Black rim, black hands, white face. But now I studied it more intently than I ever had before.

Tick 3:17, tick 3:18, tick 3:19.

Every fifteen minutes marked a fresh chunk of my confusing and still evolving new existence. That was how often the harried Navy corpsmen, overwhelmed by a steady onslaught of wounded Marines at the field hospital in Da Nang, were supposed to run a plastic tube down the hole in my throat and suction out the gunk that had collected in my lungs.

As the corpsmen scurried from Marine to Marine, each as needy as the last, I often had to remind them to suction me, spastically waving my heavily bandaged arms to get their attention, like the Tin Man before they squirted oil on his joints.

The suctioning was critical, which explained my obsession with the wall clock. I was so exhausted from days without sleep that I feared passing out and choking on my own phlegm while a corpsman, oblivious to my plight, treated another patient two beds away.

Suctioning was unpleasant, especially aurally, as the shit from my lungs gurgling up through the tube sounded like someone having a coughing fit underwater.

Keeping track of time was tricky. Some sort of discharge kept draining into my eyes, so unless I blinked furiously, I saw the clock and anything else that crossed my line of vision through what seemed like a filter smeared with goo.

Seen through the secretions, the clock itself seemed to be playing tricks on me, its face growing fuzzy, then cloudy, then vanishing entirely in the fog of glop. First went the thin second hand, then the long, wide wand of the minute hand, then even the thick black hour hand was gone.

I was distressed when the clock did its disappearing act. It was literally all I had keeping me in the game mentally, and I personified it, not as a mortal enemy determined to destroy me, but more like a playful if malevolent joker trying to trick me into drifting off to sleep and destroying myself.

Tick 7:03, tick 7:04, tick 7:05.

Each minute seemed to stretch on forever as I lay in bed, mummified and immobile. I couldn't hear the ticks in my ears but each time the minute hand spasmed and sprung from one mark to the next it screamed in my brain. Tick. Tick. Tick. Tick. A half hour of this was fine. I guess you could survive an hour of it. Tick. Tick. Tick. But a day? Tick. Tick. Tick. Tick. Three days? Tick. Tick. Tick. Tick. A week? Tick. Tick. Tick. Tick. More? Tick. Tick. Tick. Tick. Tick. Tick. Tick. Tick. Tick. Tick. Tick. Tick.

Trapped inside my ridiculous wrappings of tape and gauze, like a latter day King Tut without the jewelry and other ornamentation, I had plenty of time to brood. Why hadn't I heard from Janie? I knew she knew I had been wounded, but did she know the severity of my injuries? Did my parents? Did I? My reasonably upbeat sense of things began to erode as the sleepless days wore on, giving way to a grudging recognition that I might be more seriously injured than I had allowed myself to think. How much more seriously? I didn't have a clue as day after day I lay there helpless, fussed over by doctors, nurses, and corpsmen whose unsolicited reassurances had begun to make me cringe.

I was especially alarmed by their well-intentioned efforts to allay my fears by touting the great strides that had been made in plastic and reconstructive surgery in recent years.

"They're doing wonderful things in the field these days," one after the other would tell me.

Reconstructive surgery? Why were they talking about reconstructive surgery? What needed to be reconstructed? It wasn't like I was a Nazi war criminal who needed his looks altered so he could go to ground in Paraguay. I had seen my face during a dressing change and, yes, it was raw and red, but all my features were in place. I figured I'd look fine as soon as my skin healed. Was something happening or about to happen of which I was unaware?

Then one day—after what must have been about two weeks but felt more like a thousand hours ticked off minute by minute by that hellish clock—I sensed bustling around me. Hands shot under my body from each side, and with a heave I was hoisted into the air and onto what I guessed was a gurney. Someone told me I was being airlifted to the Air Force hospital at Clark Air Base in the Philippines. No one told me why, but clearly my condition had stabilized enough that they felt they could move me.

At Clark, a Red Cross nurse came to my bedside and chatted with me. She also offered to transcribe a letter to Janie if I wanted to dictate one. I quickly took her up on the offer. I had not been able to communicate with my wife since the explosion. Thanks to the kindness of the nurse, I was able to fill in Janie on much of what had happened, information she had tried but failed to elicit from the Marine Corps. I explained, as best I could, where I was and what seemed to be happening to me.

I tried to be optimistic about my prospects for recovery. The dark thoughts that had begun forcing their way into my mind were not something that bore sharing, especially not with a pretty young wife who had endured a rough year herself and still had hopes of resuming a semblance of the happy life we had managed to scratch out even as Vietnam cast its lengthening shadow over us.

Nor could I tell her how long I would be at Clark or where I was going from there. I thought home, but I had nothing to base that on. Patients, I was learning, are the last to know what the docs have in store for them.

The nurse dutifully jotted down my dictation and since my arms remained mostly immobile from the bandages, even signed it for me: "I love you, Bob."

Not all the nurses were that congenial. At Clark, which was a permanent hospital and far from the action, a familiar kind of stateside officiousness set in. It was generally not unkind but frequently was detached. I could hear doctors and nurses zipping past, usually in a rush to keep up with the wartime pace of casualties. It seemed at times that we patients were no more than parts on an assembly line, broken pieces of Marine Corps fighting machines that had to be put back together.

On my second day at Clark, I overheard one of the nurses. She was new, or in any case I didn't recognize her voice. But I heard the words "Where's the burn?" For a split second, I wondered myself. The burn? What burn? Then in a flash of revelation as swift and brutal as the one delivered by the land mine itself, I knew what she meant.

I should have been angry, but I wasn't. I was gripped by fright, stripped of the faux cockiness that had helped me through the previous two weeks, the web of defense mechanisms I had subconsciously constructed to protect myself against the reality of my situation. They had been swept away in little more than a second as I realized that The Burn was *me*.

With two short words, the nurse stripped me of both my identity and my humanity, revealing me as a piece of meat, and charred meat at that. No longer was I Bob Timberg, or Janie's husband, or my parents' kid; I was now The Burn, not just in the eyes of some members of the nursing staff at Clark, but in my own bleary, goopy eyes as well.

The reality of a serious wounding like my encounter with the VC land mine does not take hold all at once. There is the explosion, and the initial pain and confusion. By then, of course, the physical damage has been done, and in my case that loss alone would stay with me forever. But it's the dawning awareness, delivered in a kind of drip-drip-drip water torture of revelation that gradually lands an equally vicious psychic blow. And this, too, would stay with me forever. If I wasn't the trim, hard-charging young Marine officer, the man who worked himself out of the chaos of a troubled family, who found a gorgeous bride, who was ready to fight and kill for the ideals of his nation, who was I? I didn't know anymore.

At the end of the second day at Clark, I felt strong arms beneath my body as I was again trundled from hospital to aircraft. I was told Japan was my next stop. As I was being settled in the plane, one of my handlers, a woman I couldn't see, remarked with an audible sneer, "You must really love all this attention." The remark stunned me, as if I had gotten myself burned nearly to death merely to experience the tender mercies of military medicine. I felt like I had been spit on.

Beneath my bandages I seethed at the insult but did not react, could not react, with the fury I felt. Bob Timberg would have erupted, somehow made the woman regret her words, reduced her to fucking tears. The Burn just lay there, uncomplaining, a pathetic slab of helpless protoplasm.

Six

WASTING AWAY IN YOKOHAMAVILLE

ois-chuh, mois-chuh, I need mois-chuh."

The tinny, pleading voice was coming from the patient to the right of me, a gangly black kid named Fletcher. At least I think it was Fletcher. All I knew about him was that he was an Army enlisted man who wound up in the burn ward after his tank was blown up. A curtain usually surrounded his bed so I rarely got a clear look at him. My ability to see him also was limited because there was only a single peephole in the bandages still wrapped around my head.

His bed had high sides with vertical slats evenly spaced, like a crib, though the slats were steel, not wood painted a cheerful nursery pink or blue. He was obviously being denied water for some medical reason because the only times I ever heard him speak were to beg for "mois-chuh." It's also possible that he was getting lots of fluids but never enough to quench his thirst. Or, as it turned out, as much as he needed. He was not a docile patient in those rare moments when he was conscious. On one or two occasions he pulled out his IV, scrambled from his crib, raced screaming through the ward, and had to be forcibly restrained and manhandled back to his bed.

Fletcher and I were mates with scores of other patients on F-2, the burn ward of the 106th Army General Hospital in Yokohama. The

106th was the military's burn center for the Far East. Staffed by the Army, the facility was nothing if not ecumenical; seriously burned troops, officer and enlisted, of whatever service, usually found their way to the 106th prior to being shipped to medical facilities back in the States.

The flight from Clark Air Base took me to Yokohama and Ward F-2 in the last days of January. I was still traveling incognito, disguised as a mummy from the neck up. The trake remained in my throat. My first impression was that the 106th—most called it Kishine—was like the field hospital in Da Nang except the Army's enlisted aides were called medics, not corpsmen (though both answered to Doc). Big mistake. A lot more was going on at Kishine Barracks.

With a fellow lieutenant serving as scribe, I wrote to Janie on February 1.

> *Since my arrival here my outlook and condition seems to have improved a hundred percent. Everyone concerned seems to be competent and professional, and I believe I am getting the best possible treatment now. Naturally I can only go by what people tell me, but I believe my recovery here will be more rapid than anyplace and that it will be a full recovery.*
>
> *. . . Whatever you do, honey, don't lose your head. I'm pretty sure we're going to come out of this OK. There's just going to be a slight delay in our reunion.*

Our letters were crisscrossing in the mail, so their contents were often overtaken by events. By the time Janie received my February 1 letter, she had already set plans in motion to fly to Japan, which I was unaware of until several days later when I received the letter she wrote February 3.

> *I have been going absolutely insane not knowing where or how you are. Now I really feel better. What can I say? Just that these have been the longest two weeks in my whole entire life. . . .*

*If only I could have been with you these past two weeks. . . . I
can't bear to think of you lying there in that hospital bed—alone—
not able to talk or write or do any of the things you love to do. . . .*

*I am really excited now. I have found you and I'm coming to
you and no one will ever, ever take you from me again.*

It only took a few hours in the burn ward to disabuse me of the
notion that Kishine Barracks was the equivalent of the hospital in Da
Nang. At Da Nang, the objective was to keep me alive until I could be
evacuated for more advanced treatment elsewhere. At Kishine, the first,
crucial steps toward healing my wounds were taken though my continuing mortality remained an issue, primarily because of the threat of
infection, the biggest cause of death for burn patients who survive the
initial catastrophe.

Staving off infection dominated my early weeks at Kishine. Treatment was aggressive. It had to be. My face and right forearm had suffered third-degree burns. That means the outer layer of skin, the
epidermis, and the inner layer, the dermis, had, along with the sweat
glands and hair follicles, been destroyed. What remained looked like
steak before you throw it on the grill. The major threat was a bacte-
rium called pseudomonas, which could be deadly to severely burned
patients.

They called the treatment "wet to dry," and it was used to debride
(pronounced *de-breed*), or remove from the burn site a variety of unde-
sirable substances including dead tissue and other debris that oozed up
from below to the surface of the wound. Allowed to remain on the
burn area, these substances would provide a fertile breeding ground for
the potentially lethal pseudomonas.

Wet-to-dry debriding consisted of wrapping my most serious
wounds, meaning my face and right forearm, in several layers of gauze
that had been soaked in a solution of silver nitrate, a germicide. The
dressings were changed every six hours. For the first few hours
the dressings were irrigated with silver nitrate at regular intervals. An
hour or so before each dressing change, however, the gauze was al-

lowed to dry and stick to the wound. At the appointed time, a nurse or medic ripped off the dressing, taking with it all the bad shit that had collected under it.

I am not sufficiently talented as a writer to describe the pain inflicted by this process. I never passed out, at least I don't think I did, but that was because everything happened so quickly. Just rip! Done! In the seconds, or the second, or half second, or nanosecond it took to do this, my head exploded. I never knew what to compare the experience to until years later when I saw a porn movie in which bombs burst, rockets flared, and all sorts of other fireworks ensued at the moment of climax. Wet-to-dry dressing changes were like that, just as intense, with similar pyrotechnics, though not nearly as much fun.

— — — —

Janie, meanwhile, was making her way to Japan against doctor's advice. By then the trake had been removed from my throat so I could eat solid food and speak unaided for the first time in three weeks, which greatly improved my mood. In blissful ignorance I joined forces with the doctor to an extent, telling Janie in a letter that if she delayed her trip for a couple of weeks my appearance might be substantially altered for the better when she arrived.

"I believe at that time a major phase of the treatment will have been completed," I wrote, or rather dictated to a fellow patient.

This will make it easier for you to evaluate the situation whereas now for the next two weeks things will be in a state of flux. Additionally, I hope at that time to have most of my bandages off and be able to see you and talk to you and perhaps go down to the club and other little things which will be impossible right now.

I ended that letter by saying, "I'm making very good progress and the doctors state that I can expect virtually full recovery."

Janie arrived on February 12, Lincoln's Birthday. A cab dropped her off at Kishine Barracks as snow swirled around the unwelcoming gray stone structure.

"I'm Jane Timberg. My husband is a patient here. I want to see the commanding officer," she firmly informed the first person she encountered who seemed to have some authority.

She was not asking, she was telling, and she pulled it off. Minutes later she was ushered into the office of the hospital CO. He was briefly flustered. He had not been expecting her, but he said she could have a room in a facility for families of the seriously wounded, though only for three days since, he said, I didn't fall into that category.

I was dozing when she finally made it to my bedside.

"Hi," she said.

A one-word greeting, but the voice was unmistakable. And, against all odds, it was perky. Also warm. Also—and I never understood how she pulled this off—happy. As in happy to see me.

Because of my bandages we could not kiss or even touch hands so we made do with an awkward hug. I could see her through my peephole and my heart fluttered. The same slim figure, the laughing brown eyes, the impish, mildly suggestive grin I had always found irresistible.

At first the nurses and medics were wary of her, concerned that she might be too emotionally fragile for a place that had the ambience of a charnel house. She quickly won them over with her cheerfulness and aggressively positive attitude. It also was clear that my morale had gone up considerably since her arrival.

Soon she was pitching in to help with my treatment, irrigating my bandages every hour with a syringe filled with silver nitrate solution, thus freeing the greatly overworked staff to attend to other patients. She also fed me, though I had next to no appetite and ate little.

This was a serious problem. After infection, malnutrition is the second most common cause of death in burn patients, and I was steadily wasting away. From my normal 150 pounds, my weight eventually plunged to 110, lending my frame an appearance just this side of cadaverous, as Janie and the staff force-fed me carbs, including as much beer as they could get me to drink. Oddly enough, that wasn't much. Nothing tasted good.

Janie arrived on the ward early each morning and stayed well into the evening. She had found an unfurnished room in a boardinghouse across from the hospital, which she furnished with a futon and a space heater. She shared an outdoor bathroom—a hole flanked by two pieces of wood—with the other boarders. She showered at a nearby Red Cross facility and took most of her meals in a Chinese dive everyone called Typhoid Mary's.

On the ward, she read to me and we played endless games of Yahtzee. We occasionally tried to talk about our future, but we were immersed in so much uncertainty that we quickly dropped the subject.

━ ━ ━ ━

Fletcher, my thirsty neighbor in the next bed, was our Greek chorus with his periodic calls for "mois-chuh." At first the cries were just more sounds in a noisy ward where patients were often in great pain and new ones were coming in by chopper each afternoon. After a while, though, his pleas became worrisome. "Why isn't he being given water?" we asked a nurse. "He is," she said. "We just can't give him as much as he wants. We're trying to keep his electrolytes in balance." It didn't take long for Fletcher's appeals to become chilling.

One evening, after lights-out, I was awakened by a flurry of activity close by. I couldn't have been asleep long because Janie hadn't left yet. A bank of overhead lights was glaring down on Fletcher's bed, a curtain had been pulled around it, and I could hear several people frantically attending him.

"His blood pressure is still dropping, Doctor," a nurse said.

"Mois-chuh, mois-chuh, mois-chuh," Fletcher chanted, his voice reedy.

At intervals over the next fifteen minutes new blood pressure readings were called out. Each one was lower than the last. Janie and I were squeezing each other's hand. Equipment was being rushed to Fletcher's bedside. His blood pressure was still dropping. I heard him utter a garbled sound, then nothing.

A minute or so later, the curtain opened and Fletcher's crib was slowly pushed out into the aisle between the two long rows of beds. A small procession of medical personnel silently followed. They were heading for the elevator, taking their time. There was no longer a need to hurry.

— — — —

The one thing Janie was not permitted to witness was dressing changes. She was banished from the ward while my head and arms were unwrapped, which meant she had yet to see my face. After about a week, she rebelled, found my doctor, and said, "Tomorrow's my birthday. I want to see my husband without his bandages."

My primary physician, Dr. Giralamo, was a short, relatively young Army surgeon with an olive complexion, whose speech betrayed New York roots. He seemed to like Janie, and Janie liked him. He gave her the okay, but beforehand he briefed her and showed her slides of my face.

For Janie, the unveiling was both chilling and encouraging. A face stripped of its skin is like a lesser grade of beef, deep red in color, with little marbling, a sight so uncommon you can't believe what you're seeing. Grisly though it was, Janie didn't blink. In fact, she smiled. What she saw was a nose that looked like my nose, a mouth that looked like my mouth; in short it looked like I was wearing war paint that hadn't quite dried. She was encouraged by my seemingly intact features. Like me, she believed I'd be fine as soon as my skin grew back.

But my skin wasn't going to grow back. Unlike second-degree burns, after a third-degree burn skin doesn't regenerate itself. This was the fact that had been eluding me, the missing link that explained why the doctors and nurses in Da Nang had been touting the great strides being made in reconstructive surgery. I wasn't going to get better on my own. And things were going to get much worse before any of it got better.

— — — —

Janie may have seen the last of me in a guise that even remotely resembled what I looked like before I was wounded. During the two months I spent on the burn ward at Kishine, I underwent a series of operations in which Dr. Giralamo covered my entire face with skin grafts. The skin came, I think, from my thighs, though in the years that followed skin for grafting was harvested from my chest, back, and stomach as well. These so-called donor sites healed by themselves and did not scar, but they took on a lighter complexion than the surrounding skin, giving much of my body a checkerboard appearance.

These were split-thickness grafts: very thin, almost diaphanous pieces of epidermis, taken with a knife or an instrument called a dermatome, that are laid on wounds after they have been thoroughly scrubbed and disinfected. I can only imagine how painful this would have been since, mercifully, I slept through each procedure. Once the graft was laid into place, a pressure dressing was applied, and everyone prayed that the graft wouldn't be rejected.

There is also a full-thickness graft in which a chunk of both dermis and epidermis are removed with a scalpel from an undamaged section of skin and implanted into a slot cut in the burned area, almost like a wedge, to relieve contraction from scarring. This type of graft needs to be stitched into the wound and the donor site closed surgically.

With a single exception, all the grafting at Kishine was split thickness and done under general anesthesia. The lone full-thickness graft is the one I remember best; in fact I will never forget it.

Contraction had pulled my lower right eyelid down and away from the eye to such a degree that my vision was threatened. Dr. Giralamo decided I needed a full-thickness graft to release the eyelid so it could resume its job of protecting and lubricating the eye.

For some reason he needed me awake for this procedure, but he assured me that local anesthesia would mask the pain of the incisions. In the operating room, Dr. Giralamo and another surgeon bent over me. An injection at the donor site—my right bicep, as I recall—did its job, deadening all feeling in the area. I wasn't enjoying this, but I wasn't panicked, either.

Next was slicing open the tissue below my eye and spreading it so the graft could be inserted. First, though, the area had to be deadened. The physician assisting Dr. Giralamo told me the needle hovering an inch above my face would hurt for a few seconds, but the pain would quickly subside.

It didn't. I had the sensation of a liquid flowing down my face and neck. The assisting surgeon said, "The local's not taking. Blood is washing it away. We may not be able to deaden the site." He tried a second injection. Again liquid streamed down my face, to no effect.

Dr. Giralamo didn't panic. "We're going to have to do this procedure without anesthesia, Bob," he said. "Otherwise, you're going to lose this eye. Try as hard as you can to hold your head still."

I tried. I must not have done a good enough job because the other doctor soon had my head in a vise grip. Then I felt Dr. Giralamo's scalpel slice into the region below my right eye, and I was hurled into a maelstrom of pain and terror. I screamed. And screamed and screamed and screamed and screamed. He kept working and I kept screaming.

I don't remember how long the surgery took—a half hour, maybe less. When it was over, Dr. Giralamo apologized for causing me pain. "It was necessary," he said. His pupils were dilated and he looked drained, washed out, older.

—— —— —— ——

At this point, about halfway through the two months I spent in Yokohama, progress was being made in covering raw tissue with grafts, greatly lessening the threat of infection by providing my face and arm with a protective outer layer that performed some of the functions of skin. But the epidermis, the source of split-thickness grafts, is just a single component of the skin. The dermis, the layer below the epidermis, is the source of new skin cells, which are constantly pushing to the surface. The underneath skin also contains nerves, blood vessels, hair follicles, glands, and sensory receptors, all with individualized functions. In the areas where I had third-degree burns, the skin was totally destroyed, top to bottom. The grafts were the equivalent of brushing a coat of shellac on raw wood; they provided a covering, nothing more.

Something else was going on. Scars were beginning to form, negligible at first, but quickly becoming thick and ropelike in appearance. Then everything—grafts, scars, burned tissue—began to contract. It was as if someone had switched on a microphone and said, "Now do you see what you're dealing with?"

My features were no longer intact, as it seemed they had been only a week or so earlier. My lower eyelids now were pulled down radically, exposing the pink mucous membrane, but only my left eye was fully visible so it looked like I had only one eyeball; my nostrils were stretched sharply upward, lending them the exaggerated flare of a horse running a distance race; my mouth had closed so tightly that nothing much wider than a straw could pass through my lips; contraction had deprived my face of all definition—no valleys on the sides of my nose, no indentation between lower lip and chin. The skin, or whatever you call the tissue now standing in for my skin, was pale and mottled, with irregular red blotches swimming on the surface.

"Now I know why no one wanted me to come over here," Janie said.

"Why?" I asked.

"It wasn't that you weren't wounded seriously enough," she replied, at last putting together the pieces I had been too consumed with pain or horror or false hope to grasp. "They didn't want me to see your face."

Then she flashed a smile. "They really don't know me," she said.

Seven

LYNN

L ieutenant Timberg? Hi, I'm Lynn Ketchum."

With that breezy greeting, the trim, solidly built officer in the white smock introduced himself as he strolled into my room at the U.S. Naval Hospital in San Diego.

"I'm going to be your doctor while you're here."

Not Dr. Ketchum, not Lieutenant Commander Ketchum, just Lynn Ketchum. And he was smiling. Not a big, goofy smile, or even a kindly welcoming one, more of a sly smile, as if the two of us were privy to a secret no one else shared.

I immediately understood that, aside from Janie, this youthful, unassuming, nonetheless imposing physician stood to be the single most important person in my life for the indefinite future, as well as the one who held the key to my fragile hopes for a productive existence beyond the hospital.

First impressions rarely hold up, but some do, and this one sure in hell did.

From April 1967 to July 1968, Lynn Ketchum performed reconstructive surgery on me more than twenty-five times, each occasion under general anesthesia, at the San Diego Naval Hospital, widely known as Balboa because of its proximity to the city's famed Balboa

Park. Three years later, he operated on me seven more times at the University of Kansas Medical Center. During those years, we became friends, at least to the extent that you can be friends with someone who is going at you with a scalpel every few weeks.

Both Janie and I were convinced at that first meeting that by some novel stroke of good fortune I had come under the care of one of the nation's most eminent plastic surgeons. Lynn was unpretentious, but he carried and comported himself in a manner that bespoke confidence, competence, and personal warmth. Not a touchy-feely kind of warmth, but rather a sense that he liked you and hoped you felt the same about him. Most of all, he had a persona that said he knew what he was doing and you could trust him.

Lynn, at age thirty-two and just months removed from completing his residency in plastic surgery, did not then have the towering reputation in medical circles that he would command in the years ahead. But he was anything but a neophyte. By the time I landed in San Diego, he had been performing reconstructive surgery on wounded Marines and Navy corpsmen, many of them suffering from severe burns, for the past year.

I held a special place in his pantheon of burn victims. Many years later, in his personal journal, he wrote, "I have had many patients with facial burns in my career, but none as bad as Bob Timberg."

— — — —

I've often thought Lynn and I were destined to cross paths. I was convinced of it when I learned he was born January 18, 1936, the day on which I was wounded thirty-one years later.

Lynn spent his first twenty-eight years in New Orleans, absorbing the color and rich cultural heritage of that city's blend of French, Italian, Spanish, and African-American ethnicity. As a kid he was both smart and a fine athlete. His life changed dramatically, though, as he reached his early teens. He was infected with *Entamoeba histolytica*, a draining, occasionally deadly parasite of the colon that plagued him for the next four years. The infection left him morbidly thin and chronically fatigued. Many of the sports he had previously engaged in—such as baseball, football, and basketball—were no longer options for him. So he turned to golf, which he had played with his father since he was eight.

Distressed by his skin-and-bones frame and otherwise sickly constitution, he decided to attack his illness head-on. He took up weight lifting. Over the next two years, he put on fifty pounds, most of it muscle, and managed to rid his system of the parasite that had been siphoning off his strength and energy. His gym was not for dilettantes. One of Lynn's fellow weight lifters, an older kid named Red Lerille, was named Mr. America 1960. Lynn himself won a trophy, less exalted but symbolic of his achievement: a framed photo that showed him lifting the six-foot-eleven center of the Loyola College basketball team over his head.

Golf, meanwhile, proved an inspired choice of sports. The game ran in the family. Lynn's father, an optometrist, was also the local promoter for the Professional Golfers' Association, later for the LPGA. Lynn was named captain of the Jesuit High School golf team, which won the city prep school championship all four years he was there.

Away from sports, he turned to debating and oratory, where he again excelled, winning several competitions, including a debating tournament sponsored by Tulane University, which convinced him that he was cut out to be a lawyer.

He had all but decided to enter pre-law when he took an aptitude test that said his greatest strengths lay in science and dealing with people. He interpreted this to mean medicine, so he switched his major at Loyola College to pre-med.

Not surprisingly, he stood first in his class. He worked as a lab assistant both in college and during medical school at Tulane. The first summer in med school he interned as a scrub nurse at the Eye, Ear, Nose, and Throat Hospital.

His father encouraged him toward ophthalmology, but Lynn was not excited by it. Plastic surgery was a different matter. One of the surgeons he worked with—a pompous, arrogant but highly talented physician—rarely failed to dazzle Lynn with the deft, innovative procedures he performed. The first time Lynn observed him he was fashioning a vagina for a young woman who had been born without one.

He spent two years in the pathology department, studying chromosome aberrations in cancerous tissue, and when it came time to select a specialty, he was torn between pathology and plastic surgery. He chose the latter in large measure because he preferred working on living patients.

From med school, which he later described as "brutal, the hardest thing I have ever done," he moved on to an internship at New Orleans's Charity Hospital. His roommate was a third-year dermatology resident, Carlton Carpenter, who told him about a novel treatment of lichen planus, a skin condition that causes shiny, flat-topped bumps that often produce intense itching. Carpenter and his colleagues were using a new drug called triamcinolone, a steroid hormone also known as Aristocort, to reduce the nodules.

An aspiring plastic surgeon by then, Lynn thought the drug might work on hypertrophic scars, the thick kind that often accompany surgery or burn injuries. He tested the idea by using himself as a guinea pig.

He had had a suspicious mole removed from his right upper arm, which left a thick scar and itched constantly. He asked a fellow intern to inject half the scar with triamcinolone. Within three days, the itching stopped on the injected portion of the scar. That portion also softened and flattened in a month.

He then asked his intern friend to inject the other half of the scar. Same result. Lynn had not even begun his plastic surgery training, and he was already a pioneer in the treatment of hypertrophic scarring, which paid dividends for me a few years later.

Before he began full-bore plastic surgery training, he did a three-year general surgery residency at the Ochsner Clinic in New Orleans, where the renowned researcher and surgeon Alton Ochsner became one of his mentors.

Ochsner was one of the first scientists to link smoking to lung cancer, publishing a groundbreaking article on the issue in 1939. A dozen years later, he led the surgical team that performed the nation's first successful separation of Siamese twins. He also created the first recovery room, where patients just out of the operating room were cared for by nurses trained in postanesthesia care rather than by floor nurses lacking in such training. That led to Ochsner's development of specialized intensive care units.

A stern taskmaster, Ochsner terrorized medical students and residents with relentless cross examinations during his lectures, convinced that aspiring surgeons needed to learn early on to work effectively under intense pressure.

Ochsner did not confine his activities to medicine. He was a passionate anti-Communist and a well-known figure in right-wing political circles. Lynn told me he had no involvement in Ochsner's nonmedical activities.

In the third year of his general surgery residency, Lynn married Cindy Jeansonne. They were wed on January 18, 1964, Lynn's twenty-eighth birthday and three years to the day before my run-in with the land mine.

His general surgery residency complete, Lynn and Cindy moved to Kansas City, where he began the next stage of his career, a two-year plastic surgery residency at the University of Kansas Medical Center.

His new mentor was David Robinson, warm, generous, and distinguished. In Lynn's final year, Dr. Robinson became president of the American Society of Plastic Surgeons and chairman of the American Board of Plastic Surgery.

Dr. Robinson encouraged Lynn to continue his research into the use of Aristocort on hypertrophic scars and keloids, a grossly disfiguring condition—essentially scars heaped upon scars. In 1966 Lynn and Robinson cowrote the most extensive study of Aristocort treatment published up to that time.

— — — —

Lynn joined the Navy when he completed his plastic surgery residency, and was commissioned a lieutenant commander in the medical corps. He had taken on a two-year obligation. In return, Selective Service deferred his induction until he completed his education. This arrangement is what eventually led our paths to cross.

First he had to undergo military training. Over the years this consisted of a limited program designed for doctors, lawyers, and others recruited by the Navy for their professional skills. But this was wartime. Lynn's training was more intense, consisting of six weeks with the Marines at Camp Pendleton.

There were thirty doctors in his training company at Pendleton. Twenty-nine were shipped off to Vietnam, all but Lynn. He was told there was no billet for a plastic surgeon in the war zone—curious considering our battalion surgeon in Vietnam was a gynecologist.

Lynn was assigned to the plastic surgery department at Balboa to await a Vietnam billet opening in his specialty. One finally did. But he never made it overseas. His deployment orders were rescinded five hours after he received them. Instead, a more senior physician in the plastic surgery service received the assignment.

He never served in a combat zone, but he didn't miss the war. Nearly all the Marines and Navy corpsmen assigned to the Marines who were in need of reconstructive surgery wound up at Balboa. Lynn and the other plastic surgeons were in the operating room constantly, trying to turn once rugged and robust young men into some semblance of their previous selves.

Lynn also found time to be a student of sorts. As it happened, two of his patients were professional magicians, and if he could break free in the afternoon he dropped by the men's ward for his own private magic class.

Eight

THE SKIN GAME

S ettling himself at the foot of my bed, Dr. Ketchum asked about
my medical history, though it was clear from his questions that
he had already done more than glance at my file.

"Where do we go from here?" I asked. In response he proceeded to
give Janie and me a short lecture on skin and plastic surgery. First
off, he made it clear that all those tales of war criminals and gangsters
getting a plastic surgeon to remake their features overnight were pre-
posterous.

It doesn't work like that, he explained. For major wounds like
mine, plastic surgery was a series of small steps, each building on the
one preceding it. Sometimes you had to take a step back in order to
move forward. And nothing happened overnight; the process in cases
like mine was long, at times frustrating, and the results uncertain. And
forget looking like you used to look; we can do a lot, we don't deal in
miracles.

"Skin is like leather," Dr. Ketchum said, "and it goes through
stages."

A skin graft, in particular, goes through stages. The first is simply
getting it to adhere to the wound bed on which it's laid. It's not unusual
for a graft to be rejected.

The next stage, assuming the graft takes, is contraction. This process goes on for weeks, sometimes months. At first the graft looks perfectly smooth, not like your original skin, but something that resembles it, however remotely. It seems like something you can live with.

Contraction changes everything. It distorts, pulling features out of shape, the mouth, nose, eyelids; definition vanishes. It also creates scarring, thick, ropey, hideous hypertrophic scars. After many months, the graft may soften, but most of the scarring and distortion remains.

"That doesn't mean we're helpless," the doctor said. "We can make a real difference. It's going to take time, but if you're ready to get started, so am I."

By the time Lynn Ketchum and I got together all the scarring, pulling, and distortion had done its job. I was at my worst, visually and emotionally. By any measure, I looked like a monster.

"So what do we do first?" I asked.

— — — —

D r. Ketchum said that both my mouth and my eyelids needed immediate attention. Contraction had caused my lower eyelids to turn outward, a condition called ectropion. That kept me from closing my eyes, crucial to protecting the corneas. Dr. Giralamo, in Yokohama, had tried to deal with this problem with a full-thickness graft. It helped, but not much. Now Dr. Ketchum was saying more surgery was needed, not just to release the eyelids, but to rebuild them so they could resume their crucial function of lubricating the eyeball.

"The way we do it is we place skin grafts on the lower eyelids, then we sew them to the upper lids to prevent retraction," he said. "So both your eyes will be covered, but we'll leave peepholes so you can see. Then we wait, give the grafts time to go through the stages I mentioned. Then, when that's all over and the grafts have matured, we slice across the top of each graft and you'll have upper and lower eyelids."

"How long will all this take?" I asked.

"A few months, we'll have to see how quickly you heal," the doctor replied.

"So I'm gonna look like a raccoon for a few months?"

"Yes."

"Fuck!"

Dr. Ketchum pursed his lips slightly at my monosyllabic commentary on his game plan. Then he moved on to the next item on his agenda.

My mouth had contracted to the circumference of a small cigar. Whatever nutrition I was receiving was coming in liquid form, through a straw or vein. The doctor said it was vital that I start taking in solid food, especially protein, so he was going to have to rebuild my mouth. To do so, he said, he would slice into the sides and create a normal-size opening. For lips, he would pull out some of the rosy mucous membrane from inside my mouth and stitch it to the new openings on each side.

"That's a lot of stuff," I said. "How many operations?"

"Just one, and we have to do it as soon as I can schedule the surgery. Your eyelids and your mouth have got to be taken care of as quickly as possible."

The room was quiet. Janie, who had said nothing during the whole discussion, remained silent. Finally, Dr. Ketchum said, "Any other questions?"

"Yeah," I said. "How about letting me smoke?"

"Sure," the doctor said. "Can't hurt."

Then he pulled a silver dollar out of my ear, glanced at it, dropped it in his pocket, and walked out.

— — — —

Lynn (we were quickly on a first-name basis) was not joking when he said progress would be slow and often seem as if we were moving backward. The grafting of my lower eyelids and sewing them to the uppers fell in between; it was hard to tell if the surgery made things better or worse. The raw membrane below my eyes looked ghastly; my eyes, effectively disappearing under skin grafts, looked freakish. As I suspected, I looked like a raccoon.

Three months later, Lynn sliced open the grafts. Suddenly I had upper and lower eyelids. I even had upper eyelashes, which must have been lurking somewhere. Did my eyes look great? No. Did they still look bad? Yes. But there was no denying they looked better.

As promised, Lynn also reshaped my mouth in that first surgery, opening it, rearranging skin, creating lips from the mucous membrane. Normality restored? Not a chance. An improvement? Yes. I could finally get solid food in my mouth. At first it was just hospital food, which rarely if ever rises above bad. Soon, though, Janie was sneaking in all sorts of appetizing, if mostly unhealthy, goodies.

During those sixteen months I had an operation every two or three weeks, almost always involving skin grafting. It was like living on a conveyor belt. I'd spend the week following surgery recuperating in the hospital, then go home to Laguna Beach for a week or two, then back to the hospital for more surgery.

The hospital regimen was predictable. Check in the day before surgery, an injection before being wheeled into the OR, the starting of an IV, then a mask comes down over my face. I always panicked as I saw the mask descending. The next thing I knew, I was in the recovery room, usually throwing up from the anesthesia. There was almost always serious pain from the donor site since the harvesting of skin is the equivalent of a second-degree burn. Four or five days later, back to Laguna till the next time.

In the year and a half I was under his care at Balboa, Lynn performed amazing surgical feats. He rebuilt the top of my ears, which had nearly been burned completely off. As an abstraction, this three-stage procedure was fascinating. First he created tubes, called pedicles, from skin on both sides of my neck, leaving the tops attached so that the tubes would have a blood supply. Then he detached the bottom of the tubes, flipped them up on my neck in the direction of my ears, and reattached them. This was possible because the tops (the original bottoms) had in the interim developed their own blood supply.

A few weeks later, the tube bottoms were detached and flipped upward and attached just below my ears. The next time the bottoms were flipped and attached to what was left of my outer ears. Finally, the other ends were attached across the rims of my outer ears. This forced march up my upper extremities did make the size of my ears closer to normal, though I think Lynn and I both hoped for greater improvement.

Lynn also did a lot of work on and around my nose. He released and grafted my nostrils so they no longer pulled up toward my eyes, reducing the horsey aspect. He re-created the creases on either side of my nose to provide some definition to my face, which had been pulled so tight by scarring that it looked as if I were wearing a nylon stocking mask. Then he inserted skin below my nose to expand the distance between the septum and my upper lip.

My whole head was pulled downward by scarring on my neck, the result of burns and the incision for the tracheotomy tube. Lynn released the tension, laid in a split-thickness graft, and I could again move my head up and down, left and right.

— — — —

The skill, efficiency, and professionalism at Balboa were, with rare exceptions, incomparable. Not so the administrative machinery of the Marine Corps. Four months into my stay at Balboa and I hadn't been paid once. In fact, I hadn't been paid since I was wounded in January, and this was August. Finances were tight. No salary, and since I was no longer in South Vietnam, no more of that easy money they called combat pay. Janie had her teaching job, which by necessity had become our sole source of income.

I complained and was told that my pay record had been lost and that I couldn't get paid until it was found. The irony of the situation was blinding. I had been wounded, maimed, and almost killed trying to pay Marines in a combat zone, and here I was in sunny, peaceful San Diego and the Marine Corps was incapable of paying me.

This made no sense. Why wasn't some sort of temporary pay record created so I could be paid until my permanent record was found? I loved the Marine Corps, but this made me furious, as if some sinister coven of paymasters at Headquarters Marine Corps was conspiring to undercut the Corps' credo that it always takes care of its men. The only good thing to come out of it was that my periodic bursts of anger at this bizarre situation temporarily banished the deep depression that had taken hold of me.

Adding to my depression, a few days before I was wounded I learned that I had been selected for captain. In San Diego I was told I would not be promoted until I was fit for duty. But I would never again be fit for duty, and everyone knew it.

What comes after Catch-22?

Enter a chunky, bespectacled fireplug of a Marine colonel named Walter Moore, a much-decorated veteran of three wars. He had been our battalion commander during the last months at Pendleton and the first few months of our deployment to South Vietnam. His nickname was MuMu. That's how he spelled it, eschewing—for aesthetic reasons, no doubt—the phonetic spelling, MooMoo. Few knew where the moniker came from, and those who knew kept it to themselves.

MuMu, a lieutenant colonel at the time, took over our battalion just before we mounted out for Vietnam. He led us for several months, whipped us into shape. We were young and tough. MuMu was tougher than all of us. No one doubted that. A few months after we landed in Vietnam, he was tapped for higher command, an infantry unit, the First Battalion, Fifth Marines. We hated to see him go.

Some months after I was wounded, MuMu rotated back to the States. He came to see me in the hospital in San Diego. He had been promoted to colonel, something that never would have happened absent a war; he was not a natural on the cocktail party circuit, normally an indispensable skill for officers hoping for promotion to the loftier ranks. I was in the midst of a deep depression, but seeing the roly-poly, tough-as-nails MuMu storm into the room immediately raised my spirits.

We chatted. He filled me in on old comrades. Then he asked if he could do anything for me. I told him about my pay problem. And that the Corps wouldn't promote me. His eyes narrowed, his brow furrowed, his mood grew dark. Moments later he was himself again.

Two weeks later, he again blew into my room. I tried to sit up. "No," he said. "Just stay there." He reached into his pocket, pulled out a small box, opened it, and took something out. He pinned the double silver bars on the collar of my hospital gown, then saluted me.

"Congratulations, Captain Timberg," he said. "By the way, you'll be paid, back pay and all, next payday."

I don't know how he pulled it off. There was probably a rule, if not a law, against it. For some reason I got the impression that Lieutenant General Victor Krulak, a friend of MuMu's and the father of Chuck Krulak, my Naval Academy classmate and a future Commandant of the Marine Corps, had played a role. But mostly I think old MuMu screamed bloody murder about the way I had been treated and scared the hell out of anyone who tried to reason with him.

— — — —

Despite such small victories, my depression rarely eased, at times dipping into the suicidal, though never long enough for me to act on it. For the most part, I was able to keep my mood reasonably stable, at a manageable level of depression, though at times there would be terrifying swings downward, as if I were in a plane that had suddenly gone into a stall. Each time I would pull back on the joystick just as we were about to crash, and we would soar upward, but not to the heavens, just to the upper reaches of the living Hell that had come to define my existence.

After Lynn had performed a number of procedures, I finally accepted reality: I had been horribly disfigured and plastic surgery could only do so much. Yes, Lynn and I had taken small steps, but the path toward God knows what end seemed to roll on forever.

Oddly enough, the hospital was a sanctuary, a place where almost everyone other than staff was suffering in one way or another. There were unwritten rules for patients that most adhered to, especially those stuck there the longest. One was the need to respect the privacy of fellow patients despite often confined quarters. Another, more important, was to avoid reacting to the visible manifestations of another patient's misfortune.

Mostly I felt comfortable at home, where I spent two to three weeks after each operation, even though Janie was at work weekdays and I just rattled around our apartment. I read books, watched television, listened to records, did some drinking—more and more as time went on.

I rarely ventured out, almost never on my own. The less I saw of other people, by which I mean the less other people saw of me, the better. Janie and I took walks down to the beach, just three blocks from our apartment, in the early evening, rarely encountering anyone. When we did, I averted my eyes from them, hoping they would do the same, fearing they would not. Hardest of all for me were young kids, who would see me, point, and say something like, "Mommy, look at that man!" I tried to ignore them, and often succeeded. Not always. Sometimes I exploded.

This invariably happened when I couldn't disregard what a kid had said and I swung around to look at the speaker and saw a man with him or her. If the father had the least scent of the counterculture about him, as was almost always the case in Laguna Beach, I flared.

"Hey, asshole, how about teaching your kid not to stare?"

This usually resulted in the father hastily stepping in front of his child, no doubt to keep the youngster from being eaten by the monster glaring at him, uttering an obsequious apology, and hurrying away.

These encounters always left me shaking and unhinged. Janie was sympathetic for a time, but less so as such incidents continued.

"Honey, you can't keep turning on people who look at you funny or kids who have no idea what they're saying."

"Why not? Fuck 'em."

"Because you're never going to get beyond where you are if you don't figure out a way to handle this stuff!"

— — — —

Sometimes withholding sympathy, even when someone is crying out for it, can be therapeutic.

One of my many roommates during my time at Balboa was an Academy classmate who I didn't know at Annapolis and whose name now eludes me. He was a good guy, but a tough one. I think he was a SEAL.

One morning I was moping around our room, clearly unhappy. My roommate, who also had been wounded but less seriously than me, asked what my problem was. Mildly nonplussed at what I took to be his obliviousness, I snapped at him, said something like, "Jesus, look at me. I'm gonna have to go through my whole fucking life like this!"

After a few seconds my roommate replied, "Okay, sure. But think of it this way: You're not a girl."

I had no answer for that. My roommate had set a new standard for insensitivity. As the years passed, though, I came to think of his comment as the single funniest thing anyone said to me during the whole period of my convalescence. And for a time that morning I ceased my moping.

— — — —

Conversely, sometimes too much sympathy can backfire. Several months into my stay at Balboa, a corpsman I had not previously encountered came into my room to take me down for a routine X-ray prior to surgery the next day.

He was a friendly, enthusiastic kid who seemed to feel his every interaction with a patient should brighten the patient's day. Emotionally I was in worse shape than usual, and I revealed more to him about my state of mind than I meant to. In particular, in response to questions from him, I told him about my pervasive depression and about how deeply it pained me when I saw people staring at me.

"I've got an idea, Lieutenant," he said. "Hang on a second."

He scurried out of my room. When he returned, he was brandishing a pair of scissors and a brown paper grocery bag.

"What's the bag for?" I asked.

With that, he cut two holes about an inch and a half apart, about midway from the bottom of the bag.

"Here, Lieutenant, try this," he said, and handed the bag to me.

"What?"

"Put it over your head," he said. "This way no one can see your face. I can move the eyeholes if they're not in the right place."

I didn't know what to say. I pulled the bag over my head. The eyeholes were perfectly positioned. I climbed into the wheelchair he had brought with him and we headed to X-ray. Down one corridor, onto the elevator, down another corridor, into X-ray, then back along the same route.

Along the way people were staring at me, as well they should. Even in a hospital a patient in a wheelchair with a bag over his head is not a routine sight. My brain was spinning. Was this a terrible idea or a good one? I couldn't tell. At least people weren't reacting to my face. Did they think I was missing a head?

As it happened, Janie had pressured me to see one of the psychiatrists available at Balboa. My first appointment was that same day.

The psychiatrist was a friendly guy and clearly wanted to help me. I told him about the corpsman and the paper bag.

"Hm," he said, "that may not be such a bad idea."

Janie came by later that day. I showed her my bag. She went berserk, ripped it to shreds. Fortunately I didn't have to explain the destruction to the nice corpsman. I never saw him again. Nor the shrink.

Nine

NUT-CUTTING TIME (1)

In the fall there was a brief ceremony in the office of a general at the Marine Corps Recruit Depot in San Diego, where I received a not-terribly-impressive combat medal to go with my Purple Heart.

About this time the Marine Corps saw the writing on the wall—that I would never again qualify for active duty—and decided that I should be medically retired at the rank of captain. I went before a medical evaluation board, which determined that I was 100 percent disabled. That meant I would receive the highest possible monthly stipend, 60 percent of a captain's pay as of that year, 1967, indexed to inflation.

The board also had to decide whether my injuries were permanent or temporary. The latter status meant the percentage of my disability, upon which the stipend was based, would be periodically reassessed and reduced if my condition improved. The board said permanent, hardly a ringing endorsement of my prospects, but one that provided a baseline of financial predictability for the years ahead.

The document transferring me to the Marine Corps' medically retired rolls described my wounds as "highly repugnant." Till then, I'd never suspected the Corps of having a way with words.

I had a sense during this period that the routine of surgery, recovery, home, surgery would go on, if not forever, well into the future. By late fall, though, Janie began challenging that thinking.

You can't go on having surgery forever, she said. At some point, probably sooner rather than later, you're going to have to figure out where you go from here.

I didn't want to hear that, even though I was asking myself the same question. The problem was, I wasn't coming up with any answers. Anything having to do with the future seemed to mean getting a job, which meant leaving the safety of the hospital or our apartment, and I was in no way anxious to take that on.

"Are you talking about me going out to work every day?" I asked Janie.

"Yes," she said.

"Looking like this?" I asked incredulously.

"By then you're going to look better than you do now," she replied, "but, yes, you need to get back into the world. What's the other choice, sit around the apartment drinking beer and feeling sorry for yourself for the rest of your life?"

"I'm scared," I said.

"I know," said Janie. "We'll figure it out together."

— — — —

What could I do besides be a Marine? Did I have any skills that might carry over from the Corps to civilian life? Was anyone looking for a job applicant who could fieldstrip an M14 rifle or shoot Expert with a .45 caliber pistol? Or lead a rifle platoon in combat? The question was no longer academic by late winter when Lynn Ketchum dropped a bombshell.

"We're pretty close to the end of what we can do for a while," he said. "We've been moving at a pretty hectic pace. Time to let your skin heal."

"What does that mean? How long are we talking about?"

"A year at least, probably closer to two years, maybe a bit more."

"So, what happens to me?"

"We can do two, maybe three procedures in the next few months. By the summer, though, I'm going to discharge you from the hospital."

Stunned does not begin to describe my reaction. Discharge me from the hospital? To where? The apartment in Laguna? To sit around there for two years before I can go back to the hospital for more surgery? My head was spinning. Up till then I had a sense of progress, of moving forward, even if it wasn't especially evident. Now, it seemed, I would be dead in the water for the indefinite future.

"Actually," said Lynn, "we're going to be checking out together. The Navy's going to discharge me about the same time I discharge you."

"What are you going to do?" I asked, not making much of a show of caring; I was already starting to distance myself from Lynn, on whose judgment, skill, and friendship I had relied so heavily for the past year.

"Not sure yet, but I think I'm going to accept an offer to join a plastic surgery practice back in Kansas City."

"Great," I said, without much enthusiasm. "That's where you went to med school, right?"

"Actually, I did my residency in Kansas City, at the University of Kansas Medical Center. I went to medical school in New Orleans."

"Oh, right, I remember."

"So you need to think about your future, too."

"No shit," I replied, turning my back to him.

— — — —

Not long after, Janie dropped a bombshell of her own.
"I'm pregnant," she said, her delivery halting, as if fearful of my reaction.

"What did you say?"

"I said I'm pregnant. We're going to have a baby."

"Wow," I murmured, trying to process the news.

We just looked at each other for several seconds. Our plans for the future were at best unformed but in no way included a child anytime soon. All of a sudden I'm going to be booted out of the hospital and become a father as well.

Despite my scars, panic was evident on my face. Janie was expecting—correction—hoping for more from me.

"I thought you'd be at least a little bit excited," she said. I couldn't tell if she was disappointed or bristling. Then her eyes started to well up.

"Honey, look, I'm sorry. This is just such a shock to me. We never talked about having kids this soon. How did this happen? I thought you were on the pill."

"I was on the pill," she fired back. "It's not foolproof!"

"Obviously," I said.

— — — —

Janie and I now found ourselves confronting two issues we were monumentally unprepared to deal with. I would soon lose my relatively safe haven in the hospital, and a few months later we would become parents. I wrung my hands; Janie looked for solutions.

She had been thinking about our future for some time, long before Lynn said he was going to discharge me. At her urging, we had even batted around a few ideas, though for a long time I was a grudging participant in these discussions. We did settle on one thing: I needed to go to graduate school. And there was money for that under the VA's Vocational Rehabilitation program, a more elaborate version of the GI Bill, designed for seriously wounded veterans. The question was where to go and what to study and to what end.

As far back as the summer of 1967 we thought we had found the answer. The lead story of the July 27 *Time* magazine was entitled "Our Embattled Cities" and featured on its cover a Harvard professor named Daniel Patrick Moynihan. He was described as a pioneer in a new field, urbanology, the study of the dynamics of cities. As I read the article, I grew excited. I was a city kid and I liked cities. Urbanology seemed like something that might work for me. Soon it had moved to the top of my gauzy list of prospective professions. After reading the *Time* article, I raced to the library for a copy of *The Death and Life of Great American Cities*. I became even more excited as I read the Jane Jacobs classic.

Just as quickly the excitement wore off and urbanology was no longer an option. I came across a snippet that suggested, or flatly said, that urbanology required a significant use of statistics. I'd hated statistics at the Academy and barely made it through the course. My friends marveled at how poorly I did on statistics exams. "I don't believe in statistics," I told them.

Now, unlike the previous year, there was no time to toy with ideas. Graduate school applications were due in little more than a month, so Janie and I began a quest to find the field that I might enjoy and in which I had the potential to be productive. I thought of the academic disciplines that appealed to me—literature, history, sociology. Early on, Janie threw in a profession that had never occurred to me: journalism.

"You've always been a good writer," she said.

"I was a good writer at the Naval Academy because I could write a simple declarative sentence, which was not a common midshipman skill," I said. "My papers may have been deficient in substance, but they were not a chore to read. I think the instructors were grateful for that and I got away with a lot."

"You wrote good letters to me," Janie persisted. "You should think about journalism."

Not a chance. I was not crazy enough to choose a profession based on my proficiency at explicit or thinly veiled love letters. I summarily dismissed the idea for other reasons: I had never thought about it, never even brushed up against journalists, had never had a word in print anywhere, and was not even sure it was a profession. A total nonstarter.

Writing was a different story. I read a lot, appreciated good writing, and vaguely thought I might be a writer one day. Writers lead a solitary existence. That worked for me. There were a few graduate programs in creative writing, notably the Iowa Writers' Workshop at the University of Iowa, and one at Stanford that the novelist Wallace Stegner created in 1964. Since we were living in California, Stanford made more sense.

Rather than just applying, I wrote a letter to Professor Stegner, telling him about myself. I also sent him as a writing sample a short story I had written in Vietnam. The story was about a dragonfly that lands on a piece of flypaper on the makeshift desk of a Marine officer in Vietnam. The dragonfly struggles to free itself. The Marine watches the action and notes the resemblance between the insect and a UH-1 Huey helicopter. He blows cigarette smoke at the trapped dragonfly, trying to prod it to renew its efforts to pull itself free. Soon, though, tiny ants are marching toward the dragonfly, one after the other getting stuck on the flypaper till they form a bridge to the immobilized prey for their slower but wiser comrades. Scurrying over the helpless dragonfly, the ants quickly devour or tear loose whatever soft tissue exists. They then march back single file, across the bridge of their luckless brethren, to feast on the spoils. All that remains of the ravished dragonfly is its exoskeleton, which looks like a miniature version of a Huey gutted by fire.

Professor Stegner promptly replied with a gracious, encouraging letter. He said he found the story of the dragonfly intriguing. He recommended that I apply to the creative writing program at Stanford and left me feeling that my acceptance was likely.

Maybe it just seemed too easy, something that always makes me wary. Much stronger, though, was my sense that I was in over my head by corresponding with Wallace Stegner and thinking I could ever be more than someone who had faked his way through several courses at Annapolis by writing clean, if forgettable, prose. Perhaps if I had known more about Stegner, or made an effort to find out, I would have jumped at the chance. As it was, I had a vague sense that he was a person I'd like to know but nothing more. So I let the opportunity slip away.

Through most of my life, I had been an enthusiastic, at times aggressive, person. Now, faced with a decision that probably would define my future, I was surprisingly passive.

The truth was, I did not want to make a decision because once I did I would then have to implement it. And that meant routinely going outside and meeting people on a daily basis, which petrified me.

So in answer to Janie's brutal if inescapable question, no, I didn't want to sit around the apartment drinking and feeling sorry for myself. But better that than what I foresaw on the outside: random strangers glancing absently in my direction, their eyes momentarily widening before abruptly turning away. Folks in conversation hastily lowering their voices as they caught sight of me. Children being children, freaking me out. Street people promising to pray for me, something that happened a lot. Catching sight of myself in the window glass of a storefront.

We had reached nut-cutting time. Grad school applications were due in less than two weeks. I had to decide almost immediately what I wanted to study and where I wanted to go so I could fill out the applications, write the essays, and do whatever else needed to be done to ensure that I didn't piss away the next year.

But I was still perplexed. Conflicted would even better describe my state of mind. Janie and I haunted the public library, reading college catalogues. Almost everything seemed appealing—literature, history (especially modern history), sociology, political science. Even urbanology rallied, and writing staged a comeback. But would Wallace Stegner remember me if I wanted to try creative writing when I hadn't even acknowledged his warm letter?

I needed to make a decision. I sat in our small kitchen, leaning back in my chair, and stared glassy-eyed at the ceiling. I hadn't said a word in several minutes. I was talked out; there was nothing left to say. I finally understood the etymology of "tongue-tied." I rolled my eyes toward Janie, who was sitting on the floor, her arms wrapped around her knees.

"I have an idea," she said brightly. Christ, how the hell could she be perky at a time like this?

I didn't bother to answer.

"Do you want to hear it?"

I still didn't bother to answer.

"Here's what I think," she said, her tone curiously enthusiastic. "I think you should think about journalism again."

As I turned away dismissively, she raised her voice a few octaves. "Just listen," she said. "As a journalist you're not stuck in one field. You can be interested in all of them. Plus you get to write about all of them."

It took a few seconds for her words to register. Then they fired through my brain at the speed of light, as if it were a pinball machine, the silver ball bounding from spinners to bumpers to flippers and every other target on the game table, setting them all flashing madly.

"Holy shit," I murmured, realizing that her idea was not as crazy as it first seemed. I read the *Los Angeles Times* every morning. I liked it, even knew some of the bylines—Bob Donovan was one, Jack Nelson was another—and found their work, if not their jobs, fascinating and illuminating.

The more I thought about it, their jobs sounded pretty interesting, too. Suddenly everything except being a Marine and being a reporter seemed really boring. How crazy was that? But I needed to make a decision, fast, so all sorts of considerations flew out the window.

I interrogated myself.

Q. You've never written anything for anyone that's been printed anywhere. How do you overcome that?

A. Doesn't matter. I've done harder things.

Q. Of all the professions you've considered, this is the most public, the one more likely than any other to expose you to strangers, including kids. How are you going to deal with that? You've done a really shitty job so far in such situations.

A. I don't know. I just know that I'm gonna do it.

Q. Really, why are you doing this?

A. Gotta do something.

NUT-CUTTING TIME (1)

— — — —

I may have gotten a few of the details wrong, but that's how it happened. It came together that quickly. After weeks, actually months, of anxiety and introspection, the decision was made. When, years later, someone asked how I got into journalism, I would tell them I threw a dart and that's where it landed. Against all odds, too, because the space on the target for journalism was barely a sliver.

In truth, there were two factors that finally forced the decision. First, Lynn telling me he was going to discharge me. Second, my realization that time had run out. It was either do something now—right now!—or take up basket weaving.

In my mind, it was like a couple of burly Marines were beating the crap out of me and they kept saying, "Say it, Lieutenant!" After a while I couldn't take anymore, so I said it: "Uncle!" But the Marines kept pummeling me and demanding, "Goddammit, say it, Lieutenant!" Finally I said it.

"Journalism."

The beating stopped. I think the Marines would have accepted anything. They just couldn't tolerate a fellow Leatherneck, an officer no less, who was too fucked up to make a decision.

Ten

THE WICHITA LINEMAN

Janie and I arrived in Palo Alto in August 1968, barely a month before Stanford's fall semester was to begin. I had been accepted in the journalism graduate programs at Stanford, UC Berkeley, and UCLA. I chose Stanford in part because Janie received her best job offer from a school in San Bruno, about twenty miles north of Palo Alto. Mostly, though, Stanford just seemed to have a more human scale.

Laguna, which was hard to leave for any number of reasons, embodied the quirky side of the Sixties counterculture—an artsy hippie haven of outlandish clothes, drug varietals to tickle every palate, bizarre, often obnoxious, though rarely threatening behavior. Perhaps unfairly, I thought of most young people in Laguna as wacky, relatively well-educated beach bums screwing around until they cleaned up their acts or completely wrecked their lives.

The Bay Area had a harder edge to it. Students at the schools clustered in and around San Francisco seemed deadly serious in their determination to change the world, starting with bringing the war in Vietnam to an end. Many of them struck me as humorless, but at least they had loftier aspirations than getting marijuana legalized and keeping laws outlawing LSD off the books.

Berkeley, centerpiece of the superb University of California system, had been the breeding ground of the Free Speech Movement four years earlier, and birthplace of the Vietnam Day Committee, formed in 1965 by Jerry Rubin, Abbie Hoffman, and others. The VDC organized antiwar rallies and marches in California and elsewhere.

San Francisco State College, presided over by the fiery S. I. Hayakawa, was the site of numerous high-profile demonstrations, some violent, led by the Black Student Union, Third World Liberation Front, and Students for a Democratic Society.

Then there was Stanford, the only private institution among the three, and viewed until a decade or so earlier as a finishing school for California's moneyed youth. But by the time Janie and I rolled into town in our VW convertible, with its yellow flower-power daisy affixed to the chassis, Stanford was streaking toward the upper reaches of the nation's higher education establishment and was poised to claim a spot on the top rung with Berkeley and the Ivies. By then it also was gaining a reputation as a hotbed of student activism.

In May, three months before we got there, Stanford's Naval ROTC building was burned to the ground by an early morning fire, completing the work of a less aggressive blaze in March. In July, arson destroyed the office of the university's president, J. Wallace Sterling, a major force in expanding the reach and reputation of the school. The fire caused $300,000 worth of damage and destroyed priceless possessions Sterling had accumulated during his four decades in higher education. But as Janie and I hauled shipping boxes up to our new apartment we were barely aware, if we were aware at all, of the unrest on the Stanford campus.

— — — —

We had found the apartment during an earlier trip to the Bay Area—two bedrooms on the second floor of a two-story complex that discouraged children other than those traveling *in utero*, whom management tolerated or failed to notice. The amenities included a swimming pool and a small grassy area suitable for grilling and picnicking. We were not in Palo Alto proper but rather in what felt like a white compound in the predominantly black community of East Palo Alto. EPA, as some called it, actually was north of Palo Alto. Just a few months before we moved in, voters there had narrowly turned back an effort to rename it Nairobi.

As we settled in, I was mostly oblivious to my surroundings, lost in my own tortured thoughts as I struggled to come to grips with the breathtakingly stupid decision I had made a couple of months earlier. I had forsaken a miserable but protected life in our Laguna apartment for a year of basking in the furtive stares of my fellow students followed by a career of rushing up to people with a pen and notebook only to have them shriek, call a cop, run away, or bash me with their umbrellas.

Janie calmed my fears, talking me down, reflecting my concerns, but keeping me focused on the need not to crumble before I even began the formidable journey we both knew awaited us. Her message: Don't let this beat you; one foot in front of the other.

Janie needed the VW to commute to San Bruno, so I was going to have to come up with another way to get to school. I bought a sleek, black Raleigh three-speed. No idea how to ride it, but the guy in the bike store gave me a quick tutorial.

I anticipated the two-mile ride to school with dread. I vaguely wondered if I could outfit myself with blinders, like a racehorse, so I could only see straight ahead and avoid the shocked faces of pedestrians and the drivers motoring past me. That was clearly impractical. Almost without knowing it, though, I began to develop the first of what would grow into a complex web of defense mechanisms: During the ride, I somehow managed to short-circuit almost anything in my surroundings that related to my disfigurement.

Thanks to this fortuitous and probably fragile new talent the ride to the Communication Building, where I had most of my classes, was reasonably pleasant. I sang to myself as I pedaled, which helped even more. My repertoire contained one song, "Wichita Lineman," as rendered by Glen Campbell, words and music by Jimmy Webb.

I am a lineman for the county
And I drive the main road
Scarchin' in the sun for another overloud.
I hear you singing in the wire,
I can hear you through the whine,
And the Wichita Lineman
Is still on the line.

It was not a favorite song, just the one that popped into my head the first time I rode the bike to school. Having negotiated the two miles without crashing or causing people to run away as if fleeing a tidal wave or, more to the point, Godzilla, I stayed with "Wichita Lineman," like a ballplayer on a hitting streak who wears the same underwear day after day.

The Stanford campus was green everywhere. Soaring above it was the 285-foot-tall Hoover Tower and its forty-eight-bell carillon. San Francisco's high-rises, some fifty miles distant, were visible from the observation deck.

A few palm trees were scattered among the live oaks and elms, but to me, coming from Southern California and before that Southeast Asia, there was a distinctly eastern feel to the campus. (In fact, the founder, railroad magnate Leland Stanford, visited the president of Harvard to discuss duplicating that school in Palo Alto.) Perhaps it was in the scale or the placement of buildings since the architecture was anything but eastern, most academic buildings displaying buff sandstone exteriors, red tile roofs, and stone colonnades punctuated every few yards by muscular arches.

— — — —

This is what I knew about journalism as I began a first semester that supposedly would lead to a master's degree the following spring:

Nothing.

I knew newspapers were protected by the First Amendment, certainly understood their importance, but had no idea how to report, write, edit, or produce them. Oh, and I didn't know how to type. I had a vague sense that I was training to be a reporter. Years later, when I was a reasonably seasoned newsman, my father, who was a bona fide genius when it came to music but painfully naïve about many other things, asked about my job:

"So, Bobby, what do you do every day? Drive around in your car and look for fires?"

Frankly, that's pretty much what I figured I'd be doing as my Raleigh three-speed coasted to a stop at the Communication Building to begin classes.

Years earlier, on the first day of high school, my knees turned to Jell-O when I realized I was the only kid in biology class who didn't know what a molecule was. History was now repeating itself: Everyone in my newswriting class spoke a language foreign to me. They spoke of leads, extended leads, inverted pyramids, nut graphs, the rewrite desk, copy editors, makeup (makeup?). I quickly realized it was jargon, the language of my new profession. I had already learned the jargon of the Naval Academy and the Marine Corps, not to mention various sports, so how hard could this be?

It wasn't hard at all. In fact, after a week or so the writing exercises and everything else we did in the classroom were easy. I had never had a word in print in my life, knew no one who worked for a paper, but I was beginning to think this journalism deal just might work out. Maybe it was in my DNA or in an exotic chromosome that had been awaiting a secret signal to declare itself. For a brief time, I thought I might be a natural.

It did not take long for me to realize I was kidding myself. All it took was for me to focus on a skill indispensable to reporters: talking to people, mostly strangers. Interviewing was at the heart of what reporters do. And if you couldn't do it and do it well, you were in the wrong job. And I wasn't prepared to do it. Not nearly. On the phone, sure, but not in person.

This was a problem and I knew it. And if it was a problem in the relatively insulated confines of a college campus, how damaging would it be a year or so from now when I was hopefully working as a reporter, which meant going anywhere and everywhere to get the story, bouncing off strangers all the way.

I came up with a couple of devices to deal with the problem, at least at Stanford. First I kicked the can down the road, the Scarlett O'Hara solution, persuading myself to set the issue off to the side and worry about it when it made sense to worry about it. As Janie said, one foot in front of the other. For the time being, just fuck it!

The other device was gaming the reporting assignments. We had quite a few, and they all required reporting outside the classroom, often off campus. Implicit in the assignments was the requirement for quotes, both to enliven the copy ("copy," as I had learned, was the newspaper word for an unedited story) and to nail down key points.

I managed to get through the entire semester without ever talking face-to-face to anyone I didn't already know. Instead, I fulfilled the assignments by covering all sorts of meetings—city council, planning board, board of education—where I could sit in the back of the room, take notes of what was being said, and collect many if not all the quotes I needed.

Then if the council was discussing widening a road or cleaning up a lot or rehabbing a school, I would go to the site so I could work a physical description of it into my story. A small addition like that would take the story out of the meeting room and let it breathe (another newspaper word).

I also made several phone calls to fill in gaps in the story, thus gathering more quotes and a deeper appreciation of the issue. Finally I would write my story and turn it in.

Essentially I was covering my tracks. But I did it well. Someone would have to read the story closely to realize that although I had quoted a number of people in it, I had never gone up to anyone and said, "Hi, I'm Bob Timberg. I'm a reporter. I'd like to ask you some questions." It's also possible that my instructors knew what I was doing, but out of a kindness rarely attributed to newspaper people never called me on it.

I took similarly evasive action in other courses. In Magazine Writing, I wrote a long feature about the birth of our son, Scott, in February at Stanford Hospital. Janie and I took a Lamaze course, and she had the baby by natural childbirth. The story was a good one. It had color, tension, and humor and captured the pain and strain of the moment of birth and the exhilaration that followed. But the characters in the tale were Janie, me, the obstetrician, some random medical personnel, the members of our Lamaze class, and Scott. Another closed system.

I worked hard at Stanford and received good grades, except in what I considered a wild-card course, Communication Theory, which involved such things as cognitive dissonance, Bobo dolls, the experiments of B. F. Skinner, operant behavior, and the effect of television violence on kids. The course was mildly interesting and taught by a giant in the field, Nathan Maccoby, but for me it seemed irrelevant. I was working to become as good a reporter as I had been a Marine, so I spent only as much time on it as I had to.

—— —— —— ——

Most of my time on campus I was in class or in the common room of the Communication Building, a relatively small, stand-alone structure bereft of architectural flair. Students gathered there, but it was a manageable crowd. Some were in my classes. Through them I met other journalism students, along with those in the Communication Department's radio-TV and film programs.

At first I was uncomfortable both in class and in the common areas, but the more I met and talked to the other students the more relaxed I became. My personality and bearing, it seemed, melded with their fundamental decency. And somehow I managed to induce them to see behind the scarring, neutralizing them as threats to my fragile psyche. Some warm relationships blossomed. I was becoming more comfortable in groups, though I remained petrified in crowds.

I rarely strolled the campus, beautiful as it was. The way I figured it, the less people saw of me the better. Fewer shocked looks to endure, fewer chances of overhearing a devastating whispered comment.

Sometimes, despite my wariness, I found myself among my fellow students as I traveled from one part of the campus to another. Their appearance covered a wide spectrum. At one end were those who dressed like me, in jeans or khakis and a sport shirt, and whose hairstyles were undistinguished. At the other end were the long-haired, self-absorbed faux warriors who wore camouflage utilities and VC sandals or combat boots and lived their opposition to the war. At times I felt like I had infiltrated an alien nation inhabited by creatures with whom I had nothing in common. Where I came from blind men or disfigured men or men without legs or arms or both struggled to build some semblance of a future, never quite overcoming the recognition that in most important ways their lives had ended before they had even begun—like me, old men before their time.

This was the issue: Most Stanford men were about my age, but almost none had been in the service, let alone fought in Vietnam. A few, no doubt, had genuine physical infirmities that disqualified them from serving, but the vast majority managed to evade the not terribly long arm of Selective Service by availing themselves of a variety of deferments (an allergy to eggs was my favorite), sympathetic doctors willing to falsify medical records, a network of draft counselors, or courageously taking extended sojourns to hellholes like Canada and Sweden. Their worst fears, to my unforgiving mind, had to do with failing to get into the right grad school.

— — — —

The most important lesson I learned at Stanford was tolerance. Not tolerance as it's usually understood—the acceptance of people's differences, whether physical characteristics such as race and sexual orientation or intellectual qualities like religion and political beliefs. Tolerance in this context meant accepting people just like me, almost, whom I would thoroughly despise if I allowed myself to think about them in anything other than the most superficial way.

After a year and a half in and out of hospitals, despite enduring my own pain and observing the anguish of wounded comrades, I had developed, without even knowing it, a kind of survivor's instinct that pulled me back whenever I edged too close to an emotion that might immobilize me, even destroy me: irreconcilable anger toward, perhaps even hatred of, the lion's share of the male members of my generation.

I also had to deal with the realization that the war, unlike other wars, was not a burden equally shared and that the social contract as I understood it had been shattered. Poor kids were being marched off to war; middle- and upper-class kids, such as most of my fellow male students at Stanford, had come up with a variety of novel ways to steer clear of it.

Intuitively I understood that it was important that I not act like the stereotype of the Vietnam veteran then gaining currency in the mass media: a wild-eyed, unpredictable, short-fused, violence-prone, ticking time bomb.

My friend Eric Smith, who served in the Army in Vietnam, was attending Georgetown's law school about the same time I was at Stanford. One day he was heading to class when a student he barely knew began ragging him about his service in-country. "Hey, how many babies did you kill over there?" and "How many villages did you burn down with your Zippo?" That kind of thing.

Eric tried to ignore the guy as he seated himself at a long table in the front of the room. The guy persisted in baiting Eric, taking a seat at the far end of the same table. Eric had been in Intelligence, not a grunt, but he figured he'd never convince the guy he wasn't a crazy Vietnam vet. So he decided to play to the stereotype. Short but well built, he reached across the two students between him and his tormentor, grabbed the guy by the ears, and pulled him along the tabletop until they were eyeball-to-eyeball—so close it looked like Eric was about to bite the guy's nose off.

"Listen to me, you little motherfucker," said Eric, his voice soaked in menace. "If you ever say anything like that to me again I'm going to cut your balls off and stuff them down your throat." Then, still holding the guy by the ears, he dropped his head on the table.

No one at Stanford ever baited me like that. I'd like to think students there were classier, but I also believe none of them had the heart to berate someone, even a presumed war criminal like me, as disfigured as I was. For whatever reason, I was glad to have gotten a pass from the antiwar crowd. I was unlikely to be as gentle as Eric if my war record was questioned as his had been.

A factor other than self-preservation kept the rage I felt from blasting to the surface: the war itself. I had remained ambivalent about it. Good war, bad war—I hadn't spent a lot of time thinking about it before or during my time in Vietnam. I wasn't a "my country, right or wrong" guy, but I did believe that the United States and its leaders were reasonably wise, generously motivated, and, as important, competent. Now, after the Tet Offensive in January, Walter Cronkite's pronouncement a few weeks later that the nation was "mired in stalemate," and President Johnson's renunciation of his office in March, I became less sure that the country was on the side of the angels. And even if it was, I had become less and less confident that LBJ and Defense Secretary Robert McNamara, whom the former had just exiled from the Pentagon to the presidency of the World Bank, knew what the hell they were doing.

I was perplexed, torn between two views. On one hand, I believed if called a man should be willing to take up arms for his country, even if the cause was murky and the reasons for going to war not clearly defined. On the other hand, what should a man do if he honestly believed the war was a ghastly mistake, as so many seemed to? Go anyway, taking a chance of being killed or maimed like me or killing another man while defying his own conscience?

The truth is, I did believe that many of the men in the antiwar movement had studied contemporary Vietnamese history and concluded that we never should have gotten involved in the first place and we needed to get out as fast as we could. But I also believed that those men who had educated themselves about the war were just a fraction—much less than half—of those making up the antiwar movement. The others were fellow travelers, joining up because they viewed it as their main chance for staying out of Vietnam—either by bringing the war to an end or by becoming part of a network of middle-class kids who would help them evade the draft.

If we were to believe the party line, the hundreds of thousands, if not millions, of men in the various wings of the antiwar movement understood the complexities of the Vietnam conflict, while those of us who went were too dumb to know any better.

For a time I quietly despised without distinction members of the antiwar movement even though I knew I was playing with fire by giving in to this emotion. But I soon realized I despised the fellow travelers and hangers-on more than those whose intellect told them the war was a mistake. Viscerally I despised them, too, but not for their beliefs, which were becoming mine. In fact, I was not really sure why I felt as I did.

Who am I kidding? I despised them because I could not fathom how one part of my generation could watch from the sidelines as the other part was marched off to war! So what did I want them to do? I didn't know, I just wanted them to do something other than make noise, stage weekend circle jerks, and dodge the draft.

The answer to my dilemma materialized in the person of David Harris.

Harris, elected Stanford's student body president in 1966, was by the following year an avid and high-profile opponent of the war. He founded an organization called The Resistance and counseled young men to resist the draft, not by hiding behind deferments or fleeing the country, but by refusing to be drafted even if it meant going to jail. As good as his word, Harris refused to report when he received his draft notice in January 1968. This led to his arrest and conviction in May for draft evasion. He was sentenced to three years in federal prison. (While out on bail in March, he married another antiwar figure, the folk singer Joan Baez.)

This was my answer. If you were against the war, fine, you didn't have to go into the Army and hump the hills and rice paddies and jungles of South Vietnam. But there was no free lunch. Somehow you had to put yourself in peril in a way that mirrored the dangers faced by millions of other men of your generation. I wasn't sure which was more dangerous, the Big House or the boonies. Probably the boonies, but it wasn't an easy call and the guys willing to go to the slammer like David Harris were okay by me.

———

At times Stanford seemed like a parallel universe in which the inhabitants walked and talked and looked like me and my wartime comrades but in truth were our mirror images a little worse for wear.

I tried not to view matters in terms of them and us but rarely succeeded. They were whole and we were not. That was it in a nutshell. Not only did these guys not go to Vietnam, few even knew anyone who had. These guys were playing Frisbee on the Quad; my friends were propelling themselves around in wheelchairs and learning Braille.

I did not fixate on these things and rarely if ever talked about them. I was at Stanford for a number of reasons, none of which involved refighting a war that may not have been worth fighting in the first place or calling out those who found better things to do than wear a uniform.

For Janie, the time at Stanford might have been fun, but wasn't. She only taught in San Bruno through Thanksgiving, as school-district rules required her to take maternity leave three months before her due date. Deprived of her school-based social network, she reluctantly settled in at our apartment complex, where nearly all our neighbors were childless young professionals who were gone during the day.

A sense of isolation set in, which I failed to do much to relieve. My days were full, with classes during the day, occasionally in the evening. And if I didn't have close friends, I did have something akin to friendship with a few schoolmates with whom I enjoyed chatting between classes.

David Jones was majoring in filmmaking, not journalism, but we had something in common: We were both Marines. David didn't seem to take particular pride in his time in the Corps, and he was discharged before Vietnam, but the experience gave him standing in my eyes to oppose the war, which he emphatically did. He was a smart guy, and I liked him a lot. Through him, I learned about French New Wave films. Soon I could fake my way through discussions of Godard, Truffaut, Chabrol, auteur theory, jump cuts, and tracking shots like Godard's seven-minute visual exploration of a traffic jam in *Weekend*. I watched other Godard classics like *Breathless*, which left me confused but forever smitten by Jean Seberg. I didn't even fully understand Truffaut's *Shoot the Piano Player*, which was probably the most accessible of the French films I watched, as well as having my favorite title.

Carol and Lory Marlantes were the closest Janie and I had to shared friends, but the relationship was sporadic, our social activities sharply curtailed following Scott's birth. Lory was a doctoral candidate in economics; Carol was my classmate in the journalism program. We had dinner together a few times, either at their apartment or ours, and that was about it. The relationship was memorable, though, because Carol and Lory were, to my mind, the golden couple—smart, handsome, sophisticated, and, it seemed, invulnerable.

Lory missed the war because of an injury suffered playing football for the University of Washington, but his brother Karl carried the family standard into battle. Though he was in no way obligated to do so, Karl put the Rhodes scholarship he had been awarded on hold so he could serve as a Marine infantry officer. In Vietnam his actions earned him the Navy Cross, second only to the Medal of Honor among the nation's awards for combat gallantry. (Karl powerfully captured Vietnam combat in his highly acclaimed 2009 novel *Matterhorn*.)

Carol seemed to have stepped out of something by Fitzgerald—the beautiful, elusive woman over whom men are destined to make fools of themselves: Judy Jones of "Winter Dreams," or Josephine of "A Woman with a Past." Her voice underscored her beauty. Like Gatsby's Daisy, she had "the kind of voice that the car follows up and down, as if each speech is an arrangement of notes that will never be played again."

At times, though she never said anything about it to me, I sensed that Janie was uncomfortable around Carol, even mildly intimidated by her, not that Carol ever did anything to elicit such a response. I think it had to do with where we all were in our lives. Before Stanford, Carol had worked with Bill Moyers in Lyndon Johnson's White House, which gave her cachet, a kind of glamour that she never flaunted but that intensified her luminescence. Janie, by contrast, was either pregnant or a new mother during this time, and she seemed to feel dowdy though she never was. And once her pregnancy forced her to give up her teaching job, she was deprived of the professional and personal satisfaction she had received on a daily basis working with special ed kids.

Carol never flirted with me, which occasionally depressed me. Not that I was any less in love with or committed to Janie. I just hated being so unattractive that even the thought of straying was craziness, and temptation as out of reach as the green light at the end of Daisy's dock that Gatsby could never quite grasp.

Eleven

SYLVIA SAMURAI

My time at Stanford should have ended in the summer of 1969. By then, in theory, I would hold a master's degree in journalism and a job at some news organization, presumably a newspaper. The thought of blithely stepping out into that world, however, petrified me. So during the spring semester, when most of my classmates were applying for jobs, I was doggedly not completing work on my master's project, the final requirement for my degree.

The subject of my project was *PM*, a scrappy, mildly leftist New York tabloid started in 1940 that was perhaps best known for its policy of not accepting advertising to underscore its freedom from corporate pressure.

PM struck me as a worthy topic for a master's thesis, though hardly a compelling one. But it had a number of elements that recommended it, notably Ken Stewart, a kindly sixty-seven-year-old visiting professor from Berkeley.

Stewart had worked for a dozen papers, including the *Fresno Bee*, *El Paso Times*, *Atlanta Journal*, *New York Herald Tribune*, and *New York Times*. At age seventeen he was a full-fledged reporter for the *Humboldt* (California) *Times*.

For me, his most impressive and useful credential was his experience at *PM*, where he had been a founding member of the staff and national news editor. Of greatest importance, truly pure gold, was something I didn't know until I had committed myself to telling the story of *PM*. Stewart had an unpublished draft manuscript that chronicled the *PM* saga from birth to death.

Hard to imagine a less demanding master's project. Professor Stewart's manuscript provided an understanding of the motives of the men who started the paper, their problems and successes, money issues, and the colorful and talented characters who peopled the newsroom. So why didn't I finish up by the end of the semester, like most of my classmates?

I didn't want to. I had come to think of the Communication Department as an entity I had somehow neutralized and made safe for myself, a variation on the San Diego Naval Hospital. From time to time I imagined zapping classmates with a ray gun that caused them to see me the way I wanted to be seen. Ray gun or not, I had made friends in the department and was comfortable there. More to the point, I feared placing myself in a totally new and terrifying situation, especially if that meant taking a job, with all that portended. I was just not ready to step back into the world.

— — — —

That summer I took a film course, taught by Henry Breitrose, a knowledgeable and engaging professor, and his teaching assistant, an earnest grad student named David Denby. The course was fascinating, covering film history back before *The Birth of a Nation*, along with exercises in film criticism. "Don't assign grades," David sternly advised me when my first critique was filled with words like "good," "bad," "impressive," "weak." "Engage with the movie. Tell us about it, show us where it works or doesn't work, and why." I didn't realize it at the time, but he was teaching me a cardinal rule of all writing, one that I had somehow failed to pick up during the previous academic year but which I've tried to follow ever since:

Show, don't tell.

We had to make a movie for the class, a short one, ten or fifteen minutes, using an 8 mm movie camera. We had been studying Japanese films when we received the assignment. I had become an admirer of the director Akira Kurosawa, whose best-known films—*Rashomon*, *Yojimbo*, and *Seven Samurai*, among others—were filled with samurai warriors, lots of swordplay, and often starred the fearsome and gifted actor Toshiro Mifune. I decided I would make a not terribly serious action film in the Kurosawa tradition. Thus was hatched the immortal *Sylvia Samurai*, starring Jane Timberg as Sylvia and Scott Timberg, age six months, as The Child.

The movie was set in the backyard of my sister Pat and her husband Dan's home in the San Jose suburb of Milpitas, an irresistibly comic name that I tried to work into the movie but never figured out how. The plot involved a kidnapping gone awry. Pat and Dan, a Navy pilot, were the hapless kidnappers. Sylvia rescues The Child, then dispatches the villains with a samurai sword that my Uncle Marty brought home from the Philippines after World War II.

———

Shooting *Sylvia Samurai* was fun. Little else was that summer. Most of my friends had moved on. I remained dead in the water, doing next to nothing to advance my future. As the weeks passed, though, my inertia came to be too much even for me. And Janie, though uncomplaining as usual, began gently suggesting that perhaps I should begin thinking about my next step.

Grudgingly, I agreed. There were still enough of my friends around looking for jobs, so I threw myself into the mix, essentially following their lead. I bought a book about writing résumés and began putting one together. I had two major concerns. First, I didn't know what to say, or whether I should say anything, about my wounds. I didn't want to give a potential employer reason to reject me without even interviewing me. I also didn't want him to think I was trying to use my disability to obtain favored treatment. On the other hand, he no doubt would be stunned if I walked into his office without forewarning him that I was different from the usual job seeker.

Fortunately, my résumé guide provided the answer. If you are handicapped, it advised, don't keep it a secret. Doing so could result in an awkward interview. I took the advice, mentioned the disfigurement in my cover letter. I did not include the fact that the Marine Corps considered me 100 percent disabled. That was more than a potential employer needed to know.

The other major concern was my total lack of experience as a journalist. I did not have a single newspaper or magazine article to send to prospective employers. Nothing from high school or the Academy, not even from grad school, when I could have easily worked for the *Stanford Daily*. At the time, though I sensed it, I had no real idea how ridiculous it was to apply for a newspaper job without clippings of stories that a future boss could look at to evaluate an applicant's talent and potential. In place of news clips, I sent classroom assignments, the reporting exercises that I had pretty much faked my way through over the past year.

Perhaps if I were seventeen, as Ken Stewart had been when he was hired by the *Humboldt Times*, I might have been forgiven the absence of a track record. But I was approaching my thirtieth birthday, very much an advanced age for a cub reporter.

And I was not applying to the *Humboldt Times*. In an astonishing combination of hubris and naïveté, I had written to the editors of the *San Francisco Chronicle*, *Los Angeles Times*, *Denver Post*, *Kansas City Star*, *St. Louis Post-Dispatch*, *Washington Post*, *Boston Globe*, and *Baltimore Sun*, essentially most of the major papers I had heard of aside from the *New York Times*, the only one that struck me as a bridge too far.

I received written replies to all my letters, either from the editors themselves or their senior deputies. The responses were courteous and, to a degree, personal. No one had a job available, nor did they expect one to open up anytime soon, but I was invited to stop by and introduce myself if by chance I ever found myself in their city.

All also sent warm wishes, though no one asked me to travel at their paper's expense for an interview, which I interpreted as meaning they were nice people who wanted to be kind to a disabled veteran but were wary of being too encouraging since there was no way in hell that they were going to hire me.

Despite my ambivalence about actually getting a job, my competitive juices, numbed since the day I was wounded more than two years earlier, began bubbling to the surface when I realized I was getting the standard kiss-off letter customized for veterans. More polite than most, perhaps, but kiss-offs nonetheless.

I was angry, but there was a degree of zaniness to my anger. I didn't really want a job, but I didn't want to not be offered one, either. I had devoted time, energy, and thought to putting together application packets for some ten newspapers, including a résumé, a personalized cover letter, and classroom reporting assignments tediously copied. I wanted the papers to which I had applied to do more than blow in my ear.

What now?

The editors, as gently as possible, had delivered a crushing message. Decoded, it said, we have no job for you now and probably never will. In an abundance of generosity, though, they had failed to snip off all the loose ends. At the Naval Academy we called them "Irish pennants," and there could be hell to pay if any were found dangling off your dress blues at Saturday noon meal inspection. In this instance, the Irish pennant, the loose end, was the invitation to stop by and say hello if I ever was in their city. Flailing, I tugged on the errant thread. Most of these editors, I figured, had no expectation that I would ever show up at their office. What if I did, what if I traveled, say, to Denver or Kansas City or St. Louis or wherever at my own expense?

I discussed the idea with Janie. Why don't we just hop in the car and go to all these places? It would display seriousness of purpose and a commitment to journalism. Probably not enough to cover the absence of a single newspaper clipping, but who knew what the hell might happen if I got in the door?

I was proposing a car trip from the West Coast to the East Coast and back again with a colicky six-month-old. Janie was game, but pointed out that attempting the trip with our VW convertible was not in the cards. We need something bigger and sturdier, she said.

We didn't have a lot of money, but we had some, so we settled on a VW bus. It was larger, though not much sturdier, as I would soon learn.

Twelve

NUT-CUTTING TIME (2)

I mapped out the trip, figuring how long it would take to get from one city to the next, and alerted all my editor contacts that I would soon be in their town and looked forward to taking them up on their offer to meet with me. Then, by letter and phone call, I managed to put together an itinerary designed to take me across the country with an interview every day or every other day depending on the distance between cities.

In early October, we strapped Scott into his baby carrier in our new VW bus, piled in enough clothes and sundries to carry us through a month (about what we figured the trip would take), and headed south to Los Angeles and an interview at the *Los Angeles Times*.

The *Times* interview was encouraging, but no offer and no promises. I felt good though. I was finally trying to make something happen. My interview at the *Denver Post* was much the same, warm and friendly, but no offers and no promises.

Snow was falling when we awoke the next morning in the motel, outside Denver, where we had spent the night. We loaded the bus and headed east, next stop Kansas City, where I was to interview with the *Kansas City Star*. We were fortunate that we had made it over the Rockies two days earlier because the snow was coming down harder as we merged onto Interstate 70 and moved into hilly but no longer mountainous eastern Colorado.

The snow continued to intensify as we passed a string of small towns—Cedar Point, Limon, Wild Horse—and we considered, then dismissed, the idea of stopping at one of them. Not a well-thought-out decision. Soon the snow was blowing horizontally and the car radio was calling the storm a ground blizzard, a disquieting term I had never heard before. We were beyond the point of no return when I realized that we were in big trouble. I now understood what the weather guys meant when they talked about "whiteout conditions."

The road ahead was visible for about ten yards as our wipers labored gallantly to clear the windshield. Even so, I had to climb down every few minutes to scrape away the snow and ice that the blades had caused to pile up along the sides of the glass. And more roadworthy vehicles kept overtaking us, coating the bus with layers of slush as they blew by.

We had slowed to a crawl, which created its own set of problems. The heater, it seemed, depended on the speed of the bus, the faster we traveled the more heat, and vice versa. When we stopped, no heat. If barely moving, as we were, barely any heat. The temperature outside was in the teens, inside not much warmer. And the bus reacted like a sailboat in choppy seas and gale-force winds. It was all I could do to keep the damn thing from flipping over when I wasn't battling to keep it from sliding off the road into a ditch.

And there was nowhere to stop and take shelter. We were on as godforsaken a stretch of road as I had ever seen, with only a gas station here and there to distinguish it from the surface of the moon. Scott was amazingly docile, which was very unlike him, and I worried that his blood might be freezing in his little veins. I didn't mention this to Janie for fear of spooking her, though I did suggest she poke him to get him moving around a bit.

It seemed like a lifetime, but it was only four hours when we pulled into the crowded parking lot of a motel in Cheyenne Wells, a few miles from the Kansas border.

"I hope to hell they have a room," I said to Janie, as I turned off the ignition. My eyes felt as big as saucers and probably looked that way, too. I closed them, then let my head slump back.

overweening feeling of gratitude I gave him somewhat more. He returned the favor by giving me a spare fuse and showing me how to install it.

Our next stop was Kansas City, probably the Missouri version, but I wasn't sure. I also wasn't sure who I was interviewing with. I thought the *Kansas City Star*, Hemingway's paper, but it may have been the *Kansas City Times*, the *Star*'s sister paper that I hadn't known existed.

I interviewed with Dave Jones, who was either the managing editor or the city editor of the *Star* or the *Times*, as well as the namesake of my filmmaking pal at Stanford. Like the editors I had met at the *LA Times* and the *Denver Post*, he was friendly and seemed happy to meet me. But unlike the other two he gave off vibes that made me feel he might actually want to hire me.

We talked about Stanford, my late-blooming interest in journalism, Vietnam, and jobs. I was looking to be a reporter, but Jones, without discouraging that plan, sounded me out about a copy editor's position as well.

I had never thought of being a copy editor. My J-school friends and I joked about copy editors as guys in green eyeshades who sit around the newsroom all day smoking cigarettes and drinking cold coffee as they correct comma faults. We knew better, of course. Copy editors, who had to okay stories before they went into print, were the unsung heroes of the newsroom. They rode herd on spelling, grammar, and punctuation, but they did much more. They fact-checked stories, kicked them back to reporters when they seemed structurally deficient, awkwardly phrased, insufficiently supported, or even mildly off point. And more than once their keen eyes saved even the best reporters from humiliating mistakes. It was an important and honorable job—I just didn't want it.

Not that Jones offered me a job as a copy editor. Or as anything else. He promised to let me know if anything opened up, as had other editors, but my sense was that he meant it. I made it clear that I wanted to be a reporter, but I didn't completely dismiss the idea of copyediting.

Kansas City was followed by St. Louis and the *Post-Dispatch*, an influential and well-respected paper founded by Joseph Pulitzer. Generations of Pulitzers had run the paper and I interviewed with one of the clan. Another pleasant and promising interview, but I left feeling that only Dave Jones in Kansas City was thinking seriously of hiring me.

Eventually we rolled into Baltimore, where Janie's parents took us into their home in the northern section of the city. I still had some interviews ahead of me but getting off the road (and out of that stupid bus) did wonders for our outlook.

From Baltimore it was a short drive to the nation's capital, where I interviewed with the *Washington Post*. After that came the *Baltimore Sun*.

I should have known that the Baltimore Sunpapers, as they were known, were two papers, similar to Kansas City. There was the *Sun*, the distinguished if often tedious morning paper, and the *Evening Sun*, the lively younger sibling that had been the journal of H. L Mencken, the "Sage of Baltimore" and one of the most influential American writers.

Once again I wasn't sure who I was interviewing with, but the editors made sure I had the chance to speak to representatives of both papers. Scott Sullivan, the *Sun*'s city editor, gave me a quiz. He played the role of the city fire chief; I had to question him about a fictional fire, then write a story about it. I didn't do very well; this was my first experience with deadline pressure. I didn't disgrace myself, but I didn't impress Scott, either. It also became evident that I couldn't type. If I had not so obviously lacked that most basic skill of newspapering he may have overlooked my lack of clips and possibly offered me a job.

After we finished chatting, Sullivan took me to the other side of the newsroom and introduced me to Ernie Imhoff, city editor of the *Evening Sun*. Ernie was engaging and enthusiastic, a young old-time newspaperman. As with Scott Sullivan, though, my lack of clips and any kind of experience as a newsman seemed to be a threshold he just couldn't surmount, even without knowing I couldn't type.

"Do you know the *Evening Capital*?" Ernie asked me.

"No," I said. "Where is it?"

"It's in Annapolis."

The newspaper in the city where I had spent four full years not that long ago? Talk about being asleep at the switch—not to mention incurious, a defect harder for an aspiring newsman to overcome than not being able to type. I felt like I had blown the equivalent of the question of who was buried in Grant's Tomb.

But Ernie was forgiving. He told me that his predecessor as city editor, Phil Evans, had recently taken over as the top editor of the Annapolis paper, that he was shaking it up, and was the type of editor who might be willing to take a chance on a green prospect.

This was not in my game plan. A small-town paper in a city I didn't even like very much? I was damn near thirty years old; it was one thing to be a cub reporter on the *Washington Post* or *New York Times*, even the *Baltimore Sun*, at thirty but the Annapolis *Evening Capital*, circulation probably about twenty thousand, if that?

Ernie was persistent. He gave me a desk, a phone, Phil Evans's number, and told me to call him. He was so good natured that I didn't know how to refuse. Grudgingly I dialed Phil's number.

— — — —

From then on everything seemed a little off-center. That Sunday afternoon, I found myself, along with Janie and a porta-crib-bound Scott, in Phil Evans's Annapolis apartment, interviewing for a job. Phil's wife was there, so was his teenage daughter. Phil was tall, slim, prematurely gray, unfailingly courteous, with the faint whiff of the rake about him. Despite the bizarre setting, the interview was quite professional and seemed to go well. And despite my misgivings about the size of the paper, Phil's enthusiasm and excitement sparked similar emotions in me.

I left feeling positive about the *Evening Capital*. I still wasn't sold, but there was nothing to be sold on; there had been no job offer, though I thought one might be forthcoming.

We took the southern route back to Palo Alto, avoiding the snow to the north. Back home, I wrote to everyone I had met, thanking them for their courtesy and expressing the hope that they might find a place on their staff for me.

The letters from Dave Jones and Phil Evans arrived within a day of each other. Both contained job offers. Dave was offering a copy editor position; Phil wanted me as a reporter. The salaries were comparable. I was conflicted, perplexed. The Kansas City paper was a relatively big deal, the *Evening Capital* a little deal. And was I really determined to be a reporter? I certainly hadn't spent the past couple of years putting myself in strange settings. The fact was, I had done pretty much all in my power to avoid such situations. Now, suddenly, as a reporter, I was going to be out every day meeting new people and, let's face it, probably grossing out many of them. Dave Jones was offering a protected environment, an office that I could go to each day, do interesting and serious work, then go home to my family. I almost never would run into someone I didn't know. And after a few years as a copy editor, who knows? If I felt I could handle it, perhaps I could switch over to reporting.

Janie and I discussed little else for the next few days. Janie leaned toward Annapolis, since it was her home turf, and Kansas City, so far as we knew, had little going for it. But she didn't seem to feel strongly either way. The decision, without question, was mine.

One afternoon I was marshaling all the reasons Kansas City and the copyediting job made sense. Reporting, with all it entailed, scared me the closer I got to actually doing it.

"I really don't need to go running around the streets with a pen and notebook," I said. "At least not right now. Maybe a few years down the line."

"Sure," said Janie, which sounded like concurrence but fell a little short of that.

I closed my eyes, let my head roll back, was silent for several seconds. Finally I said, "But if I don't do it now, I never will do it, will I?"

Janie held her peace.

I picked up the phone and called Annapolis.

"Mr. Evans, this is Bob Timberg, your new reporter."

Thirteen

CUB REPORTER

I spent most of the first day at my new job filling out forms and familiarizing myself with the *Evening Capital* building, an unprepossessing two-story structure on West Street, the dowdy thoroughfare radiating away from Church Circle and the historic section of Annapolis. I was grateful for the paperwork; it gave me a few hours to find my sea legs. Even so, I was painfully aware of my journalistic shortcomings, which made it difficult to avoid the feeling that I was masquerading as a reporter and would shortly be exposed for the fraud I was.

I don't know what Phil Evans told my colleagues to prepare them for my arrival, but whatever it was effectively smoothed my entrance into the newsroom. The small staff, six to eight reporters depending on who you counted, was milling around as Phil and I walked in. The ones standing glanced in our direction; those seated looked up. No reaction other than a smile here and there. The reaction was warmer as Phil squired me around, making introductions.

"Billy, meet Bob Timberg, he's joining the staff," said Phil. "Bob, this is Bill Gregory, he covers county government for us."

I liked Billy immediately. He had a puckish demeanor and exuded an engaging work-hard, play-hard quality. I also understood that he held one of the most important beats on the paper.

"Phil tell you what you're gonna be doing, what your beat's gonna be?" he asked.

"Actually, no," I answered.

"I think we'll start him in on general assignment, give him some time to learn the city and the county and how we do things here," said Phil. "And he's an Academy grad, so we'll probably have him take a look at what really goes on over there."

"So you were a Navy man," Billy said.

"A Marine," I said.

Phil and I worked our way from desk to desk, lined up one behind the other at right angles to the wall. The space was longer than it was wide, and I was not surprised to learn that it had once been a bowling alley.

After we made the circuit, Phil ushered me into a handsome wood-paneled office to meet the publisher, Philip Merrill, who came across as bright, engaging, and energetic but with a fidgety, rabbitlike demeanor that made him seem in a hurry even when standing still and saying nothing.

Everyone went out of their way to make me feel welcome, but I was unsettled by the youthfulness of the staff. None of my fellow reporters seemed older than twenty-five, but they all talked and carried themselves like veteran newsmen, as if they had been covering the waterfront or some facsimile thereof for years. Four months short of my thirtieth birthday, I was at least five years, in some cases ten years, behind my new colleagues in terms of newspaper experience. I have a lot of catching up to do, I thought.

Oh yeah, only two staff members the older guys, Hal Burdett and Al Hopkins—and Evans had been in the service, but I was pretty much beyond resenting those who had managed to avoid serving by partaking of the tempting smorgasbord of draft deferments available. I had packed away my anger and resentment in an imaginary footlocker on which I had scrawled Do Not Open!

—————

Timberg, some woman is shouting about throwing herself off the Eastport Bridge," said Mike Lewis, the bespectacled city editor, in the clipped phrasing he seemed to employ for everything from scoldings to the all-too-infrequent pleasantry.

He slammed down the phone as he spoke. The newsroom chatter ceased. I looked up from my desk. Mike was staring at me. As his stare morphed into what seemed like a glare, I wondered if he was trying to tell me something. He was.

"Go!" he snapped.

Second day on the job, first story! I pulled my jacket from the back of my wooden swivel chair, stuffed a reporter's notebook into my breast pocket, slapped my pants pockets to make sure I had a pen, and scrambled down the stairs from our second-floor office into the frigid January day.

I considered taking my car, parked in back, but decided I didn't know the city's streets well enough so chances were I'd wind up driving in circles and missing whatever action was occurring on the Eastport Bridge.

So I ran, barely aware of the cold. My breath poured from my nose and mouth like cigarette smoke. Up West Street to Church Circle, around the Circle to Duke of Gloucester Street, then down Duke of Gloucester to the waterfront and the bridge. Perspiration rolled down my forehead into my eyes; my sweat-soaked undershirt stuck to my chest.

I passed people on the way, but I was moving too fast to register the shocked expressions I knew would be plastered on their faces as I sped by. The only thing on my mind was getting to the Eastport Bridge before whatever was going on there was over.

I didn't quite make it. The bridge was crowded with police cars, fire trucks, an ambulance, and scores of onlookers who had been herded to the side of the bridge away from the action. But there was no woman hollering about jumping into Spa Creek, the waterway the bridge traversed, or anything else.

I was not in good shape. My legs had turned to rubber, my lungs burned, and I was wheezing heavily as I staggered up to the nearest policeman.

"Sir, you'll have to stand over there," he said, gesturing toward the crowd gathered behind a police line.

I raised my hands and waved them back and forth, palms forward, signaling, I hoped, that I was not just another curious bystander and that I would explain my presence as soon as I caught my breath.

"*Eve . . . Cap . . .* ," I gasped, pulling out my notebook.

"You're with the *Crab Wrapper*?" said the cop, not unkindly but in a tone of disbelief.

I answered with a series of nods while struggling to catch my breath.

"You're a little late," he said, giving me what I took to be a self-satisfied smile. "It's all over."

I turned toward the bridge. Police, firefighters, and medical personnel scurried about, and there was plenty of activity, but—alas—no sense of urgency. It was, indeed, over. A knot began forming in my stomach; I had blown my first story.

Or had I? A light went on. Reporters rarely are present at the scene of the action while it's occurring and almost always need to reconstruct it by interviewing witnesses. Sure, I hadn't seen the action but several dozen onlookers had—in addition to the cops and other emergency personnel.

Turning back to the officer, I said, "What happened?"

"I'm not authorized to talk to the press," he said, directing me toward an officer on the bridge who seemed to be in charge.

"Look, Officer, this is my first day on the job. I just need a little help. I won't quote you in the paper; just give me some idea of what's going on so I don't sound like an idiot when I start asking questions."

A short silence ensued. Then he said, "This lady dove off the bridge. They just fished her out."

"Is she dead?" I asked.

"I don't know, I think so," said the cop. "That's all you get from me. Good luck."

They say a little knowledge can be a dangerous thing. True, but as I was to learn in the years ahead, a strand of information can be enough to unravel the most amazing tales if you tug on it skillfully enough. Over the next hour, armed only with the most general outline of events, I fleshed out the story.

I did it by talking to everything that moved, onlookers as well as officials, opening each encounter by saying, "Hi, I'm Bob Timberg from the *Evening Capital*. Can you tell me what happened here?"

Most of the people I spoke to reacted to my scars, usually with startled expressions of the sort that in other circumstances might have triggered a hostile response from me. Not now. I didn't care how spooked they looked when I first approached them; I just wanted them to tell me what they'd seen and heard. A couple of impatient cops in a police vehicle started to pull away before I was done questioning them. I pulled open the rear door, poked my head in, and said, "Hey, I've got a few more questions. How 'bout I ride along with you?"

Before they could say no, I was in the backseat, pen poised, notebook at the ready. The cops looked like they wanted to shoot me. Instead, they drove me back to the paper, answering questions along the way. I'd like to think they admired my chutzpah, but they probably were taking the path of least resistance.

The next day, the off-lead story on the front page of the *Evening Capital* carried a double two-deck headline . . .

AFTER PACING EASTPORT BRIDGE
WOMAN PLUNGES TO ICY
DEATH IN SPA CREEK

It began:

A 53-year-old Annapolis woman leaped to her death from the Eastport Bridge shortly before noon yesterday, seconds before a city police officer could reach her.

Alerted by a passing motorist who reported a woman on

the bridge acting suspiciously, Officer Sidney Diggs rushed to the scene and was stopping his car as Mrs. Lovie G. Lindsay, of 78 Clay St., plunged through the thin crust of ice covering Spa Creek.

"She saw me," Diggs said, "but by the time I got my car stopped, she jumped."

The story ran with a dramatic photo by staff photographer Joe Gruver showing rescue equipment lifting Mrs. Lindsay's lifeless body from the creek. Missing was a byline. Tradition held that a cub reporter, even one with a war under his belt and approaching his thirtieth birthday, has to earn his byline, and he can't do it with one story, no matter how good it was. I had no problem with that. Whether my name was on it or not, I knew it was my story and that I had gotten it right.

Only later did I realize that Mrs. Lindsay's watery demise marked the start of my transition from victim to something else—I wasn't sure what. I was sure, though, of a fascinating phenomenon. From the moment Mike Lewis chased me out of the newsroom until I returned to my desk and turned in my story, I had no sense of being disfigured.

Fourteen

GRILLING THE PREACHER

S o now I had a front-page story to my credit but I still couldn't type. How did I handle it? I did all my news gathering the day before a story was to run but held off writing it so the editors and my fellow reporters, pounding away at nearby desks, could not see me poking childishly at the typewriter. Instead, I fiddled around the office as if doing something productive till the workday ended, took my notes home, then sat at the dining room table after dinner and composed the story in longhand.

The next morning I would go into the office early, the longhand version of the story in my pocket, set it down beside my typewriter as if it were my laboriously gathered reporting notes, and—hunched over so it wasn't obvious I was using the hunt-and-peck method—copy it word for word.

Occasionally, for verisimilitude, I tried my hand at method acting, scrambling through a pile of unrelated papers on my desk as if in search of additional notes. At times I would mutter under my breath or let out a garden variety oath, as if a crucial piece of paper was eluding me. I looked like a seasoned reporter putting together a tough daily story; at least I hoped I did.

In time I learned to touch-type and to compose on the typewriter (though I still can't type the top row of numbers without looking). But even during my hunt-and-peck period, I had already begun a love affair with reporting that has lasted to this day. I had also inadvertently sown seeds that meant trouble when they finally took root a year or so later.

— — — —

A totally unexpected development accompanied my budding affection for journalism. I was, it seems, a good reporter. In fact, it became clear fairly quickly that I was a very good reporter.

This was a welcome surprise. I didn't have any expectations at all at the start, employing whatever mental gymnastics I needed to keep my competitive juices from bubbling to the surface.

This went against the grain since I had always wanted to be the best at whatever I did. I was, in the words of my wise Academy roommate and fellow Marine Ron Benigo, an "applause seeker," which I took to mean a person looking to do something that would win the cheers of others. But that was the old me, the one that existed before that day in January 1967 when I zigged when I should have zagged, as if my DNA had been changed by the blast as much as my face.

No, at first I wanted nothing more than to be a journeyman reporter, one who could be counted on to do the job competently and with a minimum of fuss, content to live out the life I nearly lost without any further excitement. I wanted to go home after work and spend time with Janie and Scott. I was not so foolish as to think a newspaperman could work banker's hours, but I figured the workday, if not routine, would be pretty regular.

So did Janie. After four solid years of barely relieved chaos (war, hospitals, endless surgeries, a clinically depressed husband, and more recently a colicky infant), she looked on the *Evening Capital* as a much-needed bastion of normalcy. I did, too. Except it wasn't. No newspaper is.

I started as a general assignment reporter, essentially a jack-of-all-trades, assigned to stories that didn't fall into any specific beat or thrown in with a beat reporter when a story called for reinforcements.

It wasn't long, though, before I gravitated to the Naval Academy, which until my arrival had never been given a close journalistic look from someone who knew how it worked.

I held the Academy in high regard and had no desire to write stories that would sully its image. When I found out that I'd be covering the place, I paid a courtesy call on the Academy superintendent, Rear Admiral James Calvert, a truly impressive officer, with a splendid record of achievement.

Our meeting was congenial, but I knew my role was different now; it was not that of a midshipman or even a Marine captain who had graduated from the place. I was a newspaperman, and, green though I was, I understood that I was not to be a cheerleader for my alma mater any more than I was to be a scold. My job was to find out what was going on at the Academy that might be of interest to the readers of the *Evening Capital* and tell them about it in a fair and balanced way.

My stories found a ready audience since Annapolis had a sizable military community that included many Academy alums within the ranks of the active and retired Navy and Marine officers who resided there.

I had been at the *Capital* less than a week when the story that would claim my attention more than any other for the next year blossomed on my radar screen. The coming Monday the U.S. District Court in Washington was to begin hearing a civil case brought by six Annapolis midshipmen and a West Point cadet challenging the constitutionality of compulsory chapel services at all the nation's service academies, meaning Air Force and Coast Guard as well.

All the academies required their midshipmen and cadets to attend some form of religious service on Sunday mornings. At Annapolis, there was Catholic Mass at nine, followed by a generic Protestant service at ten thirty. Jewish midshipmen and those whose sects did not fit comfortably under the Academy's Protestant umbrella marched in small groups, called church parties, to synagogues and other houses of worship in town.

Visitors seemed heartened to see their future military leaders, like soldiers of Christ, marching in lockstep to the imposing Academy Chapel, with its massive dome and gleaming Tiffany glass windows, to commune with the Deity.

Not all midshipmen shared this feeling. Some—who knows how many, but more than a few—felt bullied by the requirement that they attend chapel services. Some believed they had a personal relationship with their God that did not lend itself to ecclesiastical ritual.

Others were agnostics; uncertain about the existence of God, their doubts intensified when forced to go through the motions of worship. Other midshipmen were atheists. None of the three felt chapel services made sense for them, and they were resentful at being forced to attend. Upperclassmen of this persuasion employed a rope-a-dope strategy, marching briskly from Bancroft Hall to the Chapel, holding themselves ramrod straight as they passed through the building's massive wooden doors and filed down the aisle, then slipping into the pews on the blind side of the celebrant, and promptly dozing off. This section was known as Sleepy Hollow.

My own feeling was that compulsory chapel was without question unconstitutional. As I saw it, freedom of religion was imbedded in the Bill of Rights. I figured the midshipmen and cadets challenging the rule would quickly and easily prevail. I planned to cover the court hearings in DC.

That Sunday, the day before the hearings were to begin, the celebrated evangelist Billy Graham was to speak at Protestant services at the Academy Chapel. I decided to cover the event on the chance that Reverend Graham might address the issue in his sermon. If not, I would try to catch him after the service and ask him about it.

That was not my preferred way of doing things. At the time I didn't know the term "ambush journalism," but I was uncomfortable at the thought of essentially springing out of the shadows to grill a clergyman of Graham's stature about compulsory chapel, moments after he completed a religious service. Assuming I could even get to him.

My misgivings aside, after the service I headed to the area behind the altar where Graham was changing out of his vestments. Admiral

Calvert was the senior member of the coterie of officers surrounding him. Both men were smiling as I approached. I asked if I might briefly ask Reverend Graham a few questions.

Admiral Calvert seemed pleased by my interest and explained to Graham that I was a new reporter for the local paper and that I also was both an Academy graduate and a Marine officer who had served honorably in Vietnam. Graham smiled at me, welcoming my questions.

My first question was a softball, something on the order of, "What does speaking at the Academy mean to you?" His answer was thoughtful and gracious, and I dutifully recorded it.

I then asked him if he was aware of the challenge to compulsory chapel, and if so, how did he view it? You could have heard a pin drop. I had nailed a man of God with an offensive, if legitimate, question, one that in the eyes of some bordered on the unsavory. I looked around. The color had bled out of everyone and everything, as if we had all suddenly become characters in a black-and-white movie. And we were all quite still, frozen in place.

Reverend Graham was the first to regain his color and mobility. As he did, the others in our small group blinked back to life, as if the power had been restored to a string of previously incapacitated Christmas-tree lights.

I waited for Graham to respond to my query, wondering if posing a question that exposed me as a tasteless dick was going to pay dividends. He finally answered.

"I believe it is part of a planned attack against all chaplains, to force them completely out of all the services," he said.

My heart beat faster. Did he really say that? I asked myself. Six mids and a cadet in the vanguard of a movement to eliminate chaplains? Whoa!

I said that the men involved in the suit, while objecting to the compulsory nature of the academies' rules, maintained that they themselves held religious convictions.

"What kind of religious convictions?" asked Dr. Graham. "Communism is a religion, too."

He went on to say of compulsory chapel that it would be "the greatest possible tragedy if it were to be stopped. . . . We need it now more than ever before."

I knew I had a good story, a really good story. The nation's best-known (and probably best-loved) religious leader had literally portrayed seven service academy men in good standing as little more than Communist dupes conspiring to rid the armed forces of its chaplains. Still, I kept pressing.

"Can an atheist be a good naval officer?" I asked.

"I can't comment on that," he replied.

My story, with a byline, ran on the front page the next day, under a photo of Admiral Calvert and Dr. Graham warmly shaking hands.

I knew the story would not endear me to Admiral Calvert and his staff, let alone to many in the Academy community. Would I have written it differently if I were someone else, just reporting on the sermon and staying away from questions posed to elicit newsworthy answers? I don't know, but in pursuing the story as I did and writing it with a whiff of the smartass to it, I subconsciously signaled that whatever my relationship and affection for the Academy, I was not going to be a tame reporter. I wasn't looking for trouble, but I wasn't going to run from it, either.

Fifteen

LIKE A MARINE TO MUD

Newspapering conformed to no set schedule. I often worked past quitting time, and all too often I found myself alone in the newsroom, finishing up a story or making late-night phone calls in hopes of picking up a few nuggets to brighten my copy. My learning curve was near perpendicular, but everything seemed to take me twice as long as it took my colleagues. I was certain Janie didn't resent the extra hours I spent at the office. We were partners on the comeback trail, and I felt confident that she, more than anyone, knew how strongly I had begun to feel about catching up with my contemporaries.

After several weeks, though, success at work, such as it was, did not produce a similarly salutary effect at home. At first Janie and I were thrilled to see my byline in the paper, but before long the novelty of being the spouse of a newspaper reporter began to lose its luster. I rarely got home on time; then, after rushing through dinner, I'd clear a spot on the table so I could begin the time-consuming process of writing out in longhand the story I had spent the day reporting so I could copy it on the typewriter the next morning. Of course there were stories to cover at night, too. Weekends as well. Not always but often enough.

Part of the problem, of course, was that I barely knew what I was doing. This extended time I spent working on a story meant less time—or, more accurately, next to no time—spent with Janie and Scott, who had celebrated his first birthday and was charging headlong toward the Terrible Twos.

Janie's daily life had changed drastically as well. She was used to teaching and planned to return to the classroom as soon as Scott was a bit older. She had even had some preliminary discussions with officials at a local school for the developmentally disabled. But a few months after we arrived in Annapolis, she was again pregnant. We were stunned, literally. Scott had beaten birth control pills; this time a rogue sperm had outmaneuvered Janie's IUD.

For Janie, it was both maddening and depressing that we were having our married life, so chaotic up till then, once again taken out of our hands just as it seemed we were gaining control of it.

I felt that, too, though undoubtedly not as acutely as Janie. And I was driven, as well, by an insistent need to fight my way back into the game, whatever the game was, and to play it at the highest levels, scars or no scars. Those early days at the *Evening Capital* convinced me that life had something more in store for me, and I was determined not to let a random land mine cheat me out of whatever it was.

Was I interested in fame and celebrity? No, at least I don't think so. But I did not want to go through life with nobody noticing me, either. I wanted to count. And if I was going to count, it seemed it would be as a journalist.

I understood that there would be a price to pay; I was willing to pay it. What I didn't know until it was too late was how high that price would be. I had turned thirty. At my age guys had already written books and picked up one, perhaps even two, Pulitzer Prizes. Or were heading off to Harvard for a year on a Nieman Fellowship, the prestigious midcareer program for journalists. Midcareer? Jesus, I was still teaching myself to type!

Sixteen

KEEPING FAITH

I was in Rookie's, a high-end butcher store across from the City Dock, when I saw, through the window behind the meat counter, a sight that made my stomach clench. I hoped my first impression was wrong, that I wasn't looking at the man I thought I was. A man that I knew. That I knew very well.

My old friend and classmate Sandy Coward was ambling casually down Main Street toward the dock, stopping occasionally to look in shop windows.

Sandy, in longhand Asbury Coward IV, was not merely a member of my Naval Academy class; he had been in my company, the Seventh Company, one of the twenty-four units that made up the Brigade of Midshipman. The company is the closest thing to a family that exists at the Academy. My forty or so company mates and I had been together all four of our Annapolis years. As seniors we earned honors as the Color Company, which further enhanced our camaraderie and bonhomie.

Sandy was a friend, not my best friend, but someone I knew well and liked a lot. Tall, baby-faced, with a crop of red hair, a lusty sense of humor, and a goofy smile, he came from a military family that stretched back at least to the Civil War. During our first two years at Annapolis, Sandy's father, Captain Asbury Coward III, was the Academy's athletic director.

I hadn't kept in touch with Sandy, but through the grapevine I knew generally what he had been up to since graduation. He was a naval aviator, piloting aircraft such as the A-6 Intruder and the supersonic F/A-18 Hornet. (He would later become a squadron and air group commander and CO of the Navy's Test Pilot School at Patuxent River, Maryland.)

I got to know him best First Class year when he lived across the corridor from me on the third deck of Bancroft Hall. It was during those months that he took on a task for which his company mates would be forever in his debt.

He taught us to dance to Beatles music.

I don't know how Sandy developed this exotic skill. All I know is that when we returned from Christmas leave in January 1964, "I Want to Hold Your Hand," "All My Loving," "I Saw Her Standing There," "A Hard Day's Night," and lots of other tunes with this incredibly infectious sound were blasting from the stereo in Sandy's room.

Most of us in the company didn't have a clue how to dance to this new music that was sweeping the country. We had hardly moved beyond the Lindy Hop and the fox-trot. But we could see that learning this skill would immeasurably enhance our appeal to young ladies.

Sandy generously became our tutor. He never seemed to mind classmates dropping by his room during a free period, at night during study hour, or on weekends as we sought to acquire the arcane terpsichorean flair he had so mysteriously mastered. His room was always crowded with Gene Kelly wannabes who didn't come across as what they were: young men months away from leading Marines on combat patrols and sailors on stormy seas.

My first impulse on spotting Sandy through Rookie's plate-glass window was to rush out and greet him. That lasted no more than a nanosecond. Then I realized the situation was more complicated than the chance meeting of two old friends might suggest. And the more I thought about it, the more distressed I became.

I wondered if he knew what had happened to me. Possibly, but hardly a sure thing. Even if he knew, there was no way he would recognize me now. So what do I say to him? A riff on Jack Ruby's pronouncement in the Dallas city jail flashed in my mind.

"Hi, Sandy. You know me. I'm Bob Timberg."

So how would Sandy, confronted by a hideously disfigured man who seemed to know him, respond to that greeting?

"Huh? What?"

Maybe I needed to say more.

"Sandy, I'm Bob Timberg, your classmate. I was wounded in Vietnam. A land mine."

Sandy, I'm sure, would have handled the situation smoothly. But I wasn't sure that I could. I had been seeing and talking to midshipmen and naval officers on almost a daily basis because of my job, but either they hadn't known me prior to Vietnam or were informed of my injuries ahead of time (though not by me), so my appearance wasn't a surprise to them.

Sandy was different. He may or may not have known what had happened to me, but he hadn't seen me. I felt certain that before he put it all together his face would contort with shock, however briefly. I couldn't think of what else I could say to him. I just kept imagining Sandy trying to reconcile what I used to look like with how I looked now, the puzzled expression that would cross his face, his trying to find words that conveyed sympathy, understanding, happiness at our crossing paths, anything but what I knew he would really be feeling—astonishment and horror.

I dropped my eyes from the window to the butcher case, studying Rookie's steaks as if they were a fluid-dynamics problem I was struggling to solve, and I didn't take my eyes off them until I was sure Sandy had moved on.

— — — —

The episode with Sandy Coward was a variation on the issue I had been wrestling with since I decided to go to journalism school: As a reporter, how was I going to deal with meeting strangers on a daily basis? A reporter needs people to tell him things, not to be distracted by the way he looks.

For a brief time, I considered introducing myself by saying something like, "Hi, I'm Bob Timberg of the *Evening Capital*. Don't be put off by my appearance. I had a bad war." But that struck me as awkward. Also like I was looking for sympathy. I just couldn't imagine myself opening a conversation that way.

The way I handled the problem was by not handling it. My job didn't allow time for what I came to think of as "morose delectations," a marvelously euphemistic phrase from my Catholic upbringing that the catechism described as "entertaining impure thoughts," but which I now equated to wallowing in self-pity.

Wariness of the reaction of others to my wounds unnerved me, but working a story actually had a transforming effect. At the moment I had to introduce myself to someone, I became another person. In fact, it felt as though I became the person I once was—mildly aggressive, relatively fearless, and occasionally pushy, though friendly and unfailingly polite.

Very quickly I learned how to put people at ease or, at the very least, get them to concentrate on my questions rather than my appearance. Sometimes a joke or a gentle wisecrack did it, or a comment on the weather or the pennant race. I was tested when there were children with the person I wanted to talk to, especially small children who would slip behind their parents as I approached. I tried to defuse this situation by smiling at the kid, waving, winking, then pretending he didn't exist, even though I assumed he was staring wide-eyed at me from behind his parent's protective leg.

Oddly enough, my wounds did not come up all that often. When they did, I answered conversationally, telling people as much as I thought they wanted to know, though for sure I didn't drag out the explanation.

For those who I figured knew about such things—police, firefighters, other veterans—I'd just say that the vehicle I was riding on hit a land mine. That usually was enough for those guys, who could fill in the blanks from their own experiences.

For others, I invariably began my answer with a rueful smile and the phrase "this is a tale only Karl Marx could love," explaining that I was carrying a brown canvas bag stuffed with thousands of dollars in military payment certificates at the time of the explosion—capitalism getting what it deserved.

For the most part, my answers satisfied the questioners. A few wanted to know more, less out of curiosity, morbid or otherwise, than from sincere interest and a desire to display sympathy. I never resented such questions, though occasionally they made me uncomfortable. What I really had problems handling were strangers, usually older women, walking up to me and saying things like "God bless you, son," as if my days were numbered, and the best I could hope for was that they ran out quickly so I could be spared further pain.

— — — —

Instinctively I knew I had to steer clear of the military community, except for a few, a very few, old Academy and Marine friends. I didn't join organizations like the American Legion, Veterans of Foreign Wars, or Disabled American Veterans. My fear, which I only vaguely understood at the time, was that my wounds would spur friends, old and new, to take me under their wing, try to protect me, lavish sympathy on me.

It wasn't that I found the prospect of such treatment distasteful. But I realized that such kindnesses, however well meant, would prove debilitating.

In a way, this recognition that I needed a kick in the ass more than a pat on the back was akin to taking the reporting job at the *Evening Capital* rather than the copyediting job in Kansas City.

I also decided that reporting on the Academy was the last time I would cover the military. I knew that if I progressed in newspapering, future editors would look at my background and see a natural Pentagon correspondent.

The thing was, I was becoming a better reporter every day and knew that although I was capable of writing good, positive stories about the armed services, I also was going to find improprieties, lapses, and downright blunders, and I did not want to write stories that reflected badly on men I had gone to war with. I'd leave that to others.

I was still at the *Evening Capital* in March 1971 when Lieutenant William Calley was convicted of having murdered more than twenty Vietnamese civilians three years earlier in the course of the well-documented My Lai bloodbath that claimed the lives of several hundred unarmed villagers. The popular reaction against his conviction, among everyone from combat veterans to middle-class citizens who knew little about the military to long-haired draft evaders, triggered my only brush with the military, beyond the Academy, while working in Annapolis.

Phil Evans, my boss, asked me if I wanted to write something about the verdict. My first thought was no, I didn't need to get involved, and that's what I told Phil. He suggested I think about it for an hour or so. I did, and realized that whether I liked it or not, I had a forum others didn't to challenge the pervasive belief that Calley was no different from any other soldier. In the depths of my soul, I knew that wasn't true. There was no way I could conceive of my fellow Marines, or any soldier other than the most despicable, acting as Calley had. Unless, of course, he had lost his mind, which may have been the case with Calley.

I began the piece, which ran on the editorial page, by recounting some of the comments on the verdict voiced by Calley's defenders: "Disgraceful," "We're all guilty," "Calley is a scapegoat," "We train a man to kill, then charge him with murder when he does just that."

I stated my opinion in the second paragraph. Calley, I wrote, "is guilty, both legally and morally, beyond a reasonable doubt."

The heart of my argument was the contention that a soldier in combat, even though he kills, is not what we mean when we use the word "killer."

As to the defense that the men, women, and children systematically mowed down by Calley and his troops at My Lai may have been linked to the Vietcong, I conceded that this was a matter for reasonable speculation in a war where friend and foe were often indistinguishable.

"This defense, however, as emotionally effective as it is, is irrelevant," I wrote. "Had the prisoners at My Lai been uniformed enemy captured after a bloody battle, there is no authority which empowers a U.S. soldier, officer or enlisted man, to execute. Much as the distinction has been blurred by controversy surrounding the war, there is still a difference between a soldier and an executioner."

I have no idea how many minds, if any, were changed by my essay, though reaction to it suggested at least a few. I felt, in challenging virtually every muddleheaded comment decrying the conviction, that I had provided the readers of the *Evening Capital* another way to view what had become known as the My Lai Massacre. In more personal terms, I was glad I hadn't been silent when Calley's murderous actions were being used to portray members of the armed forces in a deplorable way. Most important, I satisfied myself that I had kept faith with my fellow soldiers and Marines, the reason I felt compelled to write the piece in the first place.

Seventeen

A FISH STORY

This time Janie would give birth at the Naval Academy hospital rather than the hospital at Stanford. She received excellent care at both, but there were two unsettling glitches in Annapolis.

She had pretty much gotten over her initial distress on learning she was pregnant and was soon happy and excited about it. Then someone on the hospital staff told her the presence of the IUD meant she was likely to miscarry. She checked with her doctor and learned the staffer was right. So Janie had to live with that knowledge for the rest of her pregnancy.

She was also frustrated and angry when her doctor told her flatly that I could not be in the delivery room with her as I had been for Scott's birth in Palo Alto. She did not back down, though, and finally persuaded the doctor to give the matter some additional thought. Then she gave him a copy of the article I had written on Scott's birth at Stanford. That seemed to soften his attitude. Finally he relented.

I was lying on the couch, watching a boxing match, on the evening of October 31. Most of the trick-or-treaters had dispersed when Janie alerted me. Time to go to the hospital. We barely avoided a Halloween baby. Craig was born no more than two hours after midnight on November 1, 1970.

"What about the IUD?" Janie asked the doctor, having successfully given birth a second time without medication.

"Let me look," said the doctor.

He found it, gave it to Janie, told her, "It looks like it came out in his hand." Jesus, I thought, Craig really wanted to be born. Janie said she was going to mount the IUD in resin and present it to Craig on his twenty-first birthday.

We brought him home two days later. Scott, by now twenty months old, was waiting at the door in anticipation. We lay Craig down on the couch and motioned Scott over to meet his new little brother.

Scott stood over Craig, silently staring down at him. Then he balled up his fist and punched him in the face.

Janie and I agreed our sons' relationship had nowhere to go but up.

— — — —

Working hours didn't seem to matter much to my fellow reporters, so I couldn't afford to let them matter to me. Most, of course, were in their early twenties and unmarried. I was past thirty, married to a woman who had been through hell with me, and the father of two very young sons.

I wanted to be a good husband and father. Janie deserved no less. Not to mention the kids. But I also needed to distinguish myself in my new profession. Reporting was not just a way to pay the bills; in my mind it had become crucial to my ability to ring down the curtain on my run as a sideshow attraction.

I did not have a long-term plan, just the belief that if I kept pushing myself hard enough good things would happen for me and my family. I also believed—no, knew—that if I backed off even a little, I would be throwing in the towel on the rest of my life.

But an unfamiliar tension had crept into my relationship with Janie. The problem, I knew, was my job, and I promised repeatedly to ease off. But there was always another angle to explore, another phone call to make, another thread to pull, another file to check.

I sensed that I was playing with fire. Much too late I realized that my work habits had the power not just to benefit my family but to destroy it as well.

— — — —

About that time, Bill Gregory left the paper and I took on the county government beat. My competition now represented no less than six big-city newspapers. Three Baltimore papers, among them the highly regarded *Baltimore Sun* and its sister paper, the *Evening Sun*, covered Annapolis and the county. So did the spunky *Baltimore News-American*. Three papers in the nation's capital, including both the vaunted *Washington Post* and *Washington Star*, made all-too-frequent forays into what I had begun to think of as my territory.

Their reporters were big-timers in training: young, highly capable, well educated, energetic, occasionally sneaky, most of all ambitious. No question they would spend a couple of years as local reporters then join the national or foreign staffs of their respective newspapers.

I liked them all, even those who were better reporters than me, though I chose to think it was just a matter of time until I closed the gap.

There was rarely any doubt about who did the best job on any story. If it was you, you accepted kudos graciously, while giving the impression that trashing the competition was nothing new, in line with the old sports homily "Look like you've been here before." If you were the one grinding your teeth, you congratulated your rival on his achievement while trying to convince yourself that you could have done as well or better had you thought the story worth the effort.

Getting beaten on a run-of-the-mill story is like stubbing your toe; it hurts but the pain passes quickly. Getting beaten on a big story is like having your pants pulled down in public. I hated it. You plaster a smile on your face, but everyone knows you're mortified. Out of sympathy, your colleagues keep their distance, except those who don't like you and find a way to rub it in just enough to salt the wound without provoking a physical confrontation. At home, unless you're an easy-going soul who leaves the job in the office, the fallout is usually a moodiness that infects the whole family. Or else you pretend that nothing is bothering you when quite clearly something is.

And it carries over to testiness as you go about domestic chores such as bathing the kids, reading to them, and putting them to bed.

Truly, those three tasks were just about all Janie asked of me. Problems arose when I got home too late to perform them, which was all too often. Instead of me walking in the door at six, as Janie expected, the phone would ring just about that time.

"Honey, things are running late. This is a bitch of a story, and a big one, too, and nobody is calling me back. I'm not going to be home for at least an hour. Kiss the kids for me."

"Not again? Can't you hurry it up? The kids really want to see you before I put them down. I'll keep them up if you're sure you can make it in an hour."

"Okay, good. I'll try. Keep the kids up."

"Try? You'll try?"

"Well, what do you want me to say?"

"I want you to say you'll be here in an hour."

"Okay, I'll be there in an hour."

Sometimes I was. Sometimes I wasn't.

Janie later said: "It was as if the kids and I were stranded on a desert island and you occasionally paddled over and threw us a fish."

Eighteen

SCARSDALE GALAHAD

Before Vietnam, Janie and I thought of my Marine uniform as a costume to be worn with great pride for a few years, then mothballed as we revealed our true nature, an unconventional young couple akin to Scott and Zelda splashing around in the fountain at the Plaza.

But the journey that I began on that aging troopship did not include port calls at Five Star hotels. Instead, it took me to battlefields in South Vietnam, a succession of frigid operating rooms, the leafy glades and intellectual ferment of Stanford University, and finally back to Annapolis where it had all begun for us.

Now Janie used the words "normal life" to describe a future she would happily settle for. That didn't seem too much to ask. As it turned out I couldn't even give her that.

— — — —

In hindsight it wasn't fair of me but at the time I felt that a line from a song in the Broadway musical *Guys and Dolls* described the man Janie wanted me to be: "*You have wished yourself a Scarsdale Galahad, a breakfast-eating, Brooks Brothers type.*"

That mocking line, sung by the gambler Sky Masterson to Sister

Sarah, the Salvation Army lady, flashed in my brain too often for comfort or, as it turned out, my own good.

There was no apparent reason for my reaction any more than there was an easily explained reason why I balked at wearing Bermuda shorts or hated the idea of mowing the lawn even though I actually kind of liked mowing the lawn. I now know that I was trying to figure out who I was and where I was headed.

Unscarred, I probably would have been happy being whatever Janie wanted me to be. But no matter how much alchemy Lynn Ketchum and his fellow surgeons might perform on me, I knew I would be scarred, grotesquely scarred, for the rest of my life.

My hostility to Bermuda shorts and mowing the lawn, along with the Scarsdale Galahad line rattling around in my head, was trying to tell me something.

I finally understood that they were telling me I didn't want to be a Scarsdale Galahad, or, more precisely, that I couldn't pull it off even if I wanted to. Sure, I could buy myself a few pairs of Bermudas, even make my lawn the pride of the neighborhood, but I'd still be the guy down the block who scared the shit out of little kids. And whom their parents pitied.

In truth, it seemed the frequency of such spirit-crushing occasions had dropped off in recent months. I concluded not that they were occurring less often, but that I was not noticing them as much.

And the reason, I came to believe, was the complex network of defense mechanisms I had subconsciously fashioned to insulate me from painful situations: the way I held someone's gaze in conversation, as if warning them not to let their eyes leave mine and drift over my face, or rubbed my nose and gnawed conspicuously on a fingernail, or used my cigarette as a distraction, or simply ignored the curious passersby who peered in my direction, then did an embarrassed "Eyes Front!" when I turned to challenge their gaze.

The most important of these defense mechanisms, I had no doubt, was my job. I was, within limits, functioning as an able-bodied man because I was a newspaper reporter. Without the job, I believed, I would crawl back into myself, a very dark place, no visitors welcome.

And it wasn't just that I had a job. The crucial element was that the job I had lent purpose to my life. I needed to view what I was doing as something that mattered, that affected peoples' lives in a positive way. Reporting mattered. And because I was a reporter, I mattered. And that meant I was no longer a victim.

One thing I couldn't get over was my age. I was competing with reporters from big-city newspapers, papers I hoped to work for someday, and all my rivals—the good ones, at least—were seven or eight years younger than me. I have to catch up, I told myself, though I wasn't quite sure what I meant by "catch up." I'll know it when I've done it, I told myself.

There was also this: Deep down I was angry, prideful, and bitter. I had gone to Stuyvesant High School, one of the best in the country, attended the U.S. Naval Academy, stood high in my class, chosen to be a Marine infantry officer, taken one of the hardest punches a war can deliver, and was still standing.

And I had done most of this as unbloodied members of my generation demeaned my service and that of my comrades. Whoever I was before rolling over that land mine was now reclaiming me. So no, I didn't want to be a Scarsdale Galahad. I wanted to be a kick-ass reporter and give some back. I don't think I wanted to make anyone pay, but I wouldn't swear to it.

— — — —

I don't believe any of that was a problem for Janie. But there was a complicating factor: I wanted to be one of the best at whatever I did. This was something of a compromise on my part. As a teenager in New York City, I believed that I could be the best at anything I put my mind to. Back then that meant academics and football. The first of those conceits was shattered when I entered Stuyvesant, a public high school with a towering reputation, rigid entrance requirements, and a demanding curriculum. For a time I found myself wondering if I had gotten in under false pretenses. Soon, though, I gained my sea legs and did just fine, making ARISTA, the New York City chapter of the National Honor Society. But I was not valedictorian or salutatorian, and dozens of kids stood higher than me.

I was disabused of my gridiron delusions by a kid from DeWitt Clinton High School named Lenny Rochester. Lenny was a running back like me, but that was all we had in common. He was bigger than me, though not by much, faster than me, by a lot, shiftier and more elusive than me. By any measure, he was better than me and no matter how hard I worked at it I knew he would always be better than me.

So by now, thanks to humbling encounters with Stuyvesant and Lenny Rochester, I had long since lowered my sights: "Among the best" worked for me. Striving for anything short of that, though, was intolerable. But more realistic aspirations did not change my work habits or make life less difficult for Janie. And gradually I was absorbing her unhappiness, which wasn't healthy for either of us.

Janie's unhappiness mattered to me. I loved her. I also was grateful to her in ways too numerous to count. I carried the scars of ground combat, but she did not make it out of the war unscathed.

Six months after our marriage I mounted out for Vietnam. She lived alone, carrying her fears for me for more than a year. Then our world changed forever thirteen days before I was scheduled to rotate back to the States. In my absence she had returned to teaching. Now she had to take care of me in addition to her classroom duties.

At home she changed my bandages, kept me from lapsing into a clinical depression, and bullied me into cutting back on my escalating alcohol consumption. At least once a week after work she drove me from Laguna Beach to the San Diego Naval Hospital and back, a good fifty miles each way, for an operation or post-op treatment.

There were similar issues during the year and a half at Stanford when I continued to lean on her, though perhaps not as much as before. For one thing, our son Scott was born and required much of the attention previously reserved for me. But she still had to deal with me, mostly cooling me out on days of major and minor indignities.

So, yes, I had suffered the pain, absorbed the ridicule, and struggled mightily to restore meaning to my life. I wasn't there yet, might never get there, but I had come a very long way from that day when I lay helplessly in a rice paddy exhorting a Marine NCO to set up a perimeter defense.

But I never could have done it without Janie. At great cost to herself, she gave me the strength and love that I needed. Along the way she rekindled my ambition. Now she was paying the price for her kindness and generosity of spirit.

— — — —

At work, meanwhile, I was becoming a better reporter, thanks to a previously unsuspected talent for reporting nourished by the wide variety of stories I was assigned to cover. I also profited immensely from the tutelage of a new colleague, Dick Levine, a veteran investigative reporter who taught me how to research and read documents like deeds, mortgages, and incorporation papers along with many other exotic tricks of the trade.

The first time I met Dick, before he even said a word, I thought he might be a madman. Slight in stature, almost rickety, he had wild white hair that had long since broken off any relationship it may have once had with a comb or brush. His demeanor called to mind a misbegotten combination of an Old Testament prophet and Doc Brown, the wacky inventor played by Christopher Lloyd in *Back to the Future*.

"The records tell a story, Bob," said Dick in what I had come to think of as his trademark conspiratorial tone. "Listen to them."

Nineteen

KANSAS CITY HERE I COME

W hen Lynn Ketchum discharged me from the hospital in San Diego in 1968, he said my appearance would profit from more surgery but he couldn't continue operating until the work he had already done completed the stages of healing, essentially the contraction of the skin grafts, then their relaxation and softening. He estimated it would be at least two years before more surgery could be productively undertaken. Well, it was now nearly four years out. If there was to be more surgery, this was the time to do it.

I had left the *Evening Capital* the previous fall, not long after my friend and mentor Phil Evans had quit after one too many run-ins with the publisher, who had always struck me as too enmeshed in local political dramas to oversee a newspaper that aspired to impartiality. Though I didn't plan it this way, my break from reporting allowed time for a long-delayed and final round of surgeries. There was still one serious problem: Dr. Ketchum was now at the University of Kansas Medical Center, in Kansas City, and I was living in Annapolis, but Janie, Lynn, and I were determined to make it work.

This was the plan: I'd fly to Kansas City in the morning and check into the University of Kansas Medical Center that afternoon. Lynn would operate the next day. He would discharge me four or five days after surgery, and I'd make my way home. Back in Annapolis, Janie could drive me to the Bethesda Naval Hospital for follow-up treatments, mostly dressing changes.

Working out the financing was not simple. I couldn't rely on savings because we had none. I did, however, have my Marine Corps disability pension. I also applied for and received a modest monthly Social Security disability stipend. Lynn's fees and the hospital charges, which I'm sure were staggering, were covered by a program called CHAMPUS (Civilian Health and Medical Program of the Uniformed Services), which paid medical costs if needed services were not available at a military facility. Somehow I persuaded officials that I required treatment by a civilian surgeon at a civilian hospital in Kansas City even though the two gems of the military's medical establishment—Bethesda and Walter Reed Army Medical Center—were within easy driving distance.

I took care of the airfare. I didn't try to get the government to cover it even though I thought it should. I knew better than to press my luck. Overreaching had the very real potential to rouse the bureaucracy into asking questions like "Hey, why in hell are we sending this guy to Kansas City when we have . . . ?" You get the picture.

My solo flights from Washington to Kansas City were not terribly grueling except for the plane change at Chicago's O'Hare, a side dish I would happily have passed on. The return trip, though, was a trial. Not always, but most of the time my head was wrapped in layers of gauze and tape so that I once again resembled a mummy, often leaving me only small eyeholes from which to see, and then only straight ahead. This meant I had to negotiate the crowded Kansas City airport like a racehorse wearing blinders. I didn't walk into many walls, but I did bump into more than my share of people as I hustled to make a flight. And the injuries to my eyelids, though largely corrected with skin grafts, caused my eyes to water, requiring me to frequently blot the eyeholes to clear my vision. When my eyes weren't tearing, they secreted a gelatinous gunk that completely clogged them and forced me to retreat to the men's room to irrigate them.

Getting around the airport in Kansas City was tricky, but it was nothing compared to changing planes at O'Hare, the world's busiest airport. To make my visually impaired way from one terminal to another I almost always found myself falling back on my days as a running back, abruptly cutting left, then right, then barreling straight ahead when I glimpsed a sliver of daylight, only to have the hole close when an unsuspecting fellow passenger filled the gap, occasioning the inevitable collision.

Between my airport misadventures, Lynn Ketchum demonstrated that his return to civilian life had not lessened his surgical skills. Month after month I was wheeled into the OR and greeted by Lynn decked out in green scrubs and his trademark cocky smile. Moments later something horribly bitter was sprayed down my throat, presumably a local anesthetic to ease the insertion of a breathing tube that would run from my mouth to my trachea, maybe farther. I cringed each time a mask came down over my face. Then nothing.

I invariably woke up in the recovery room sick to my stomach from the anesthesia, usually vomiting on and off for the next several hours. At some point Lynn would materialize at my bedside and provide a report, always upbeat, on the outcome of the surgery. Nurses administered pain medication, normally Demerol, at four-hour intervals for the next several days, mainly to ease burning at the donor site.

It didn't take long for me to conclude that hospitals were hazardous to the health of anybody confined to one for more than a day or two. By my lights, you take a healthy man (or woman), put him in a hospital room for a week, do nothing to him, and he will come out wrecked. It's something in the air, and I don't mean germs. Mostly it results from what I came to think of as "the patient mentality," a state of mind you fall into about the time you change out of your everyday clothes into a hospital gown, the kind that ties in back and leaves your butt hanging out. It's as though you've morphed into a being lacking any control whatsoever over your own life. You are, once again, a child.

Roommates rarely ease the psychic chill that along with the ambient odor of disinfectant I came to associate with hospitals. They're patients, too, and have their own problems so it's not like you're in a locker room cracking jokes, slapping asses with towels, and lying about women. One of my roommates back at the hospital in San Diego was a young naval officer who had been a few years behind me at Annapolis. He was a good guy, the kind you immediately like, and he had a lovely wife whose visits lit up the room. He had cancer. We weren't always roommates since I would go home between operations and was assigned to whatever room was available when I checked back in. He didn't go home, but I'd always look in on him if we weren't in the same room.

One day when my friend and I were again sharing a room, I was chattering away about nothing that mattered, hoping the sound of my voice might ease the distress I could tell he was experiencing. Frail as he had become by then, he seemed to be reacting to my words, but I couldn't be sure. Then a corpsman came in and wheeled his bed out of the room and down a long corridor. I had no clue where the corpsman was taking him or why.

The space his bed had occupied remained vacant for the next several hours. I wondered when he would return. Late in the day a bed was rolled back in. It was empty. Not long after I had a new roommate.*

Another roommate, in Kansas City, was an older guy, maybe late forties. As a youth, he explained, he had serious acne issues that were treated with X-rays, a common practice well into the 1940s. In his case, and I gather thousands of others, the result was like destroying the village in order to save it: The X-rays took care of the acne but caused skin cancer, the malignant kind.

Looking at him, you couldn't tell that his face had suffered any kind of trauma. He looked like a normal guy. When I said so, he told me most of his face was composed of prosthetics. I wasn't curious, but he must have thought I was, because he proceeded to show me what he was talking about.

---

* I have not used my friend's name. I have long since lost touch with his wife, but on the chance that she or one of her acquaintances reads this book I don't want to stir painful memories. But I haven't forgotten him or his name.

First, he removed his nose. Then a cheek. I'm not sure what came next, maybe his chin, because I mentally checked out about then, refusing to let myself see what I was seeing even though I was looking right at him. It was like I was looking into his head.

To this day, I'm not sure I didn't imagine the whole thing.

— — — —

I remember as a kid watching movies in which some villain has his features radically altered overnight by a plastic surgeon. Usually the patient was a Nazi on the run, occasionally a mob boss. He'd lie down on the operating table a Boris Karloff clone, pop up looking like my old Vietnam buddy Glenn Ford.

As I learned, reconstructive surgery in the real world is a far more time-consuming process, almost always taking more than one operation to achieve a desired result, for example, a crease in the chin. Even then, it takes a considerable period of time before the swelling goes down and the graft (or grafts) completes the postsurgical cycle of contraction, relaxation, and softening. Only at that point can the success of a procedure be judged. It can take months before the result of any single surgery declares itself. Sometimes it takes years.

I didn't think of Lynn Ketchum as a miracle worker, but I believed that any chance I had of regaining an unfrightening visage rested with him. Lynn understood, and helped me understand, that restoration of the puzzle that had once been my face had to proceed step by painful step.

Lynn took his scalpel to me in Kansas City for the first time in January 1972. I was on the table for three and a half hours. In that time, Lynn worked on my eyelids, lips, and mouth. In March he dermabraded my forehead and covered it with skin taken from my back. According to the record of the procedure, the graft was applied only after "homeostasis was achieved," meaning when I stopped bleeding. Lynn dermabraded and grafted my left cheek in May. June was a double dip: hair transplants in the office the day I arrived, then dermabrasion and grafting of my chin the next day in the OR.

One time Lynn worried that a graft he had just applied might be rejected so he harvested a second piece of skin as a backup, put it in a cardboard cup with some dry ice, and told me to give it to the physicians at Bethesda when I went for a dressing change. Priceless is as close as I can come in describing the look that flashed across the features of the perky flight attendant when I told her what the cup contained and asked if she would please put it in the fridge for the duration of the flight. As it turned out, the extra skin wasn't needed.

When we had six months under our belt, we were satisfied that the convoluted plan we had come up with was working. Then it all fell apart.

Not long after I had returned home from my June sojourn to the land of blues and barbecue, as I thought of Kansas City, my face started secreting a suspicious fluid. I think it started in one spot but soon spread to my entire face. Janie and I conferred with Lynn by phone. In conversations with him, with medical personnel at Bethesda, and through the requisite lab tests it was determined that I had acquired a staph infection, a pernicious one.

Hospitals are the usual source of staph infections though the germ that causes it can be found on many healthy people. The germs are harmless unless they find a way into the bloodstream. At that point they can become lethal, even for the fittest individual.

I didn't know how I acquired my staph infection, though I strongly suspected the hospital. But it didn't matter; I'm not sure I had even heard the term "medical malpractice" in those days. For Janie and me, the issue was how to beat the goddamn bug, not how to profit from it.

We never did beat it. It kept us at battle stations for nearly four months. My role in the fight amounted to little more than swallowing massive amounts of antibiotics. But the staphylococcus bacteria were combat hardened foes and repelled everything we threw at them.

Janie was the one on the front lines. Almost daily she washed my face with bandages soaked in saline, then wiped away the pus that had been exuded overnight. She also punctured pustules as they came to a head and cleaned up the mess after they burst.

That was our summer of '72, and it badly disrupted my surgical schedule. By fall Lynn was growing increasingly worried that the staph might damage the gains we had made. In October he turned the heavy artillery on the bug, dermabrading my entire face and lancing the abscesses that survived the sanding. This time I spent more than two weeks in the hospital. Large areas of my face were raw from the dermabrasion and had to be treated with an antibiotic ointment, a topical antiseptic, and saline compresses. The outer layer of skin had been scraped away by the dermabrasion and it was not a sure thing that it would regenerate itself. When it began to do so, both Lynn and I breathed a sigh of relief, and he sent me home.

It was during this unusually long time in the hospital that I read a book I think of to this day as the finest of all chronicles of the Vietnam War, especially the fuzzy, and at times cynical, decision making that got us into it. I don't know how I found David Halberstam's *The Best and the Brightest* in the hospital, but once I did I couldn't put it down.

I read all 665 pages, doing so with great difficulty, partly because of the exceedingly small print, mostly because I could only see through a single peephole and gunk was constantly draining into it. When I finished, I knew that David Halberstam and *The Best and the Brightest* had become the standard against which I would measure any future achievements as a reporter and writer.

— — — —

During one last surgery, in January 1973, Lynn kept me on the table for three hours. He used every minute of it. First he relaxed the contraction that afflicted both eyelids and caused their inner surfaces to turn out. To do so he cut into the area below each eyelid to release the tension caused by the heavy scarring. Into the gaps created by the incisions he inserted thick skin grafts taken from my right leg.

Next he performed a vermilionplasty, a procedure for evening out and reshaping the curvature of my lips. In the process, he removed a defect I wasn't even aware of in the left corner of my mouth.

Throughout the three hours, Lynn resurfaced, released, sliced, created flaps of skin and of muscle, rotated them, and sutured them into place.

When I made it to the recovery room, I thought about this operation being the last one, that I was finished with reconstructive surgery. Nothing to cheer about, just recognition that I had reached a milestone; whatever could be done to salvage my features had been done over the previous seven years.

The thought was anticlimactic. Three hours earlier, after I had been sedated by injection, a mask came down toward my face. This was nothing new. The mask was a fixture of all my operations.

The first time the mask dropped down on me was in Japan. I felt only mild trepidation then. How many times since had I been operated on under general anesthesia? I counted thirty-five. I don't remember each of those operations, but I do remember intensifying fear each time the mask clamped down on my nose and mouth.

This time I was in a full-blown panic. As the mask came down, I shouted to myself, Never again, motherfucker. Not going to do this again. No fucking way.

Twenty

RICHARD

I started work about a month later at the *Evening Sun*, the afternoon newspaper in Baltimore that engaged in relentless fraternal combat with its better-known, higher-toned morning sibling, the *Sun*. The staffs of the two papers, who existed within spitting distance of each other in the same newsroom, were the bitterest of rivals.

My job, after a short stint on general assignment, was covering City Hall. My adversary from the ranks of the *Sun* was another newcomer with the pretentious name Richard Ben Cramer.

With his kinky black beard, Richard resembled a swashbuckling pirate, one whose threats of dismemberment or worse were offset by laughing eyes that seemed to say, Hey, I'm not serious about the stuff I just said. Or, when talking to a news source, I know you're bullshitting me, but I don't mind, I'm going to find out what's going on anyway. This way may even be more fun.

To me Richard had a goofy demeanor, but I must have had it wrong because he was irresistible to women judging by the way they flocked to him. He also personified a word just then coming into vogue—charisma. Everyone felt it, this larger-than-life quality. Once Richard and I were invited to a local political gathering on a yacht docked on the Baltimore waterfront. I arrived on time. Richard was late.

"Where the hell's Cramer?" someone asked. It wasn't a friendly question. A few days earlier Richard had written a story raising questions about the ethics of one or two of the men on board. The others were pals of the guys he nailed.

Richard was ten minutes late, fifteen minutes late. . . . At last he came sauntering down the pier, sporting this white, broad-brimmed Panama hat he always wore, smiling broadly, clearly unapologetic about his tardiness. As he neared the yacht, he picked up some grumbling that he knew came from the targets of his story and their cronies. As he climbed aboard, he swept the hat from his head with a flourish and flung it high in the air as if launching a Frisbee. I watched, as we all did, as the hat spun lazily over the water. Finally it settled on the surface, bobbing happily, an image that said whoever had been wearing it now slept with the fishes.

"Hey, look guys," said Richard, pointing to the hat, "You got me."

With that he let loose a guffaw so boisterous and infectious that everyone, including men who moments before were thinking the darkest of thoughts about him, could not keep themselves from joining in.

I laughed, too. But for the first time since I had become a reporter four years earlier I worried that I may have met my match.

— — — —

Richard had many strengths as a reporter, among them a taste for the offbeat, an eye for the telling detail, and an ear for the marvelously discordant quote. He could make a story of minimal significance a must-read just because he made it so much fun. Take his story about the legislative race in a section of South Baltimore known as Pigtown, remembered to this day as "Bip's deathbed endorsement" story. It began: "Pigtown is alive with the news that its beloved senator left a political legacy that will live on in the new 47th district."

Richard reported that the recently deceased state senator William L. Hodges, known as Bip, had shaken the political firmament of the district by blessing from his deathbed the long-shot candidacy of Cornell Dypski, who was running for his old senatorial seat.

One of Senator Hodges's sons told Richard that after his father received last rites he gathered the family around his hospital bed and murmured words destined to live after him, certainly for the few weeks until Election Day.

"He said, 'Back Dypski,' and that's what we're doing," Richard quoted the son as saying. The story read as if Richard was standing with the grief-stricken Hodges clan as Bip drew his final breath. For all I know, he was.

In the same story Richard introduced readers to a promising first-time candidate named American Joe Miedusiewski. Rendering the outlandish as if it made all the sense in the world, Richard explained that the former Joseph Miedusiewski had legally changed his name so the habitués of his father's East Baltimore watering hole, American Joe's Bar, would realize he was Big Joe's kid when they entered the voting booth.

Richard touched all the bases in that story, in the process bringing to the *Sun* a splashy, unconventional style of journalism just then coming into vogue within the profession.

This is how most reporters would have described the East Baltimore political powers that anointed American Joe:

The Staszak-Hofferbert-DiPietro coalition, the dominant political organization in East Baltimore where almost 60 percent of the 47th district voters reside, has the clout to elect just about any candidate it chooses to support.

This is how Richard wrote it:

In East Baltimore, where almost 60 percent of the 47th district votes are found, the Staszak-Hofferbert-DiPietro machine could probably make a respectable showing for an albino duckbill platypus if it chose to endorse one.

Christ, not just a duckbill platypus, but an albino duckbill platypus! This is what I didn't know about the Bip Hodges and American Joe stories until I read them: I didn't know there was a section of South Baltimore called Pigtown; I'd never heard of Cornell Dypski; ditto for American Joe; ditto for the Staszak-Hofferbert-DiPietro political machine. I'd heard the name Bip Hodges, but that was about it. It wasn't like I was stupid or lazy; I had been living a sheltered existence.

Twenty-one

PUNCH-DRUNK

Richard Cramer was a bachelor. He made it a point to get around the city when he wasn't at work. He hung out where political people hung out, chatting up sources and gathering string—newspaper jargon for collecting scraps of information of the sort that come in handy down the line.

I was married and the father of three small children. (Yes, there were now three, Amanda arriving in August 1974.) Janie expected me home for dinner in the evening, not wandering the city with no clear purpose. I didn't want Janie to be unhappy. I loved her. I owed her too much. I went home as soon as I finished work.

But there was also this: I hated getting beaten on a story. I especially hated getting beaten by Richard. Not sure why. He was cocky as hell, but he also was one of the nicest guys I knew. It didn't happen every day, either, but for a time it was happening all too frequently.

Over the next year, as Richard and I exchanged punches at City Hall on a daily basis these factors and others were coloring my life. It didn't help that I began to feel as if I was fighting with one hand tied behind my back.

No doubt Richard was an extraordinary reporter and writer. Like my high school football *bête noir* Lenny Rochester, he probably was better than me. But I couldn't tolerate that prospect. Richard would have to prove it in the ring, there was too much riding on the outcome. With my assignment to the high-profile City Hall beat I sensed I was closing on my peers and might finally pull even with them. I wasn't going down without a fight.

Maybe I was looking for a fight. My editors seemed pleased with my work at City Hall and often praised it. None suggested that Richard was doing a better job than me, though it was evident to me that he was. Perhaps if I had been content with the status quo, the inevitable spillover into my personal life could have been avoided.

But, really, there was never any chance of that, not for someone as competitive as me and as bruised as me who had come to believe that if I worked hard enough and outperformed everyone else, I might be able to neutralize the horror that had befallen me. At least that's what I tell myself on those rare occasions when I wonder if perhaps I wasn't completely to blame for wrecking a seemingly indestructible marriage.

— — — —

Richard had a devoted audience of political junkies who relished his Runyonesque tales of the Baltimore political demimonde. I didn't contest him on that turf, at least not right away. My job as City Hall correspondent was to cover the mayor, William Donald Schaefer, as well as the City Council and the city government, not to report on the small-bore state legislative races that Richard couldn't seem to stay away from.

Schaefer was a man of many eccentricities. A confirmed bachelor, he lived with his elderly mother, irresistibly named Tululu, in his childhood home, a modest two-story dwelling on Edgewood Street in West Baltimore. By the time Schaefer became mayor, he and his mother were the only white people left in the neighborhood. He didn't drink, he didn't smoke, he didn't womanize. He did have a lady friend, the no less irresistibly named Hilda Mae Snoops, who materialized on those occasions when he would have seemed underdressed without a woman by his side. He tended roses in the small patch of dirt in front of his home and cultivated exotic orchids in his City Hall office. His defining quality, all agree, was his unadulterated love for Baltimore and his indefatigable efforts to transform it into one of the nation's greatest and most livable cities.

Even those who held him in the highest esteem, however, would concede that William Donald Schaefer was not an easy man to work for. Or to cover—as Richard Cramer and I and a legion of other reporters who preceded and followed us would attest. Richard, no surprise, wrote the story that revealed the telling nickname the mayor's subordinates had bestowed on him: Mayor Annoyed.

Rhymed, Richard pointed out, with paranoid.

Schaefer, as the nickname suggests, did not trust many people. First among the many people he didn't trust were reporters. When I was first assigned to City Hall, I wrote a long story about a highway project that had been bogged down in controversy for no less than thirty years. An old story but one that regained currency when Schaefer announced he was going to build the thing, the opponents be damned.

I interviewed the leaders of the opposition. I also spoke to the mayor's planners and public works officials. I requested an interview with the mayor but was turned down.

The story I wrote was balanced and complete. I let each faction have its say. The story broke no new ground; it just brought readers up to date on the status of the project. As stories go, it had no edge, couldn't have been more vanilla.

At this point, little more than a week on the beat, I still hadn't met the mayor, even though I'd dropped by his office repeatedly in an effort to pay a courtesy call and introduce myself.

One day a fellow reporter alerted me that Schaefer was coming down the hallway outside the City Hall pressroom. I blew through the double doors into the corridor and planted myself directly in his path. He kept coming at me, probably expecting me to move out of his way. I didn't. He stopped when we were nose to nose.

He looked, uh, annoyed by my presence, as if I was invading his personal space, when, technically, he was invading mine. I smiled at him and said brightly, "Mr. Mayor, I'm Bob Timberg, the *Evening Sun*'s new City Hall reporter. I just want to introduce myself."

"Oh, I know who you are," he replied in an unnaturally deep voice that recalled the Big Bad Wolf threatening to blow the house down. "I've read your story. I used it to wallpaper my toilet."

"What?" I asked, unsure that I had heard what I'd just heard.

"I said I read your story and wallpapered my toilet with it."

I stood there, flabbergasted. After a second or two, I shrugged, stepped aside, and he went on his way.

— — — —

At first I thought I was overmatched in taking on Richard. Certainly, as I grudgingly conceded to myself, he was the better writer. But I was learning from him. Painful lessons sure, but soon I was challenging him on his own turf. Like Richard, I covered a ten-dollar-a-plate tribute to a city public works superintendent named Buddy Palughi, a colorful if dubious character whose records had just been subpoenaed as part of a city kickback probe.

Richard provided a marvelous description of the guest of honor as "resplendent . . . in an emerald green double-knit suit, dark green shirt, white tie, and green patent-vinyl slippers."

He further enlivened his story of the event, held at an East Baltimore banquet hall, with small details, noting, for example, that a local band named The Romanos serenaded the guest of honor with the theme from *The Godfather.*

I had The Romanos and *The Godfather* theme in my story, too, but I also had the East Baltimore Sandwich King and Richard didn't.

Mr. Palughi reached in his pocket, flashed a $100 dollar bill and, pointing to the tall man beside him, said, "He just give me this."

"Why'd you do that?" the man—who identified himself

as Lou Patti, proprietor of the Sandwich King on Eastern Avenue—was asked.

"Because he's a boy who made good in this world," Mr. Patti said.

About five or six weeks into my time covering City Hall, I found myself working the room in the aftermath of a Council meeting, filling in the blanks on one or two of the more interesting issues the Council had taken up. I then started back to the office, hustling north on Calvert Street toward the *Sun* building four blocks away. Under a street lamp at Calvert and Saratoga Street I saw two men, both well dressed, quietly conversing.

As I approached I recognized them as two of the most important officials in the administration of Mayor Schaefer, both of whom I had seen and said hello to at the Council meeting. I had paid courtesy calls on each of them shortly after taking over the City Hall beat. Those conversations were brief, but I found both of them engaging and press savvy. Once I knew them better, I thought, they could be quite helpful to me.

As I crossed the street, they turned and greeted me pleasantly. Both were intensely loyal and admiring of Mayor Schaefer, but unlike so many in his administration they did not view him with what sometimes seemed to me lapdog devotion.

We soon found ourselves conversing, probably on some issue that had come up at the Council meeting. As we talked, I noticed a bedraggled woman approaching. She wore little more than rags and was unsteady on her feet. Unbidden, she joined our circle and studied each of us from head to toe like an officer inspecting her troops. And then she started screaming.

"LOOK AT HIS FACE! LOOK AT HIS FACE! LOOK AT HIS FACE! LOOK AT HIS FACE! LOOK AT HIS FACE!"

Twenty-two

THE OCCASION OF SIN

I was getting flashier, partly, I guess, from going head to head with Richard. And it felt good. I had been on the ropes, even a bit punch-drunk, but now I was throwing some leather and working my way back toward the center of the ring. To get there, though, I had to take more time away from Janie and the kids. Not a lot, but more than I had been taking, which already had been deemed too much.

The truth was, I was improving as a reporter, but I seemed to be getting worse as a husband and father, and that was taking its toll on Janie and me. No question we still loved each other, but our relationship was changing. We had fun with the kids but rarely as a couple. To a measurable extent, the warmth that had sustained us through long separations and years in hospitals was slipping away. And with it the passion that had always been a vital part of our relationship.

I tried, and I know Janie tried at least as hard, to reverse the heading we were on. But the momentum was almost all in one direction. For any number of reasons, notably the demands the three kids made on her time, she stopped regularly reading my stories. There was one issue she never could get beyond: her belief—despite my attempts to dissuade her—that when she was at home cleaning house and taking care of the children I was off living what she called more than once a "gay, exciting life."

"It's nothing like that," I'd say. "My life is an open book. If you want to know what I'm doing all day, just read my stories."

— — — —

I realized as far back as the latter part of my time at the *Evening Capital* that Janie and I were starting to come apart. My job was always to blame. It infuriated Janie that I never seemed able to get home on time. She needed help getting our three kids to bed. They needed to see me more. So did she. Sometimes she would call me at the office, asking when I'd be home, scold me when I said I'd be a little late, often in an angry voice that could be heard by the reporter who sat across the double desk from me in the newsroom.

Something else, I now know, was at play though I didn't give it much weight at the time. Janie and I almost never discussed my job except in terms of the personal problems it was creating for us. I may have written a good story or a lame one—it didn't matter. Both went unremarked at home. It was as if I spent my days in a world that had little or nothing to do with the one I found myself in when I stepped through the front door in the evening.

Neither of us was thinking of a separation or divorce. We had been through so much together that we didn't believe anything could come between us. But looking back I see that this attitude bred an arrogance that masked the peril hanging over us until it was too late.

I felt guilty and helpless. I still loved Janie. And I knew I would never be able to repay her for everything she had done for me. I wanted her to be happy, for her sake, sure, but also for mine. I wanted to be happy, too. Instead, I had an unhappy wife, which was making my life miserable. I kept telling her things would get better, but I had no confidence that they would. My job was not going to change and I wasn't going to start cutting corners in the way I did it. I still had a lot to prove. That hadn't changed.

Something else had entered the mix, though for a long time it seemed like nothing more than a mischievous thought with which to tantalize myself at odd moments. Was it possible, I would idly wonder, that a woman other than Janie might find me desirable? As the rift in Janie's and my relationship widened, I toyed with this idea more and more. I was playing with fire and in different circumstances this might have been cause for alarm. Each time such wayward thoughts threatened to gain traction, though, reality intruded and I came to my senses: Who was I kidding? Women liked me, maybe even admired me, but I had no doubt they still pitied me, an emotion with zero potential as an aphrodisiac.

At this point I wasn't looking for trouble, at least I don't think I was, but there was little doubt that I had wandered onto that dubious terrain that Catholics call the Occasion of Sin. And though there seemed little chance of anyone joining me on my meanderings, I knew now that I was available in the event anyone volunteered.

And someone did.

— — — —

There's no way to defend what happened next. Only context. Janie was not a shallow person, and for me to ascribe the deterioration of our relationship solely to my work habits strains credulity well beyond the breaking point. Something else was going on, and I think we both knew it without actually understanding it. This was where our differing approaches in dealing with a problem revealed themselves. Janie, as always, thought about possible solutions. My instinct was to gut it out.

Janie suggested that we seek counseling. In retrospect, I guess that made sense. A neutral setting might have brought some unexamined issues to the surface. At the time, though, I said, flatly, no. My only experience with a psychiatrist had been the quack at the San Diego Naval Hospital who thought it might be a good idea for me to wear a bag over my head.

I knew better than to extend the insensitivity of a single doctor to all psychiatrists. But there was another reason I rejected the idea of counseling. I did not want anyone—psychiatrist, psychologist, therapist, well-meaning friend—messing with my head. I had put myself back together with bubble gum and sealing wax; I couldn't take the chance that it would all come apart if some shrink spotted a tantalizing thread or a rogue Irish pennant and decided to tug on it.

I've tried to explain what happened next by saying that professional success was not enough for me, that to feel I had completed my return trip to life before Vietnam I needed to be desired by a woman other than Janie. The first and, as it turned out, the only person to whom I offered this explanation at the time was one of my friends from *Evening Capital* days, the Old Testament prophet Dick Levine.

He listened to my story, thought about it for some thirty seconds, then asked, "Are you sure you just didn't want to get laid?" I flared, started to protest, but changed my mind. The truth is, I wasn't sure then; I'm not sure now.

At the time of that conversation I had been having an affair for about six months. The woman was smart, capable, and attractive. I liked her very much, and she seemed to feel the same way about me. Among other things, we found a lot to talk about, including jobs, hers and mine. We were, for a time, very good together.

For us to be together, of course, I had to do what men who cheat on their wives always do, become a world-class liar. And I had to live with the dreadful realization that the reason Janie believed my lies was because she trusted me. And that she would be hurt beyond measure if she found out.

She finally did. She put a lot of puzzle pieces together, discerned a pattern, confronted me, and I admitted it. Not long after, in tears, I threw some clothes and toiletries into a suitcase and moved out.

Twenty-three

ON MY OWN

After moving out I bounced around a bit, finally settled in a ground-floor apartment in a two-story colonial house on Murray Avenue, in an older section of Annapolis just outside the city's historic district. It had a living room, dining room, bedroom, kitchen, bathroom. The apartment pretty much met my needs, at least once I got it furnished. Every piece of furniture, all the dishes, everything, was from yard sales or Goodwill.

Janie insisted that I take all three children every weekend from Friday evening till Sunday evening. Without exception. This meant that for the foreseeable future I would either be working or taking care of the kids every free moment of every day except for the few hours on weekday evenings after work. To my mind, the arrangement was punitive, but I was too guilt-ridden to object.

My life now split into two parts: Weekdays were for work; weekends were for the kids. And the affair ended. No time to give it the care it needed to move beyond what it was.

During the week, newly liberated, I covered every political event I could get to, no matter how insignificant—fund-raisers, bull roasts, oyster roasts, and crab feasts—all fixtures in the state's marvelously polyglot, often tasty political universe.

Sometimes the event yielded a story, but not usually. It didn't matter. I met people, got to know them, made myself a recognizable figure, someone whose phone calls they would answer and to whom they would tell things others didn't want me to know. I expected my efforts to pay off down the line, and they did. As they had, no doubt, for Richard Cramer.

There was a human quality to politics in Maryland that made it a delight to cover. Exhausting but fun. In Washington, as I would later learn, just about anyone you wanted to talk to—the president, senators, congressmen, even barely significant bureaucrats—was walled off from reporters by a coterie of aides. And everyone watched his or her words so closely that what was said was only occasionally helpful, and usually deadly.

Things were different in Maryland. Everyone was accessible, from the governor on down. And they were far less guarded in what they told reporters. Really, you never knew what someone was going to say; often it was priceless.

One day, for example, George Santoni, a member of the House of Delegates from Baltimore, was indicted for allegedly shaking down small contractors who turned out to be FBI agents.

The next day, the Santoni indictment was the talk of the General Assembly. Ray Dypski, a chunky delegate and the brother of state Senator Cornell Dypski (the beneficiary of Bip Hodges's deathbed endorsement), rose from his seat with the Baltimore delegation and started lumbering toward the front of the House chamber where I was sitting with other reporters.

He was heading for me, a perplexed expression on his face. When he reached me, he leaned down and whispered, "Can you believe it, Bob? The man is a high school graduate!"

———

Weekends were different. I struggled to come up with ways to entertain the kids. We went to the movies a lot. Mandy loved *Grease*. We must have watched it seven or eight times. In a theater, not on TV. None of the other movies playing around seemed appropriate for children and the boys didn't object. We saw it so many times I started seeing John Travolta in my sleep. I would have preferred Olivia Newton-John, but so it goes.

That first year Janie told me I had to take the kids for Thanksgiving. I panicked. That meant cooking a turkey, which, of course, I had never done before.

Starting small seemed the wisest course, but I knew there was no way the kids would be satisfied with a turkey the size of a pigeon, so I bought a regulation-size bird, a fourteen-pounder. I had a big surprise when I reached into the chest cavity and pulled out this deep red slimy stuff. Plus—a bonus—the neck.

Struggling to control my gag reflex, I wrapped it all in a newspaper, stuffed it in a paper bag, and disposed of it in a neighbor's garbage can. Not the next-door neighbor's, either.

I had a James Beard cookbook, which would have gotten me through the roasting process, but I was victimized by what these days we'd call too much information. I prepared the turkey according to the directions in the cookbook, then put it in the preheated oven. The question was, how would I know when it was done? I had three ways to tell.

First, I inserted a meat thermometer in the turkey's thigh. When the thermometer read 165 degrees, the turkey should be done. At least that's what the cookbook said, and I trusted James Beard.

Second, a table in the cookbook said a fourteen-pound turkey, unstuffed, would take about four hours.

Third, the place where the turkey came from—I shied away from the word "slaughterhouse," and I don't think the euphemism "processing plant" had yet been coined—had inserted a little red button into the chest. It was supposed to pop up when the turkey was cooked.

The kids set the table, I made mashed potatoes, then we gathered around the television and watched football. Mandy was great. She never complained. The turkey smelled wonderful.

At the four-hour mark I checked the meat thermometer. Sure enough, it had just hit the 165-degree target temperature.

By two measures, time and temperature, the turkey should have been ready. Except the pop-up button hadn't yet popped up. I figured the people at the turkey place knew the turkey best so I decided to wait a little longer for the button to do its thing. A half hour passed and the button remained firmly implanted in the turkey's breast. Then an hour. I told the kids we probably should let it go a little longer. At the two-hour mark, the kids huddled, then announced a consensus: The pop-up button was a dud, it was never going to pop up. The turkey, they declared, was cooked. Let's eat!

Hold it, I said. The last thing we wanted was underdone turkey. I grow faint when I spot little rivulets of blood on poultry so I decreed another half hour.

The pop-up popper never popped. I finally took the turkey out of the oven. It looked wonderful, a perfect golden brown. I let it rest for about twenty minutes, to let the juices settle, as James Beard instructed.

Time to carve. I grasped the left drumstick and was about to cut it loose from the breast when it came off in my hand. Odd. Usually you had to twist and turn a drumstick and cut through the joint to free it up.

I then began to carve the breast, anticipating lovely slices of white meat neatly arrayed on the platter waiting below. Instead, that whole side of the turkey crumbled under my knife, sliding down the breastbone like an avalanche shaken loose by the sound of an explosion. A powdery white pile that resembled a snowdrift, but could only be a mound of turkey dust, formed on the plate below.

Moral of the story: Always have a package of hot dogs in the fridge.

Twenty-four

THE PINK BATHROBE YEAR

J anie called 1977, the year I moved out, her Pink Bathrobe Year. I left in January. For months after, gripped by a remorseless depression, she spent much of the day in her pink chenille robe, trying to make sense of what had happened, wondering if somehow it could be undone.

The depression might have paralyzed her if it wasn't for the kids, whose needs still had to be met, though now by one parent, not two.

Fortunately, she was as tough and resourceful as she was kind. Still reeling from my departure, she soon began substitute teaching at the local elementary school and in special education classes elsewhere in the district even though she had not taught for ten years. And within a few months she had begun work on a master's degree in special education at Loyola College in Baltimore.

She was in no hurry to tell people about our separation. That included her parents, from whom she withheld the news until months later, when they returned to Maryland from Florida, where they spent their winters.

"I'm going to get you a good Jewish lawyer," was her father's first reaction. (An attorney himself, he had never fully made his peace with my mixed parentage.)

But Janie deferred seeking legal advice. She feared I might be having a nervous breakdown or suffering from a war-related affliction of the sort that we now call PTSD. If so, she did not want to abandon me. And though still raw from learning of the affair, she refused to give up on our marriage, continuing to hope it could be saved.

One wonders why. She had gotten me through several agonizing years, nursing my wounds but more important reviving my sense of myself. I don't think anyone who had seen me near death in Da Nang or Yokohama would believe that little more than a decade later I would be a top reporter for a major metropolitan newspaper and the father of three children.

To this day I think of Janie as the person most responsible for my recovery. Even Lynn Ketchum comes in second. So how did I repay her? By having an affair and blowing up our marriage.

— — — —

A few of Janie's friends rallied around her, not many. Gradually she realized that some of those she used to talk to regularly were no longer calling her. She thought of it as just another feature in a world that seemed to be crumbling around her, of a piece with the chilling sense of aloneness that had taken hold of her life. Around this time, she remembers saying to someone, "I'd have more support if Bob had died in Vietnam."

There was another element, a related one that she only became aware of years later and that taught her the meaning of the adage that no good deed goes unpunished.

It seems that a few of our acquaintances—no more than a handful as far as she could tell—blamed Janie for our separation. The reason, so the story went, was that she could no longer tolerate my scarred face and had forced me to leave.

On one occasion a woman we barely knew saw me picking up Amanda at preschool on successive Friday afternoons, a time when most men were usually at work. She put two and two together and spread the word within her circle that I was no longer living at home, which was true, because Janie could no longer endure my appearance, which couldn't have been further from the truth.

Janie didn't realize for some time what the woman, and probably others, had said about her. It was so far from the truth that it never even occurred to her that people, especially those who had been even remotely close to us, would entertain such a possibility.

There were clues though. Janie sensed a chill when she ran into old acquaintances, but not till long after did she understand what was behind it.

Some ten years later, it all became clear during a conversation with a friend with whom she had lost touch. "We thought you had kicked Bob out," the friend told her.

Twenty-five

BLOWING MY CHANCE

My apartment on Murray Avenue fell into the category of "good enough for me," which meant that it did the job and that I felt I deserved nothing better. During the year and a half I lived there, though, something inexplicable happened: Against daunting odds, Scott, Craig, Amanda, and I developed a closeness that endures to this day, more than three decades later. We had always been close, but we grew closer. In fact, many years later as we were sitting around the dinner table, Craig, by then a teenager, referred to this time as "the good old days." I was flabbergasted. I couldn't decide if this was sarcasm, irony, or what. Another possibility was that he was serious. My first reaction was to ask him what he meant, but I let it lie, not sure I could handle the answer.

It helped, of course, that the kids were so young. Scott was seven, Craig six, Mandy two, so they didn't understand exactly what had happened between their mother and me. They knew I wasn't living with them, but because Janie didn't tell them, they did not know I was the one who had precipitated the breakup.

Despite Janie's complaints, I'd never felt like an absentee father. True, I often got home late, but I gave a lot of baths, read lots of stories, played plenty of games. Even so, the time we spent together during the Murray Avenue years—every weekend, Friday evening till Sunday evening—fostered a remarkable bond between the kids and me. We were doing something together every waking minute of every weekend.

Sleeping arrangements were spare. I had the bedroom. Scott and Craig shared a futon mattress in the living room. Mandy slept there, too, on a cot. The rest of the living room furnishings were a TV, TV stand, and a slightly ratty easy chair that a neighbor across the street had put out at the curb for Goodwill and that I appropriated with only minor pangs of guilt.

The apartment had plenty of heat in the winter, but there was no air-conditioning to offset the sweltering temperatures and stultifying humidity of summers in Annapolis. Calling on my slim knowledge of thermodynamics, which I barely passed at the Academy, I convinced the children that we should make our way around the apartment by crawling along the floor. The reason, I explained, was because hot air rises, so the air nearest to the floor was cooler.

I never understood why a midshipman had to take thermodynamics if he was going to be a Marine. Now it made sense.

This should have been a wrenching time for me, and it was, but not when I was with Scott, Craig, and Amanda. I mostly had fun, not adult fun, but fun nonetheless. And I think it was the same for them.

Perhaps the most fun was dancing to LPs I played on my battered record player. I didn't have much in the way of furniture, but I had books and records.

I had several Beatles albums, a Billy Joel, the Gerry Rafferty album with "Baker Street" and the great sax solo, the *Saturday Night Fever* sound track album, Elton John's *Greatest Hits*, and lots more.

Elton John's music was great to dance to, plus we told Amanda that the song "Bennie and the Jets" was "Mandy and the Jets." That made her really happy. She probably knows the truth now, but she didn't get it from me and I doubt Scott or Craig told her.

I worked at making the kids' weekends with me fun. To an extent I think I succeeded. What I didn't fully understand then is that this period was taking a toll on them that was serious and long-lasting.

Scott, Craig, and Amanda had ringside seats at the explosion of a marriage. Craig remembers hiding in his bed, sometimes with Scott, as Janie and I screamed at each other for what seemed like hours. This usually occurred on Sunday evenings when I brought the kids home.

All three displayed great resilience, coming through these stormy years so well that my doubts about the existence of an Almighty lessened considerably. But whenever I'm tempted for some reason to pat myself on my back, I'm reminded that I have at least as much to be ashamed of as to be proud of.

— — — —

In April 1978, as my coverage of the annual ninety-day legislative session of the Maryland General Assembly concluded, I realized I had been running in place for two years. It had not been an unpleasant two years. Anything but. I had been moved to a bigger beat as the *Evening Sun*'s state political reporter, and I had written some good stories—a few exclusives, some features I was proud of, and two or three investigative pieces. I could not imagine any other assignment that I would enjoy as much.

At the same time I knew that I was getting too comfortable, which was fine if covering politics in Maryland was the extent of my ambitions but an insidious affliction if I wanted something more.

I did. I wanted to be a Washington correspondent for the *Baltimore Sun*. Two reasons: I wanted to test myself at what I thought of as the highest, most competitive, level of reporting. More than that, I wanted to plant my battle colors at the top of my profession or as close to it as I could get.

I guessed that Pat Furgurson, the Washington bureau chief, respected me but probably didn't like me. We butted heads at the 1976 Democratic National Convention in New York, the one that nominated Jimmy Carter.

Pat brought his whole bureau to New York, eight or so veteran correspondents in addition to himself. The *Evening Sun* contingent consisted of Norman Wilson, a dogged reporter and close friend with whom I had covered the previous year's city elections, and me. Neither Norman nor I had ever been to a national political convention. We had never covered national politics, either.

The odds were nine against two, which mattered only if you were an *Evening Sun* chauvinist like me and you had gone to New York determined not to be bullied by the *Sun* or embarrassed by it. For their part, Furgurson and his henchmen went to New York barely aware that Norman and I existed.

The coin of the realm at the convention was floor passes. You needed one to get onto the convention floor and interview the delegates. Without one, you were stuck in the grandstands surrounding the action below, pissing and moaning, thinking dark thoughts, and plotting ways to make it onto the floor.

Furgurson controlled the passes allotted to the Sunpapers, the *Sun* and *Evening Sun* both. I asked Pat for our share. He said it didn't work like that. He was going to hang on to the passes. If Norman or I wanted one, he said, just ask him and he would accommodate us as best he could.

"Why don't you give me our two passes and we won't have to bother you," I said.

"Nah, nah, I'm going to hang on to the passes until I see how many we get in total and then you'll get yours," Pat replied.

Pat was hard to dislike. For one thing, he was a courtly Virginia gentleman. He also had been a Marine. As a newspaperman, he had done it all, reporting from Baltimore, Annapolis, Moscow, and Vietnam. And finally, for whatever reason, possibly because he was a decent person despite his corporate coloration, he did not want me to feel he was screwing Norman and me. So it did not go over well with him when I said, "Pat, I think you're gonna screw us."

After that, the atmosphere in the Sunpapers press area grew tense whenever Pat and I came within five yards of each other. One afternoon, my only friend in Furgurson's crew, Tom Edsall, my predecessor as the *Evening Sun*'s political reporter, drifted over to my typing station and, in a conspiratorial tone, whispered, "Hey, Bob, I thought you should know this. Pat says he's really going to fuck you and Norman tonight."

Before I could react, Tom grinned, which told me he was probably joking. Actually, Pat was quite evenhanded in distributing the passes. I can't remember a time when Norman or I needed one and he didn't have one for us. Since I considered it our due, I never thanked him when he gave me a pass, just took it and walked away. At best our relationship was cool when the convention ended.

———

Only after the fact did I think about the opportunity I had blown at the convention. I wanted to go to the *Sun*'s Washington bureau. Pat Furgurson, the Washington bureau chief, did the hiring for the bureau. At the convention I might have developed a relationship with him, a professional friendship. No obsequiousness. Nothing that smacked of ass-kissing. Just dealing with him as the high-ranking Sunpapers colleague that he was rather than as someone I was afraid to turn my back on. Swallowing my suspicions, treating him politely, and writing some good stories might have advanced my prospects considerably.

Well, too bad, I told myself. By going to the *Sun* bureau I would have finally completed my comeback. Now, in the two years since that convention, Furgurson had hired two new reporters into the bureau and shown no interest in me. As the legislature adjourned for the year, I was painfully aware that my chance to break the plane of the goal line—as I had come to think of making it to Washington—was growing ever more dim. I needed what today we would call a game changer, and there was none in sight.

And then there was. A Nieman Fellowship. Winning one was probably less likely than Furgurson hiring me into the Washington bureau, but there was no less prestige connected to it. Maybe more.

Twenty-six

QUESTION, ANSWER, *SQUISH*

The *Sun* was always in my way. No sooner had I decided to go for a Nieman and cleared it with my boss—*Evening Sun* editor Phil Heisler—than I learned that two of the *Sun*'s crackerjack foreign correspondents were also applying for one of the dozen fellowships awarded to American journalists each year.

I was wary of going against them. Whether I liked it or not—and I didn't—the *Sun* was by far the more prestigious of the two papers owned by the A. S. Abell Company, at least in the eyes of outsiders. The *Sun* had a well-stocked Washington bureau and a much-admired network of foreign correspondents. The *Evening Sun* had neither. In fact, the dispatches of the *Sun*'s big-deal correspondents did not even appear in the pages of the *Evening Sun*. We could take on the morning paper at the local level, but we weren't even in the game outside of Baltimore.

There was also this. Both of the *Sun*'s candidates were superb reporters. Fred Hill covered large swaths of Europe, Africa, and the Middle East from London. Years earlier, as a local reporter, he wrote a stunning series on suspicious zoning decisions in Baltimore County that remains to this day a model of investigative reporting. Hal Piper covered the Soviet Union and its satellites from Moscow, the *Sun*'s most important foreign posting. He had the added cachet of getting booted out of the country for writing a sympathetic story about a Soviet dissident that angered the Kremlin crowd.

My credentials were slightly less impressive. I had covered a bunch of suburban counties, Baltimore City Hall, and Maryland politics.

I briefly thought about forgetting the whole thing. Since Fred, Hal, and I were essentially from the same news organization, there was no way more than one of us would land a Nieman. And if I had to choose between Fred, Hal, and me, I certainly would not select me. Fred and Hal were prizewinning foreign correspondents. They were stars. I was a good local reporter, nothing more.

— — — —

The Nieman Fellowships, based at Harvard in Cambridge, Massachusetts, were established in 1937 with a million-dollar gift to the college from Agnes Wahl Nieman, widow of Lucius Nieman, the founder of the *Milwaukee Journal*. Her stated purpose was to "promote and elevate the standards of journalism and educate persons deemed especially qualified for journalism."

The gift came in the depths of the Great Depression, when many reporters—nearly all men—lacked a college education. Harvard president James Conant, after consulting widely, finally came up with an idea that seemed just short of heresy to many of his colleagues: a sabbatical fellowship for experienced journalists. About a dozen were to be invited to Cambridge for an academic year at Harvard and permitted to audit any courses that appealed to them—undergraduate or graduate. If, for example, one's interest was in the American presidency, he could sit in on a course of that name likely taught by Richard Neustadt, a professor widely considered one of the foremost authorities on the subject.

President Conant announced the program in 1938, still beset with doubts that newspapermen would benefit from a year of Harvard-style acculturation. He called it "a very dubious experiment."

Almost immediately the Nieman program became anything but

dubious and Fellows took Conant's dismissive description as a badge of honor.

— — — —

O ne of the first things I did as I set about applying was confer with the two Nieman alumni in the newsroom, columnist Peter Jay and editorial writer Jerry Kelly. Naturally both were on the *Sun* staff. They were encouraging even though they knew Fred and Hal also were applying. Peter provided a crucial bit of intelligence that, had he not done so, probably would have torpedoed my chances early in the process.

"Bob," he said, "it's Nieman, N-i-e-m-a-n, not N-e-i-m-a-n."

I also learned something else encouraging. There was a noblesse oblige flavor to the Nieman Foundation's search for worthy Fellows. The foundation, counterintuitively, did not tilt toward graduates of such highly selective schools as Princeton, Yale, Columbia, or, for that matter, Harvard. In fact, it appeared that an Ivy League education not only did not advance one's chances of winning a Nieman; it may have worked against the applicant. Jon Larsen, a Nieman who bucked the trend by gaining a fellowship while holding two Harvard degrees, viewed the foundation as infatuated with unearthing diamonds in the rough. As he put it, "I've always had the notion of Harvard playing Pygmalion to the unwashed city editors of the world."

In addition to work samples and letters of recommendation, the application called for two essays, the first a proposed course of study that explained how the applicant planned to utilize his or her time at Harvard. There were no restrictions and nothing that required taking courses that related directly to the applicant's beat or specialty.

For example, a diplomatic correspondent might choose courses in art history, an investigative reporter might decide to study the Renaissance poets, and, uh, an unwashed city editor might scratch a long-standing aesthetic itch at the Graduate School of Design. I didn't stray far from my beat. I proposed exploring the impact of money on politics.

The second essay, clearly the more important, called for describing one's experience, career plans, and aspirations. Also sought was an account of how events in one's life had shaped the applicant and his or her commitment to journalism. I had never leaned on my war wounds in seeking a job or anything else other than to acknowledge that they existed. Now, though, there seemed no way I could write this essay without explaining what had happened to me and where it led. My essay started like this: "The path that took me to my first city room began January 18, 1967, about twenty miles southwest of the Vietnamese city of Da Nang."

I was not feeling optimistic when I completed the application, though I felt I had a chance. I knew that my story, as hellacious as it was to live through, was compelling. But after I wrote it I thought it read like a sob story, a plea for special treatment. I was about to scrap it when I realized that like it or not, it was my story. I finally stopped beating myself up about it and mailed off the damn thing with the rest of my application materials in January, just as the 1979 session of the Maryland General Assembly was commencing.

This session was not as much fun as the other three I had covered. A wave of political corruption had rolled over the state in the previous couple of years, its relentless undertow ending the career of Spiro T. Agnew, the Vice President of the United States, and of numerous lesser officeholders. In January, as legislators gathered to begin work in the state's capital, Billy James, the Senate president, deadpanned, "A suffocation of honesty has descended on Annapolis."

By early April, as the session wound down, I began obsessing over the Nieman. If I didn't get one—and considering the caliber of the in-house competition I put the odds at eighty to twenty against—I would have to accept that I had reached my high-water mark: a good local reporter, nothing to be ashamed of but falling well short of one of the two goals I had established to symbolize my return trip to normalcy, either a posting to Washington or a Nieman Fellowship. The first seemed unlikely. Furgurson and I hadn't spoken since the Democratic Convention nearly three years earlier. The Nieman was still in play, but barely. I hung on to the fact that I hadn't been officially informed that I was no longer in the running, though the silence from Harvard seemed telling.

I had about decided I was kidding myself in thinking I could ever qualify for a Nieman when I received a call from Cambridge. The sweet voice on the other end of the line belonged to Tenney Lehman, the executive director of the Nieman Foundation. She told me I was one of the applicants chosen to interview with the Nieman Selection Committee and asked if a visit to Cambridge on such and such a date was convenient for me. If so, she said, she would reserve a room for me at the Harvard Square Hotel.

Yes, I said, that would be convenient for me.

— — — —

I checked into the hotel in midafternoon for an early evening interview at the Harvard Faculty Club. I turned on the TV, stripped down to my socks and underwear, and lay down on the bed to try to relax. I didn't feel intimidated—after Plebe Year at the Naval Academy, a year in Vietnam, and more than thirty operations not many individuals or situations intimidated me—but I was tense. There was a lot riding on this. Winning a Nieman would mean that I was finished playing catch-up.

The eight-person selection committee was comprised of distinguished journalists and important Harvard faculty members. Of the newsmen, the best known were Gene Roberts, editor of the *Philadelphia Inquirer*, and Michael Gartner, publisher of the *Des Moines Register*. Roberts was already well on his way to becoming a legend. He was national editor of the *New York Times* in 1972, when he was lured away to become editor of the *Inquirer*. Almost overnight he transformed the paper into one of the nation's finest and began accumulating Pulitzer Prizes at a head spinning pace. The man who ran the Nieman program and carried the odd title of curator was James Thomson, a former State Department official who had been a source for David Halberstam when he was reporting and researching *The Best and the Brightest*.

I didn't know any of the selection committee members personally, but a few weeks earlier I received a call from John Carroll, one of Roberts's senior editors at the *Inquirer* and previously a *Sun* White House and Vietnam War correspondent. Carroll, a Nieman himself, said he had been helping Roberts sift through the fellowship applications and thought I should know that his boss had been quite impressed by mine. I may have imagined it, but I think Carroll also told me that Roberts planned to support me in the selection committee's deliberations.

I took a shower about an hour and a half before my scheduled interview. It relaxed me. I was feeling kind of jaunty, encouraged by John Carroll's words and the fact that I had been chosen for an interview—more than I ever expected.

My jauntiness almost did me in. I was traipsing around the small hotel room in my bare feet when I ripped the small toe on my left foot on the metal TV stand. I knew it was more than a scratch because, one, it hurt like hell and, two, it was bleeding. The blood wasn't gushing, but it wasn't oozing, either. More of a slow, steady flow.

I pressed a washcloth on the wound to try to stop the bleeding. That worked briefly, but it started up again when I removed the washcloth. Then I combined the washcloth with elevating my foot.

By now I was sweating. And the clock was ticking. Time to get dressed if I was going to make my interview. I was surprised to find a Band-Aid in my toiletry kit. It didn't fully cover the cut, but it came close. I taped it as tight as I could, then worked my sock up over it. So far so good.

I figured the less I walked the better, so I took a cab the few blocks to the Faculty Club. I arrived about fifteen minutes before my interview. Although some forty candidates had been chosen for interviews, there was only one in the waiting area. Jim Thomson, the curator, escorted him upstairs to the interview room before we had a chance to do more than shake hands.

The candidate who preceded him—a beautiful woman named Jan Stucker—came down a couple of minutes later. Jan was a reporter for

SAMMY
TIMBERG

My father, Sammy Timberg, among his other musical achievements, composed background music for Fleischer Studios cartoon characters Popeye, Betty Boop, Olive Oyl, Casper the Friendly Ghost, and Superman, but as a young man he was also a vaudevillian. Young ladies in the audience called him "Fancy Pants."

My mother, under her real name Rosemarie Sinnott or the stage name Collette Ayres, was a model, a cover girl, and a featured dancer in shows mounted by the legendary Florenz Ziegfeld. A 1929 ad in *Good Housekeeping* said "her lovely face attracts a million eyes to magazine covers."

I had an Irish Catholic mother and a Jewish father. To keep things simple, they were married in July 1938 at the Franconia Hotel on West 72 Street in New York City. They then headed for Atlantic City, where they made a handsome couple strolling the famous boardwalk.

The first year at the Naval Academy, known as Plebe Year, is not meant to be fun. Sometimes it is, though, as this photo from 1960 of my roommates and me attests. From left to right, Tom Richman, Frank Spangenberg, Dave Ahern, me.

My June Week date, Jane Benson, later my wife, and me. It's 1963 and I've just become a Naval Academy first classman. It was a happy time, but the world would soon change for us.

My dad and me at June Week 1964, the end of my First Class year at the Academy. In a matter of days I would graduate and be commissioned a second lieutenant in the United States Marine Corps.

My picture in *The Lucky Bag*, the Academy yearbook, during my First Class, or senior, year.

On patrol in Vietnam in 1966.

This is me writing either a letter home or an after-action report.
I wrote lots of letters home. Lots of after-action reports, too.

Books were a great escape for me during my year in Vietnam. I seem to be enjoying what I'm reading. Could be a well-regarded novel. Might also be one of many tales of sexual hijinks that found its way to us from a shadowy publisher called the Hong Kong Press. My guess is it was something by Proust or Tolstoy.

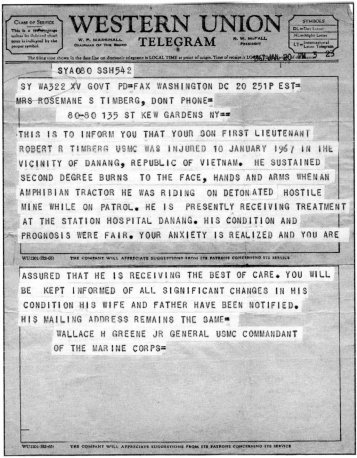

News from the battlefield.

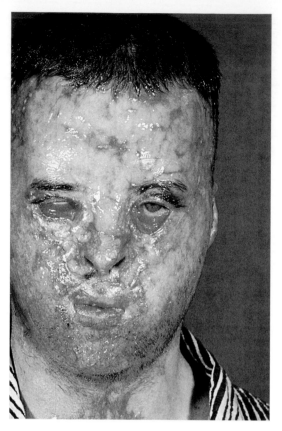

This is how I looked when Dr. Ketchum first saw what he would be dealing with.

Dr. Lynn Ketchum, who performed nearly all my reconstructive surgery, was a lieutenant commander in the Navy's medical corps and stationed at the U.S. Naval Hospital in San Diego when we first joined forces.

This is how I looked at Stanford University in 1968 when I entered the graduate school of journalism and began learning how to be a reporter.

During my five years covering the White House for the *Baltimore Sun* in the 1980s, President Reagan from time to time would meet with a small group of reporters for an hour of off-the-record conversation. I'm in a blue suit directly across from the president and to the left of the fireplace.

Senator John McCain seems to be going to great pains to tell me something. It could be his position on an issue of national importance. It's just as likely that it's one of his nutty jokes. Cindy McCain, the senator's wife, is on his left.

My mother, Rosemarie Sinnott Timberg, and me on the day Kelley Andrews and I were married in her parents' backyard in Lewes, Delaware, in September 1981.

Kelley on our honeymoon on Cape Cod in September 1981.

My dad, Sammy Timberg, a gifted musician, entertains his namesake, Kelley's and my son, Sam, at our home in Bethesda, Maryland, in the mid-1980s.

My daughter Amanda's marriage in April 2002 to Matt Horine, her high school sweetheart, brought the whole family together. From left, Sara Scribner, my son Scott's future wife, Ruey Timberg, my son Craig's wife (holding Cecilia, the first of their three kids), Craig, Kelley, me, Scott, Amanda, Matt, Sam, Kelley's and my son, Janie, Amanda's mother (and my first wife), and Lee Spence, Janie's husband.

My four kids, Craig, Amanda, Sam, and Scott.

Kelley and our son, Sam, at the 2004 wedding in Pasadena, California, of my son Scott and Sara Scribner.

Sam and I at the Cape of Good Hope while visiting Craig and his family in Johannesburg, South Africa, over the 2006 Christmas holidays. At the time Craig was a foreign correspondent covering sub-Saharan Africa for the *Washington Post*.

Janie's and my four grandkids perched in front of the fireplace at Janie's and her husband Lee's home in Severna Park, Maryland, over the Christmas holidays in 2011. From left, Cecilia, the flirtatious Natalie, and Andrew—all Ruey and Craig's children—and Ian, Scott and Sara's son.

My grandson Ian—Scott and Sara's son—and me in 2009 at a playground in Laguna Beach, California, where Janie and I lived when I was a Marine. Ian's sweatshirt is from Stuyvesant, my New York high school alma mater.

My granddaughter Natalie—in one of her many princess dresses—is on the swing, I'm doing the pushing.

My friend Lynn Ketchum, the surgeon who rebuilt my face, and I had lunch at Arthur Bryant's Barbecue, a Kansas City landmark, when I went there to interview him for this book in June 2009. The restaurant more than lived up to its splendid reputation.

the *Record*, a daily in Columbia, South Carolina. We chatted briefly. She was very self-assured. And did I say beautiful? That had to count for something.

Then Jim Thomson came for me. He was engaging, dapper, and for a few seconds my nervousness subsided. It had reasserted itself following the mugging by the TV stand. As we climbed the stairs, though, I felt wetness in my shoe; the Band-Aid had given way.

The interview room was clubby, the selection committee members seated on comfortable chairs. I shook hands with each of them; all greeted me warmly. For the next half hour or so, they peppered me with questions, mostly about my proposal to study money and politics. Michael Gartner, the *Des Moines Register* publisher, was the most pointed in his queries. Gene Roberts was a skilled interrogator, asking questions designed to elicit interesting answers from me.

The interview was going smoothly except for one problem. My left shoe was filling up with blood. I could squish it through my toes the way I used to squish Jell-O through my teeth when I was a kid. I feared that it would soon seep through my shoes. How would I explain that? The questions kept coming, and I think I answered them cogently but I couldn't keep myself from squishing. I developed a rhythm, punctuating each answer with a squish.

Question. Answer. *Squish*. The squish was like hitting the carriage return on a manual typewriter.

As the interview was concluding, Jim Thomson asked me if I had any questions for the committee members. "No," I replied. "I just want to get the hell out of here." Everyone chuckled.

On the way back to the hotel I stopped in a drugstore and bought some gauze and tape. In the room I washed my toe and wrapped it tightly. I thought of going out to dinner to celebrate, or at least mark, the end of the application process, but I was wary of walking on my wounded foot. So I ordered room service, watched some television, and went to bed wondering how long it would take the selection committee to make its decisions.

— — — —

It didn't take long. A week or so later I received a call in the *Evening Sun* newsroom from Tenney Lehman. She told me I was one of the dozen candidates selected as Nieman Fellows for the 1979–80 academic year. She sounded happy when she gave me the news, as if she had been rooting for me.

The spring of 1979 was a fruitful time for the *Evening Sun*. In addition to my Nieman, our science/medical writer Jon Franklin won the first Pulitzer Prize ever awarded for feature writing. And my *Sun* competition, Hal Piper and Fred Hill, also scored fellowships, to Stanford and the University of Michigan, respectively.

At the same time, my old rival Richard Ben Cramer, who had been hired by Gene Roberts and John Carroll at the *Inquirer*, won the Pulitzer Prize for international reporting for stories he had written in the Middle East.

Not long after the awards were announced, *Sun* reporter Karen Hosler, a good friend of Richard's and mine, gave a lovely outdoor party at her home in Annapolis, celebrating the two Pulitzers and my Nieman. Richard came down from Philadelphia. It was great to see him.

On balance, I think a Pulitzer is a bigger deal than a Nieman, and I was happy for Richard and Jon. But I was happy for me, too. I was on my way to breaking the plane of the goal line. It wasn't quite time to go into an end zone dance, but I didn't need to. I knew now I could run with anyone.

Twenty-seven

THE NIEMAN EFFECT

W e freshly minted Fellows had barely arrived in Cambridge in late August when it became evident that Harvard liked having Niemans around. We weren't the brainiest individuals in Harvard Yard, but it seemed we provided a welcome whiff of the real world, a quality reputed to be in notoriously short supply in academia. We were bright, amusing, politely skeptical, and refreshingly irreverent.

Our arrival, it seems, was cause for a small celebration. A lawn party was held in our honor that first day at Walter Lippmann House, home of the Nieman Foundation, an impeccably maintained white clapboard structure built in 1836 just off the Yard.

Several Harvard dignitaries were among the crowd sipping white wine and sampling the impressive spread of hors d'oeuvres. I was chatting with a couple of other Fellows when a high-pitched female voice behind and above me chirped, "Hello." I turned and looked up into the smiling face of America's favorite chef, Julia Child. It turned out she lived just down the street and wanted to meet the latest crop of Niemans.

So did another tall person whom I only noticed as he was taking his leave: John Kenneth Galbraith, former ambassador to India and probably the nation's best-known economist.

My Nieman classmates were not without some glitter of their own. In addition to the lovely Jan Stucker, the class included two Pulitzer Prize winners—reporter Acel Moore of the *Philadelphia Inquirer* and *Boston Herald* photographer Stanley Forman, who had won the Pulitzer twice. Stanley was the most colorful member of our class of twelve American and six foreign journalists. He went everywhere with his dog, aptly named Glossy, and slept with a police scanner on.

The six foreign Nieman Fellows were most distinguished. They included Aggrey Klaaste, a crusading black South African newspaper editor who had been detained without trial and jailed for nine months amid an antiapartheid insurrection.

Suthichai Yoon was another newspaperman who had challenged his government's policies. He owned and edited the *Nation*, an English-language daily in Bangkok. Suthichai and his wife, Nantawan, lived with their two kids in the same apartment building on Harvard Street that I did.

The Yoons became close friends of mine, in Cambridge and since. I think they questioned my survival skills when it came to such practical matters as cooking. They pretty much adopted me, treating me as if I were a unmoored boat person who had washed up on their street and needed caring for. Almost every night either Suthichai or Noi (Nantawan's nickname) would call and announce that it was time to come up for dinner. Noi was a noted magazine writer but to me she was the Thai counterpart of Julia Child.

A major element in the Nieman experience was the "wine and cheese parties," which were held once or twice a week. These were afternoon get-togethers in the common room of Lippmann House where well-known figures from government, politics, journalism, the arts, and academia spoke to the assembled Niemans.

Sometimes the speaker was a journalist such as Ben Bradlee, editor of the *Washington Post*, or another *Post* luminary, David Broder, the dean of American political reporters. Other times it might be a novelist like John Updike or John Irving, playwright Arthur Miller, or *New*

Yorker magazine writer John McPhee. We also heard from academics—Matina Horner, president of Radcliffe College, law professor Laurence Tribe, and presidential scholar Richard Neustadt. Linguist and radical political gadfly Noam Chomsky stopped by from nearby MIT, where he taught. During the question-and-answer period that followed his presentation, I told him I didn't think much of his philosophy. In fact I seem to recall saying I thought he was full of shit. He invited me to lunch. We ate at a luncheonette on Massachusetts Avenue near MIT. We didn't resolve our differences but we parted on friendly terms. At least I liked him.

Harvard captivated me, most of all because it was there that I met and fell in love with Kelley Andrews. Kelley was a graduate student at the Kennedy School of Government, working toward a master's in public administration. A tall, radiant blonde with a sparkling personality, she was smart, organized, liked by everyone. Many were smitten by her, me among them.

In her early thirties, Kelley had just spent a decade in Washington as a senior aide to GOP senator Jacob Javits of New York and Democratic congressman (and later U.S. Secretary of Transportation) Norman Mineta of California. There had been a few other stops along the way, including jobs in two presidential administrations. We met in September, in Richard Neustadt's course on the American presidency, when she stopped by my desk to bum a cigarette. By May, when the academic year ended, we were an item.

Kelley was a veteran of Washington's political and social scene. Just how much of a veteran became clear at the final Nieman event of the year. It was a farewell dinner at the Faculty Club. The speaker was David Halberstam, the journalist I admired above all others.

During the cocktail hour, a receiving line formed to meet Halberstam. Kelley and I stood in line, slowly edging forward. Finally we reached him.

"Hi, David," I said, "I'm Bob Timberg of the *Baltimore Evening Sun*. And this is . . ."

"Oh, hi, Kelley," said Halberstam.

Kelley and Halberstam, it turned out, had been an item a few years back, well before I barged onto the scene.

As my fellowship year was ending, the *Evening Sun* decided to open a one-person bureau in Washington. I was tapped to fill it.

My workstation (it would be pretentious to call it an office) was a desk in Pat Furgurson's domain among a dozen *Sun* correspondents and editors on the twelfth floor of the National Press Building in downtown Washington. His team of correspondents was a fixture in the capital's journalistic community. Two of them—military writer Charles Corddry and diplomatic correspondent Henry Trewhitt—were frequent panelists on the PBS news program *Washington Week in Review*, must-see television for government junkies on Friday nights. Fred Barnes was one of the hottest political reporters in town. Furgurson himself was among the city's most respected newspapermen.

I spent the next year as a one-man gang, using far too many of my working hours explaining to Washington heavies (which for a time was how I viewed nearly everyone I spoke to) that, no, I didn't work for the *Sun* but for its sister paper, the *Evening Sun*.

It didn't help that the *Evening Sun*, unlike the *Sun*, did not circulate in Washington. You just couldn't get it. To remedy the problem, I took to mailing my stories to men and women mentioned in articles I'd written. I didn't want my sources to think of me as some sort of pervert masquerading as a newspaperman and refuse to speak to me the next time I called. Sometimes, if I had a really hot story, I would actually go to people's offices and drop off the paper.

My early months in Washington, a city in which I had always gotten lost, were greatly eased by Kelley, who had joined me in an apartment on Capitol Hill not long after my arrival there. She seemed to know everyone, at least in the political community. She also knew Washington, even the goddamn Whitehurst Freeway, the mysteries of which to this day I haven't figured out.

More important, she understood my frustration at being a small fish in a big pond and came up with a variety of ways to lift my spirits.

At her suggestion we started meeting after work almost every day at a pub near our apartment called Gallagher's where we would have a drink and a burger and she would talk me down from whatever experience—a story missed, a painful slight, my inability to get some politician to return my call—had me spinning that day. She was, and is, the most levelheaded person I've ever known, a quality that more than once kept me from making an ass of myself.

My return from Cambridge meant reinstituting the custom of taking the kids Friday to Sunday. It also meant a total of four hours on the road each weekend since Janie's home in Severna Park was an hour from my apartment on Capitol Hill. Kelley liked my kids and related easily to them, and after a short period during which they seemed unsure what to make of the new woman in their father's life, the kids threw in the towel and decided she was terrific. And she never once complained that we never had a weekend to ourselves. By then I could not imagine life without her.

Fairness compels me to say that everyone in the *Sun* bureau, from Pat Furgurson on down, did what they could to make me feel comfortable. That included providing guidance when I needed it and asking me along when one or more of them went for a drink after work. Their obvious warmth toward someone who did not look like he belonged with them reminded me of one of my favorite ballplayers as a kid, PeeWee Reese, the Brooklyn Dodger captain and a son of the South, putting a protective hand on the shoulder of Jackie Robinson on a day during his historic if often lacerating rookie season when he was enduring especially vicious racist heckling from fans and opposing players.

Meanwhile, back in Baltimore, my editor and fellow Vietnam veteran Bill Hawkins never let me get too down on those occasions, all too frequent in the early days, when I felt—and truly was—over my head.

Eventually I wrote some good stories, notably a series on a political movement known as the New Right that was becoming a powerful force in national politics. Hawkins and other senior editors decided to nominate the series for a Pulitzer. I didn't win—I don't think I even came close—but I appreciated the pat on the back.

One day, after I'd been in Washington for about a year, Pat Furgurson asked me to stop by his office. He was, he said, considering three reporters as possible hires. Because I knew all three, he wanted my opinion of their talents. I was caught off guard. I wasn't used to conferring on personnel matters. I started babbling but managed to say that I thought all of them were highly capable and would be worthy additions to the bureau.

Back at my desk, I was mystified. Why was Furgurson consulting with me on potential hires? I reviewed in my mind the three candidates he had mentioned. All, I knew, could do the job. Then I thought, Hold it! What about me? How come Furgurson saw me as a consultant and not as a candidate?

A few days later, Pat called me back into his office. He said he wanted to continue our earlier conversation. Grumpily, I sat down and glowered at him across his desk as he began discussing those under consideration. I guess I should have felt flattered that he wanted my opinion on a matter as crucial as filling a slot in the bureau, but, truly, I wanted to scream at him, *What about me?!*

"What about you?" Pat said.

A John Alden moment. My mouth dropped open as I tried to process Pat's question. I managed to respond with my most eloquent "Huh?"

"What about you, Timberg?" he said. "Do you want the job?"

Of course I did. As much as I loved the *Evening Sun*, I knew that as a Washington correspondent for the *Sun* I would be playing and testing myself on a larger stage.

I told Pat, yes, I wanted the job, which set off a week or so of in-house fireworks as the *Evening Sun* resisted Furgurson's alleged high-handedness and my treachery. I was sympathetic. I would have screamed bloody murder if I had been an *Evening Sun* editor and the *Sun*'s Washington bureau chief launched a cross-border raid to shanghai one of my best reporters, a Nieman Fellow to boot.

Eventually tempers cooled and the *Evening Sun* graciously released its hold on me. Less than a month later I was the *Sun*'s congressional correspondent. A year or so after that I became the White House correspondent, a position I held for five years of the Ronald Reagan presidency.

By then Kelley and I were married, a lovely ceremony in the yard of her parents' home in Lewes, Delaware. Scott, Craig, and Amanda were there, of course, Mandy a lovely little flower girl. A year or so later, we had a son, Sam, who by his teenage years would become the athlete I always aspired to be and to this day the sunniest person I know.

Twenty-eight

OLLIE, BUD, AND JOHN

The Iran-Contra scandal, Ronald Reagan's Watergate, splattered all over Washington in early November 1986. Within days the phrase "arms for hostages" became verbal shorthand for the crime, if that's what it was, and everyone in the nation's capital and much of the rest of the country knew the names of the three men fingered as culprits.

Ollie, Bud, and John. Two Marines and an admiral, all three Naval Academy graduates. Oliver North and Robert "Bud" McFarlane were the Marines. Both had seen combat in Vietnam. Vice Admiral John Poindexter never made it to Vietnam but fell victim to the Vietnam-inspired distrust of politicians and journalists that infected so many of his comrades-in-arms.

When the scandal broke, I had been covering the White House for the *Baltimore Sun* for three years. During that time, Reagan participated in three U.S.-Soviet summit meetings that promised major reductions in each side's nuclear weapons arsenal and a much welcome thaw in the hostile relations between the two superpowers.

Stunning achievements, solid building blocks for a legacy any president would be proud to claim, but the Iran-Contra affair overshadowed them for the better part of two years as it transfixed the nation with a parade of colorful characters, poisonous rhetoric, military jargon, computer shorthand, and indecipherable acronyms (1 747 N/50 Hawks & W/400 Tows = two AMCITS). Along the way it indelibly stained Reagan's second term.

Iran-Contra changed my life, too, setting me on a seven-year odyssey in which I was forced to confront a gallery of post-Vietnam demons whose existence I previously refused even to acknowledge.

At a certain point, in fact, my past, a past that I had struggled for years to keep at bay, seemed intent on reclaiming me.

— — — —

A curious report drifted out of the Middle East on Election Day 1986. The speaker of the Iranian parliament, Hashemi Rafsanjani, was quoted as saying that Bud McFarlane, Reagan's former national security adviser, had made a secret trip to Iran, a nation with which the United States had not had diplomatic relations since 1979. The purpose, Rafsanjani said, was to trade weapons for Americans being held hostage in Lebanon.

At first Reagan administration officials brushed off the report. McFarlane's successor, John Poindexter, traveling with the president on Air Force One, reacted to the story as if it were unworthy of comment when White House spokesman Larry Speakes handed him a message pertaining to the report. (Speakes would later describe Poindexter's poker-faced response as an Academy Award performance.)

But officials were quick to confirm the central elements of the report. Yes, McFarlane had flown to Iran on a diplomatic mission of enormous sensitivity. Yes, he was accompanied by Oliver North, a little-known Marine officer on the National Security Council staff. And yes, there were discussions about selling arms to Iran—then at war with its neighbor, Iraq. The weapons would be in return for Iranian help in gaining the release of six Americans being held hostage by Lebanese terrorists thought to be under the control of Iran.

But the overarching purpose of the negotiations, officials insisted, was to create a diplomatic opening to Iran that might lay the foundation for a resumption of normalized relations with the strategically situated, oil-rich nation that had been estranged from the United States since the 1979 revolution that overthrew the shah.

As administration figures explained, any exchange of weapons and hostages was the equivalent of earnest money, essentially a display of good faith by the two nations that they truly desired warmer relations.

Many members of Congress, Republicans as well as Democrats, were not buying that explanation. They saw it as nothing more than an arms-for-hostages deal. And if so, the administration was abandoning the seemingly immutable position it had taken in earlier hostage crises throughout the Reagan years: *The United States will not negotiate with terrorists.*

That dictum had been restated so often and in so many different situations that it had taken on the trappings of holy writ. By violating it, the United States and the Reagan administration stood accused of hypocrisy both at home and abroad.

Reinforcing the uproar among a disbelieving public was this: Millions of Americans despised Iran and its supreme leader, the Ayatollah Ruhollah Khomeini, largely because radical Iranian students had taken fifty-two American diplomats hostage and held them in the capital city of Tehran for more than a year following the revolution.

Those diplomats were finally released in 1981, after 444 days in captivity, but six other Americans subsequently became hostages in the Middle East, and their continued detention further enraged their countrymen and haunted Reagan, who asked aides about them each morning at his daily national security briefing.

There was a second major issue at play. Half a world away, in Central America, the United States had been supporting a ragtag force of anti-Communist guerrillas—the Contras, as the rebels were known—that was attempting to overthrow the leftist Sandinista government in Nicaragua.

Reagan was determined to assist the Contras, whom he dubbed "freedom fighters," with supplies and funding, but Congress, controlled by Democrats, not only opposed the president's efforts, but enacted legislation designed to keep him from doing so. Many members voiced fears that Nicaragua would become another Vietnam.

The Contras had received some funding from the United States early on in Reagan's first term. Now, though, with Congress refusing to allocate any more money, the rebels had grown increasingly needy.

In the days that followed the administration's confirmation of the McFarlane/North trip to Iran, I was picking up clues that something else was at play. My sources didn't seem to know what that something was, but they passed on to me their suspicion that before long a second shoe was going to drop.

Amid this air of expectation, Reagan made a surprise visit to the White House press briefing room. It was a few days before Thanksgiving. Mounting the stage, he announced without preamble that his national security adviser, Vice Admiral Poindexter, had resigned, and that Poindexter's closest aide, the still-obscure Oliver North, was leaving the NSC staff and returning to duties more befitting a Marine infantry officer.

A clamor ensued as reporters shouted questions at the president. In journalistic shorthand this was a bona fide *"Holy shit!"* moment.

Having spoken his lines, Reagan, never comfortable with details, ignored the shouting and exited the briefing room stage right, leaving Ed Meese, his faithful attorney general, to fill in the blanks.

At that point the mysterious second shoe landed as Meese detailed an audacious two-headed scheme of mind-numbing complexity. Not only was the United States selling weapons to Iran, a nation against which it had maintained, for the past seven years, an arms embargo because of its support for terrorism; it was also secretly diverting a portion of the profits from those sales to the Nicaraguan Contras.

This became known as the "diversion," and its revelation enraged Congress, which had thrice enacted legislation designed to prohibit U.S. assistance to the Contras. Now, it seemed, the administration had hatched a scheme to fund the Contras behind the back of Congress.

Overnight the atmosphere in the nation's capital turned toxic.

Angry Democrats, joined by many of Reagan's fellow Republicans, demanded to know if the president was aware of the seemingly illegal diversion. The administration answered no. Horseshit, responded the Democrats. For them, Reagan's denial didn't pass the smell test. And they were not alone.

Talk of impeachment suddenly was in the air. The only thing Democrats and Republicans seemed to agree on was the culpability of the three Annapolis men, whom Meese had all but indicted at the press conference.

North, McFarlane, and Poindexter knew they faced a lynch mob. But when they looked to see who they could count on for support, they saw . . . no one.

— — — —

For the next year, I was part of a two-man *Baltimore Sun* investigative team covering the convoluted Iran-Contra saga as it unfolded. My partner was a young, energetic, irrepressible reporter named Michael Kelly, who was so good he belonged in the same league as Richard Ben Cramer and my new *Sun* bureau colleague, our national political correspondent Paul West.

Mike and I were a good combination. We were both aggressive and inventive reporters. We also liked and respected each other. Our stories almost always carried double bylines. We did our reporting separately, conferred on what we had come up with, then one of us wrote the story, subject to the approval of the other. I was about fifteen years older than Mike but because of my late start as a newspaperman not that much more experienced.

The age difference notwithstanding, we shared traits indispensable to investigative reporters: We were indefatigable in tracking down anyone we needed to talk to and skilled in persuading that someone to talk to us whether he or she wanted to or not. Mike was better at it than me, but not by much.

Of the two of us, I was the more cautious. Mike was never reckless, but sometimes he would get ahead of himself, convinced we knew more than we actually did and thinking we should get it in the paper the next day. I thought my role as the senior member in the partnership obliged me to keep us from going off half-cocked.

Almost from the beginning, though, there were elements of the story that gnawed at me. First of all, I knew McFarlane, North, and Poindexter, not well, but well enough to suspect that the portrait being painted of them was distorted. The public was seeing them in bold primary colors, with no shading to soften the picture. I knew they were not, as many were suggesting, living embodiments of the conspirators in the book (and movie) *Seven Days in May*, in which a military cabal attempts to remove the president and his cabinet and take over the country.

As I would later write of those early days of Iran-Contra:

> I picked up a familiar and troubling aroma. Others saw greed, naked ambition, abuse of authority, a breathtaking disdain for Congress and the federal bureaucracy. I saw those things, too, but what I smelled was cordite, burning shitters, the disinfectant odor of hospitals.

What I smelled was a faraway war that had ended more than a dozen years earlier, but which to my mind had scarred the nation no less than it had scarred me. And for many Americans, those scars had neither faded nor softened.

To my surprise, I turned out to be one of them.

Twenty-nine

THE BANALITY OF EVIL

You won't find three more unlikely conspirators than Bud Mc-Farlane, John Poindexter, and Ollie North.

McFarlane had been a Marine artillery officer and a good one, but by the mid-1980s he had moved well beyond the mud and the blood of his Leatherneck days. He went from duty in Vietnam to Geneva, where he did graduate work in international affairs under the tutelage of Louis Halle, a prominent strategic thinker and onetime State Department colleague of Dean Acheson and George Kennan. He worked in the White House for two national security advisers, Henry Kissinger and Brent Scowcroft, and held the post himself before turning it over to Poindexter.

By then he was no longer thinking about how to deploy 155 mm howitzers and other heavy artillery pieces; he saw himself as a global strategist, his ambition nothing less than crafting an agreement with the Soviet Union to end the nuclear arms race. In fact, McFarlane played a crucial role in facilitating the historic arms control deals set in motion by Reagan and brought to fruition by his successor, George H. W. Bush.

John Poindexter may well have been a genius. If not, he didn't miss by much. At Annapolis he was the brigade commander, the Academy's top leadership post, and stood number one in his class among close to one thousand graduates. After a year at sea, he was shipped off to Caltech where he hobnobbed with Nobel laureates and earned a PhD in nuclear physics.

He wasn't the only national security adviser to hold a doctorate. There were five others, but he was the only one whose doctoral thesis did not focus on foreign affairs. His was entitled "Electronic Shielding by Closed Shells in Thulium Compounds."

Oliver North graduated from Annapolis in 1968, four years after me and, like me, chose to become a Marine infantry officer. We didn't know each other at the Academy or in Vietnam and did not meet until years later when we found ourselves at the White House in vastly different roles.

Ollie came home from the war with a record of heroic combat leadership, earning a Silver Star, two Bronze Stars, and two Purple Hearts. Most of his superiors, Ronald Reagan included, viewed him as nothing short of indispensable, the go-to guy when you needed a tough job done with a minimum of fuss. Conversely, many of his fellow officers considered him a showboat, a talented showboat and a likable one, but a showboat nonetheless.

"There's not enough mustard in the world for that hot dog," a Marine colonel, Dave Haughey, told me.

In the early days of Iran-Contra I knew some of these things about McFarlane, Poindexter, and North and intuited much of the rest. In the years ahead I would learn much more—some good, some bad—but none of it would shake my initial reading of them: They were decent, capable men who had devoted their lives to the service of their country. But they were in over their heads when that service took them into the septic drain field otherwise known as the nation's capital.

— — — —

The Reagan/Meese press conference set Mike Kelly and me, along with scores of other reporters, on the trail of Ollie, Bud, and John. I was in full reporter mode in those first weeks of the hunt. I wanted to know everything the three had done, and I wanted to know

nam's Arizona Valley, was gritty and bloody and at times painful to read. But unlike nearly every other book about Vietnam up to that time it did not apologize for the war or the men and women fighting it. In fact, Webb was critical of men of his generation who slipped across the border to Canada or made their way to Sweden to avoid the draft.

"Fuck 'em, just fuck 'em, fuck anybody who doesn't come out here and do this," says his protagonist, a Marine lieutenant much like Webb, as he struggles to keep his troops alive in the Vietnamese outback.

The message of that quote, if your ears were tuned to the right frequency, was hard to miss. He was talking about able-bodied men of his generation who found ways to sit out the war, to not "come out . . . and do this."

Critics gave the book strong positive reviews, focusing on Webb's vivid combat writing. He had since written two other novels, both of which looked at the impact of the war on the home front.

Webb's literary output and reputation, combined with the boxing match with North, was enough to get Hirshey's editor's juices flowing. But there was a potentially sensational element playing into his mounting excitement: Jim Webb had just become Secretary of the Navy.

This meant Webb was suddenly atop the chain of command of the legally vulnerable Oliver North, a fellow member of the Naval Academy Class of 1968 and, as it happened, one of his least favorite Marines.

"There's a helluva story there," David said. "I'd really like you to take a shot at it."

"I don't want to do it," I replied, and repeated my reasons for refusing.

"Think about it overnight, okay? Call me in the morning."

"Fine," I said.

I lay awake for much of the night trying to figure ways to penetrate the wall around Ollie North.

In the morning, I called David Hirshey. "Okay," I said, "I'll do it."

—   —   —   —

"The Private War of Ollie and Jim" ran five thousand words and filled nine pages in the March 1988 issue of *Esquire*. The blurb in the table of contents said: "They go way back, back before Vietnam, to a boxing ring in Annapolis. Now one is Secretary of the Navy, the other a colonel in trouble."

On the surface Webb and North were polar opposites. North was flamboyant, Webb flinty and controlled. North smiled a lot, Webb rarely did, at least until he decided you could be trusted. No one described the difference between the two men better than Jake Laboon, a Navy chaplain who knew both men well.

"Jim is a much deeper thinker," Father Laboon told me in an interview for the article. "I think he doesn't show his emotions as easily as Ollie does. I wouldn't say he is unemotional, but Jim is very reserved."

And North? The priest paused, then grinned, and said, "Ollie is champagne."

Unwittingly, Bud McFarlane aided me enormously in terms of formulating what I was slowly coming to realize would become a central theme of any book I might write. In a March 1987 television interview with Barbara Walters, he said: *"I think, Barbara, that in a year's time, a curious and haunting factor that will come out in this episode is the Vietnam War."*

With that remark, McFarlane made the magazine article I was working on more than a personality profile of two colorful men and placed it on a canvas that I had thought would serve as a backdrop but now knew demanded much greater prominence. As it would in the book I was struggling to conceptualize.

It was about this time that I asked myself the question I would spend much of the next seven years attempting to answer:

Was Iran-Contra the bill for Vietnam finally coming due?

— — — —

With the *Esquire* article out of the way, I admitted to myself something I had been trying to ignore. Jim Webb belonged in the book I wanted to write. The problem was that the three original stakeholders—Ollie, Bud, and John—were joined at the hip by the Iran-Contra affair, on which I still figured the book should pivot. But Webb had nothing to do with Iran-Contra. The idea that North's case could someday bubble up to Webb's SECNAV suite was an interesting factoid, but by itself it lacked the thematic heft to carry a book.

The thing was, I wanted Webb in the book not because of his relationship with North but because he fascinated me. Aspects of his personality recalled both Hemingway and Churchill, with a trace of MacArthur thrown in. Ollie North may well be champagne, but Webb, in the words of one of his Marines, had a look that could crack rock. Ollie, Bud, and John went together. But Ollie, Bud, John, and Jim? There probably was a way to tie them together, but I sure in hell couldn't figure out how.

Then matters got more complicated. My day job had me at the White House one morning, staked out on the circular driveway off the West Wing with about two dozen other reporters waiting for a group of senators who were meeting with President Reagan.

Neither I nor any other reporter cared much about the senators; we just wanted to know what Reagan said to them. White House reporters had to use all sorts of tricks to find out what the president was thinking, and ambushing anyone who had just spoken to him was a time-honored tactic.

The senators had been with the president for about an hour when the Marine sentry at the door to the West Wing stepped aside to allow them to exit.

As they flowed onto the driveway, groups of five or six reporters closed around individual senators and commenced peppering them with questions.

Reporters tended to gravitate to the more senior senators, usually the majority leader if he was there, and others known for being forthcoming and savvy. Committee chairmen also were frequent targets, or a senator known to be an active player on the issue under discussion, in this instance the Contras.

John McCain, the freshman senator from Arizona with a trademark head of white hair, fell into that last category. Four or five reporters huddled around him. I joined them, hoping he might have something to say that differed from what I had already picked up from other senators.

This was the first time I had seen McCain in person, though I knew he had been a Navy pilot and had survived several years in North Vietnamese prisons. I also was aware that he graduated from Annapolis and was the scion of a distinguished Navy family. His younger brother Joe was my classmate, though academics tripped him up Plebe Year and he flunked out.

I was dutifully taking notes, when McCain looked at me and said, "Where'd you get that ring?"

He meant my Naval Academy ring, evident on my left hand, which was holding the notebook in which I was recording his remarks.

"Same place you did, Senator," I replied.

"No kidding?" he said, a big smile on his face.

"No kidding, Senator," I said.

"Well, come up and see me sometime, okay?"

"Sure, absolutely, Senator."

I called his office, made an appointment, and a few days later I was ushered into his office by his knockout press secretary Torie Clarke.

We spent a half hour alone together. McCain was the most unpretentious politician I had ever encountered. Also the funniest and most engaging. But he was thoughtful as well. At one point I asked him about Webb and North, both of whom he knew. His answer—pungent and perceptive—cited what he saw as a crucial distinction between the two men.

"Despite Webb's condescension toward elected officials, he doesn't have contempt," said McCain. "I think Ollie has contempt."

It was happening again. My brief encounter with McCain caused me to do some research, not a lot, just enough to thoroughly screw up my head.

Not only had McCain spent five and a half years in North Vietnamese prisons, he had spent much of it in solitary, his few visitors the guards who stopped in from time to time to beat the shit out of him. And if I was searching for irony, which I wasn't, there was this: McCain and John Poindexter were Academy classmates. Poindexter was the number one man in the Class of 1958. McCain stood fifth from the bottom. Now, though, Poindexter was in the dock; McCain was in the United States Senate.

If anyone belonged in my book, it was John McCain. So now I had Ollie, Bud, Jim, John One, and John Two. Three of them fit together neatly. The other two were off on their own, dancing in the moonlight, driving me nuts.

Then along came Agent 99.

Thirty-one

THE NIGHTINGALE'S SONG

D o you want sympathy or a solution?

That's the choice Kelley would always drop on me when I went to her with a seemingly insoluble problem like, for example, what the hell is this book I'm supposed to be writing going to be about?

At the time, she was working at the U.S. Labor Department. It was never quite clear to me what she did. She had a badge (but no gun) and often was involved in union elections. She made a better salary than me, which would mean more in the months and years ahead than it did at the time.

We talked a lot about my job at the *Sun* and what I had taken to calling "my so-called book." As White House correspondent, I was covering things Kelley was interested in and occasionally reporting on people she knew. I don't recall her ever complaining that I was giving short shrift to her and Sam, then little more than a toddler, though I'm sure I was.

We owned a home in Wood Acres, a Bethesda community just over the District line distinguished by towering trees and safe, walkable streets. Kelley went into work early so she could leave her office at five and relieve our babysitter, who had a child of her own to get home to. When I had to work weekends, which was often during the five years I covered the White House, Kelley became the default parent. That meant her responsibilities expanded to include Scott, Craig, and Amanda, as well as Sam.

We spent a lot of time talking about my so-called book. I had five characters, all men who had gone to the Naval Academy, been touched in one way or another by the Vietnam War, and these days were either riding high (McCain, Webb) or facing hard time (Ollie, Bud, and John). But was there anything that truly tied all five together, some unifying theme? I kept telling myself there had to be, but my belief that I could find it was crumbling.

Leave it to Kelley to see the pattern.

I was home, a rare afternoon off. Kelley was running a Labor Department conference called Work and the Family that had drawn participants from across the country.

I was slumped in a chair in front of the television, depressed as hell, when she walked in the door late in the afternoon. Normally I would have gotten up and kissed her hello. On this day I just gave her a halfhearted wave and mumbled something I hoped would pass for a greeting.

"I can see you're having a wonderful day," she said, her voice tinged with just enough sarcasm to tell me that she knew I was feeling really low.

I looked at her with a blank expression on my face. I had five great characters and I didn't know what to do with them. Richard Cramer would know, I thought.

"I've got something for you," said Kelley, flipping a small rectangular object toward me. A videotape landed on my lap. The label said "Work and the Family Conference, Washington, DC, 1988." I looked up at Kelley, my expression going from blank to double blank.

"Just watch it," she said.

"I will later," I said.

"No, watch it now."

Rolling my eyes, I dragged myself the few feet from the chair to the TV like it was the last leg of a trek across the Kalahari, and inserted the video into the tape player. Coming into focus as the screen slowly brightened was Barbara Feldon, Agent 99, the svelte, savvy sidekick of Maxwell Smart, the bumbling secret agent—part James Bond, part Inspector Clouseau—who spoke into a phone shaped like a shoe in the TV comedy series *Get Smart*.

On the tape, Feldon was speaking to a Labor Department symposium in her capacity as president of the Screen Actors Guild. I gave Kelley a "you've got to be kidding" look.

"Keep watching," she said.

So I did. Feldon's speech was mildly interesting, but what did it have to do with me and the issues I was wrestling with? Then she told a little story.

"Did you know," she asked, "that a nightingale will never sing its song if it doesn't hear it first?" It can hear robins and wrens, she said, and never sing a note. "But the moment it hears any part of a nightingale's song, it bursts into this extraordinary music, sophisticated, elaborate music, as though it had known it all the time.

"And, of course, it did."

She explained that scientists had learned that a newly hatched nightingale has a template in its brain that contains all the music it will ever need but can't sing a note until its song is triggered by the song of another nightingale.

I turned my gaze to Kelley. She was looking at me expectantly. And then I got it.

"Holy shit!"

Suddenly it came together. All five of my characters had been swaying to the song of a nightingale, a complex, insinuating melody that beckoned its listeners down one of two paths—the first leading to good fortune, the second to ruin.

And the nightingale? Who else? Ronald Reagan.

— — — —

At last I knew what the book would be about. My premise would be that all five men responded to Reagan with actions that amounted to answering calls to his rendition of *The Nightingale's Song*, as I planned to call the book.

The lyrics to Reagan's song went like this: Welcome home. I'm proud of you. You deserve the nation's thanks and respect. You're men and women I can count on. Wear your uniforms with pride.

Reagan's words were nothing less than a call to arms. He was challenging the assertions as well as the passion of the antiwar forces that had been on the ascendancy in politics, the arts, academia, even segments of the press, for the better part of two decades.

As I envisioned it, *The Nightingale's Song* was intended for a special audience—the men and women who had fought the Vietnam War, troops who on returning home had been spat on, reviled as baby killers, more often pitied as saps because they were too dumb to figure out how to beat the draft.

That audience included North, McFarlane, and Poindexter. Their voices, once lusty and full throated, had been stunned into silence by the ferocity and ridicule of the antiwar movement. Now, on hearing the Nightingale's Song, they responded with a vigor and enthusiasm that resulted in several notable achievements, but perhaps Iran-Contra as well.

As for Jim Webb, he had never been silent, and he didn't spot the antiwar movement anything, but the message he delivered in *Fields of Fire*—"Fuck anybody that doesn't come out here and do this"— harmonized with and gained resonance from Reagan's song, which set him on a path to the upper levels of government and eventually the United States Senate.

John McCain gave Vietnam a wide berth. He resisted being typecast as a POW. He was thirty-six and crippled when he waved goodbye to the Hanoi Hilton, but he was a long way from throwing in the towel on life.

"Just as I didn't enjoy my Plebe Year at the Naval Academy, I didn't enjoy my five years in prison," he said. "But it's over."

Over? Not quite. The North Vietnamese had taken a young, healthy man and transformed him into a physical wreck. Shoulder, leg, knee, arm—they all were treated to the tender mercies of his jailers.

So, no, McCain still had places to go and things to do and the Nightingale's Song would be his mood music and, when the time was right, it would also serve as his fanfare.

I now wrote another book proposal, this one incorporating Iran-Contra into a broader tale of what I called the generational fault line between those who went to war and those who used money, wit, and connections to avoid going.

Flip circulated this latest proposal to several New York publishers. Simon & Schuster gave *The Nightingale's Song* a home.

Thirty-two

IDENTITY CRISIS

A contract with Simon & Schuster in hand, I began what was supposed to be a one-year leave of absence from the *Sun*. Having a publisher in my corner gave my exertions a legitimacy previously lacking, and I happily expunged "my so-called book" from the glossary of stock phrases I fell back on when people asked what I was up to.

By then it was November 1988, two years since Iran-Contra had surfaced as the scandal of the decade, and I was ready to begin my leave. My book would tell the story of five men who at times had acted heroically, at other times unwisely, at still other times—and this was certainly a possibility—scandalously.

But there was one more actor that had to be accounted for, one that could chew up scenery as savagely as it had once chewed up men: the Vietnam War.

So, in addition to illuminating the action of my five principal characters, I had a separate but related motive. I reduced it to a thesis that went like this: You can't march a generation, or a portion of a generation, off to war, have its members suffer the pain and anguish that accompanies all wars, then tell them that it was all a big mistake, without sooner or later paying a price. Especially when much of the rest of that generation came up with novel ways to leave the fighting and dying to others.

In the case of Vietnam, that price was inflated by the grim statistics of the battlefield: 58,000 Americans dead, 270,000 wounded, 21,000 disabled, including 5,000 who lost one or more limbs.

A ghastly casualty count made all the more horrific when set against the recognition that 16 million of the 27 million men eligible for the draft during those years had used a variety of legal and illegal means to avoid serving, according to Lawrence M. Baskir and William A. Strauss, in *Chance and Circumstance*, their classic 1978 study of the Selective Service System during the Vietnam era and the source of the casualty figures just cited.

There was also this to think about: I had to find my place on this war-torn terrain. Until I did, I faced the prospect of an immobilizing identity crisis: Was I a Marine who shared many of the experiences of the five men I planned to write about or a reporter who didn't pull his punches and gloss over inconvenient facts?

I decided I was first and foremost a reporter, but one who brought special skills to the game. As Ollie North once said of Ronald Reagan, I knew more about what had happened than I knew I knew.

— — — —

M any Americans were ready to move on from Vietnam as soon as the last helicopter lifted off from the U.S. embassy in Saigon, in April 1975. But for many veterans of that war, moving on was not an option. For them, Vietnam had not been, in Erica Jong's inspired phrase, a "zipless fuck," a frenzied encounter quickly and easily forgotten.

There was too much to forget. Orphaned arms and legs, friends killed and maimed, some maimed themselves, pain that defied description, suffering that reshaped the mind and sandblasted the soul, arrayed against members of their own generation who had relied on world-class duplicity to avoid duty in Vietnam. And then claimed the moral high ground.

Those who gamed the system, of course, had to freeze-dry their humanitarian impulses so they could ignore niggling facts, like if they didn't go someone would have to go in their place, probably kids less capable of plugging into the antidraft apparatus they had been both clever enough and affluent enough to avail themselves of. Or misfits like Calley.

"I think the people who went to those schools—Harvard, MIT, whatever—are collectively responsible for William Calley," said Jim Webb. As he saw it, too many Ivy Leaguers and their brethren didn't show up, so the Army took Calley instead.

— — — —

I had been too busy putting my life back together to worry about men who had figured out how to avoid serving in Vietnam.

There was also something else, something painful to confess, dishonest to ignore. As a reporter I was someone to be reckoned with, not a freak to be pitied.

Of course from time to time I couldn't help thinking dark thoughts about members of my generation who had managed to avoid the combat boots and jungle utilities worn by millions of young men who might have been their next-door neighbor or high school classmate or the kid who bagged their mom's groceries at the supermarket.

In truth, though, since Stanford I'd hardly ever thought about the war and who went and who didn't. It was as if I had been vaccinated against such ungenerous thoughts.

The other Vietnam veterans I knew in the Washington press corps—and there were several—must have undergone a similar immunization regimen because we rarely if ever discussed the war or our role in it.

I knew there was nothing to be gained by fixating on the injustice of it all. Jimmy Carter, echoing God knows how many others, said life is unfair and that pretty much nailed it for me. I had put Vietnam in a box in the attic, on a shelf you needed an extension ladder to reach. By the time I became a White House correspondent I assumed my onetime comrades-in-arms had done the same. Then Iran-Contra broke, the shelf gave way, and the whole fucking mess came crashing down on me.

Suddenly I wasn't writing stories about natural gas deregulation or the budget or taxes or Mrs. Reagan's "Just Say No" antidrug campaign. I was reporting on three men—two Marines and a Navy admiral—I didn't know that well but with whom I felt an unmistakable and increasingly uncomfortable kinship.

So even as Mike Kelly and I worked night and day to ferret out what Ollie, Bud, and John had been up to, I suspected that the opprobrium hurled at them related at least as much to the fact that they were military men as to their alleged misdeeds.

This led me to do an about-face so I could get a better look at their critics. What I saw were scores of senators and congressmen and members of the press angrily firing for effect at men whose very existence was an affront to them, forcing them to ask painful questions of themselves, maybe answer even more painful questions from their kids.

This was when the anger I had so long controlled, whose existence I had refused even to acknowledge, broke through the vaccine that had allowed me for so long to ignore the actions of much of my generation.

A few years later, Milt Copulos, an Army veteran of Vietnam who received last rites seven times, put it to me this way: "There's a wall ten miles high and fifty miles thick between those of us who went and those who didn't, and that wall is never going to come down."

By then I had resolved my identity crisis. Newly armored, I began my voyage into what Scott Fitzgerald called the "secret griefs of wild, unknown men."

On this journey, in scores of homes and offices throughout the country I would see and hear what I needed to see and hear, the opening notes—perhaps the most haunting notes—of what had now become *The Nightingale's Song.*

Angry men. Disbelieving men. Men in pain. Men who extended their left hand when they greeted me. A man in a wheelchair under a framed photograph of a strapping kid in a football uniform. Another man in a wheelchair beside a photo showing him standing ramrod straight in the striking high-collared dress blues of a Marine Corps officer. I imagined a mantelpiece stretching as far as the eye could see, littered with the detritus of war, men memorialized in picture frames who outgrew their youth but left behind too many of—what to call them?—the essentials with which they began their lives.

Thirty-three

THE CROWN PRINCE

Friends and colleagues look at me like I'm nuts when I tell them John McCain is the funniest guy I ever met. Their image of him dates to the closing weeks of his 2008 presidential campaign when he came across as a cranky, ill-tempered old man snapping at the heels of Barack Obama. By then, though, he was struggling to recover from a self-inflicted wound named Sarah Palin.

I had come to know another John McCain, and he was anything but a cranky old man.

Starting in late 1988, I interviewed McCain at least once a month for the better part of two years. Rarely did the interviews, which usually lasted an hour, play out as planned. Not that it mattered—they were all great. And mostly fun, even those when he was telling me about his imprisonment.

Looking back, I think of every interview with McCain as beginning the same way. They didn't, of course, but there was a goofy sameness to the first few minutes of most meetings that makes it feel as if any one of them could stand in for the others.

I would be shown into McCain's office. We'd greet each other. I would take a seat on a couch. He would flash a welcoming smile from behind his large senatorial desk. Then I would begin my first question.

"Senator, can you tell me . . . ?"

That was usually as far as I got before he interrupted me.

"Hold it, Bob, hold it," he'd say, his voice low, as if preparing to let me in on a very hush-hush government secret. "I've got to tell you this story."

His stories never failed to delight. On one of the days I remember best, we were whisked away on what I had come to think of as McCain's magic carpet. Our first stop was the French Riviera where a young lady of uncanny appeal awaited us. We briefly socialized with her, then sped off to a smoky casino in Monaco, where he would introduce himself to the majordomo, à la 007, as "McCain. John McCain." Where next? No idea, just that it would be someplace fun, probably sexy, but not seriously so. Only after we landed back in his office did the business of my visit finally commence.

— — — —

McCain was willing to tell me about much of his five and a half years as a prisoner of war, but he shied away from discussing times when he might be seen as acting heroically or promoting himself. He even seemed uncomfortable talking about his extraordinary ability to survive treatment that crossed the line into the truly inhuman.

One day I went to his office determined to get him to tell me about an episode I had come upon in *P.O.W.*, John Hubbell's magnificent chronicle of the Vietnam prisoner experience. In the section that interested me, Hubbell describes prison guards administering a beating to McCain so horrific that just reading about it left me limp.

I wanted to include the story in my book, but I didn't want to rely solely on the work of another writer, so I asked McCain to tell me about the beating in his own words. He didn't actually refuse, but he wouldn't fully engage, either. I'd ask about a passage, but all I got back were shrugs, grunts, and a variety of other signals that I read as him telling me he didn't want to talk about it and I was starting to piss him off.

The problem was, I needed him to talk about it. The incident was so telling in its brutality that there was no way I could ignore it. No one could understand John McCain without knowing what he had gone through both physically and emotionally, and I was determined to portray those dark days as vividly as I could. But Hubbell couldn't be my only source on that particular beating, especially when I had what reporters call a "horse's mouth source" sitting a few feet from me. At the very least I needed him to confirm the details of Hubbell's account.

Finally I said, "Senator, do me a favor. Here's the book that talks about the stuff I want to know about. Just read these pages I've clipped together and tell me what's true and what's not true."

He snatched the book from me, opened it, and began reading. As he flipped through the pages, he paced in circles around his office. He nodded frequently, which I interpreted as confirming some passage. Now and then he would turn to me and glare, as if I was the guy in the book who had just broken his arm.

The pacing and reading continued for about ten minutes. Then he tossed the book back to me and said, "All true." End of discussion.

— — — —

Nearly everything I discovered about McCain that carried even the faintest aroma of heroism came from someone else. The most striking episodes related to his refusal to go home when his captors told him they had decided to release him. Just him, no one else.

He said he wouldn't go. He told his jailers he was bound by the Code of Conduct, principles developed by the military after the Korean conflict to govern the behavior of Americans captured in wartime. The Code dictated that POWs accept release only in the order in which they were taken prisoner. By that standard the first man eligible to go was Navy pilot Everett Alvarez, shot down in August 1964, three years before McCain.

Alvarez and scores of other aviators of similar vintage were still in prison when the offer of early release was made to McCain. By then, however, three Americans had jumped the line and gone home, charter members of what those left behind christened the Fink Release Program.

For McCain, there were constraints other than the Code. He knew the North Vietnamese had dubbed him "the Crown Prince" when they learned that he was the son of one of the Navy's most senior admirals. The *New York Times*, in fact, reported his capture on its front page, reflecting his father's prominence.

"Adm. McCain's Son . . . Missing in Raid," the headline read.

He knew his captors considered him a major catch, so he saw their offer to release him as a ploy to embarrass his father. What he didn't know at the time, though the North Vietnamese most assuredly did, was that President Johnson had just named Jack McCain commander in chief of all U.S. forces in the Pacific, including Vietnam, so the embarrassment and its attendant propaganda value stood to be intensified.

McCain could have justified taking early release. The POWs had construed the Code of Conduct as providing an exception for those seriously sick or injured. They were to receive priority if anyone was to be sent home ahead of others.

At the time McCain was in such dreadful physical condition that he doubted he could survive another year of incarceration. He weighed less than a hundred pounds, he was in a body cast, and he seemed to have shriveled up inside it. His cell mate, Air Force Major Bud Day, remembered him as "bug-eyed, like you see in those pictures of the guys from the Jewish concentration camps."

His closest friend in prison, Bob Craner, urged him to take the North Vietnamese up on their offer. McCain quotes his explanation to Craner for why he could not in *Faith of My Fathers*, the 1999 memoir he wrote with Mark Salter, his longtime senatorial aide.

> *I would be disloyal to the rest of you. I know why they're doing this—to make every guy here whose father isn't an admiral think the Code is shit. They'll tell all of you, "We let McCain go because his father's an admiral. But your father's not and nobody gives a*

damn about you." And I don't want to go home and see my father,
and he wouldn't want to see me under those conditions. I've got to
say no.

The North Vietnamese certainly had it in their power to ship Mc-
Cain home against his will. But their prisoner release program was
designed to persuade world opinion—especially opinion in the United
States where many viewed the Vietcong as peasant saints—that the
POWs were being treated humanely. McCain made it abundantly clear
he would not play that game. Send me home, he told prison officials,
and I'll blow the whistle on the beatings, the torture ropes, and all the
other shit you don't want the world to know about.

Jack Van Loan, an Air Force pilot, said he was looking through a
peephole in his cell door one day when a contingent of North Vietnamese officials entered the cell that McCain shared with two other
prisoners. Minutes later, Van Loan told me in an interview years later,
he heard McCain erupt in a torrent of world-class obscenities.

"It was some of the most colorful profanity that you would ever
hope to hear," Van Loan recalled. "He was calling them every name in
the book, and telling them that he was not going home early, that he
wasn't going to ask for amnesty and not to ask him that again and to
get out and, furthermore, screw you and the horse you rode in on.

"John was just shrieking at them. Those guys came tumbling back
out of there, I mean, they were backing up and John was just fighting
back as best he knew how. They came out of there like tumbleweeds. I
was laughing and crying at the same time. They would have lugged
him out of there that day and let him go. And here's a guy that's all
crippled up, all busted up, and he doesn't know if he's going to live to
the next day and he literally blew them out of there with a verbal as-
sault. You can't imagine the example John set for the rest of the camp
by doing that."

The North Vietnamese, for their part, were not as appreciative as
Van Loan of McCain's spunk. Not long after that episode, they threw
him into solitary and kept him there for the next two years.

The interview in which McCain told me how he was forced to confess to war crimes was the most painful for me. It wasn't a joyride for him, either.

We started talking in midafternoon. His office was bright, lit by the sun shining through the windows.

His refusal to take an early release had triggered a period of relentless torture. It began about a week after he had told the commander of the Hanoi prison system that he would go home only under duress.

Throughout this ordeal, the guards demanded a confession from him. He finally gave in. Years later he would write, "I had learned what we all learned over there: Every man has a breaking point. I had reached mine."

In his handwritten confession McCain described himself as a "black criminal" who had committed the crimes of an "air pirate." He worked in misspellings, stilted phrases, grammatical errors, and Communist jargon, anything to signal to the outside world that his confession was forced from him.

At the time, he did not know that others had been broken, including those viewed as the most courageous: Bud Day; Jim Stockdale, who disfigured himself by battering his face with a stool rather than make a public confession; Jeremiah Denton, who spelled out t-o-r-t-u-r-e in Morse code by blinking his eyes at a television camera.

It probably wouldn't have mattered. Alone, back in his cell, McCain could not free his mind of the feeling that he had betrayed his country, its flag, and his comrades.

His family as well. The McCains had an illustrious military heritage that included not just his father but his grandfather, Admiral John "Slew" McCain, who commanded "Bull" Halsey's fast carrier task force in the Pacific, fought the Japanese from Guadalcanal to Tokyo Bay, then stood on the deck of the battleship *Missouri* as the defeated enemy signed the surrender documents that ended World War II. And there were other McCains who had distinguished themselves in service to the country, a line that stretched back as far as the Revolutionary War.

Beaten, battered, diminished in his own eyes as never before, he was inconsolable. More than inconsolable. Much more.

His eyes settled on the small stool in his cell. It was so low to the ground that he had to squat to sit on it, but it was tall enough to do what he needed it for now. He took off his blue prison shirt, rolled it into a makeshift rope, draped one end over his shoulder, and fed the other end through the louvers of the window high up in his cell.

Just then a guard burst in and pushed him away from the window.

— — — —

That interview lasted longer than any of the others. It had begun in midafternoon. By the time we were through the light was dying, but neither of us moved to switch on a lamp. There was no trace of cockiness in McCain's demeanor, none of the wise-ass quality that over the past weeks and months was so often on display.

"Would you have done it?" I asked.

He took a few seconds to consider his answer.

"I don't know whether I would have gone through with it or not," he replied. "I have no idea. I kind of doubt it."

"Could it have happened?"

"It could have."

"But you're beyond any feelings of guilt now, aren't you, Senator? You know about the others, right? Bud Day and Stockdale, Jerry Denton, all the others who had been broken?"

"I still believe that I failed," he murmured.

I was starting to feel spooked. And unhappy with myself, maybe even a little ashamed. Over the years I had become an accomplished interviewer, and I was proud of that skill. But not that day. With no qualms at all I had led McCain to a place he never wanted to revisit. Christ, he takes me to the Riviera and I bring him back to a cell in North Vietnam where he almost hung himself.

By now the office was not just getting dark, it was getting crowded.

His father and grandfather, both dead for years, had slipped in when he was talking about confessing. To me they seemed interested observers, nothing more. But McCain, I think, saw disappointment and disapproval in their eyes.

"I'm convinced that I did the best that I could, but the best that I could wasn't good enough," he said. I think he was talking to me. I wasn't sure.

As I was packing up, he said, "It's the only blemish. I'll never get over it."

— — — —

As I walked across the Mall toward Union Station and the Metro, I couldn't put the last sixty minutes out of my mind. It was rush hour and federal workers were streaming out of government offices. How many of you went to Vietnam? I silently asked. Did any of you do the egg allergy routine? Do you know, do you even care, what it was like over there?

I felt a sudden surge of anger. Just as quickly it faded, replaced by a stark and horrifying image.

This is what I saw: a man I had come to respect as much or more than any man I had ever known, dangling from a homemade rope, his legs thrashing madly for a few seconds, then growing still.

Nearby a small stool lay on its side.

Thirty-four

HOOSIERS

John Poindexter, in a note composed in an unexpectedly elegant hand, informed me at the start of my work on *Nightingale* that his legal difficulties precluded him from agreeing to the series of interviews I had requested.

It was hard to argue with him. He had been indicted several months earlier on an array of felony charges—among them conspiracy, lying to Congress, and destruction of evidence—a daunting set of accusations that made telling his story to a reporter he barely knew seem well beyond stupid.

No one had ever accused John Poindexter of stupidity, at least not until now. He flashed his intellectual candlepower early. As a high school student in the small Indiana town in which he grew up, he had a flattering if decidedly unsexy nickname: Brain.

At the Naval Academy, he stood first in his class, the Class of 1958, a ratification of his academic brilliance, and commanded the three-thousand-man Brigade of Midshipmen, a rare achievement and a tribute to his leadership qualities.

Poindexter's academic achievements continued beyond his Annapolis graduation to include the PhD in nuclear physics he earned at Caltech. Now, facing an array of criminal charges that could make his next assignment the federal pen, he was confident in his belief, one that he had adhered to throughout his career, that nothing good could come of talking to a reporter.

Even if reporters could be trusted—to his mind, a barely conceivable concept—they were vulnerable if the government decided they had something it wanted.

Poindexter's view of reporters calls to mind a saying of my grandmother's that crystalizes for me one reason his career crashed and burned: Too smart is half-stupid.

As we shall see, his distrust of the press played an important role in taking an enormously intelligent man and making him half-stupid.

— — — —

I didn't give up trying to persuade Admiral Poindexter to let me interview him. Every few months I dropped him another note renewing my request. I invariably received a short, pleasant response citing his continuing legal difficulties as the reason it was impossible for him to even consider talking to me.

I also spoke with many of his associates and urged them to use their influence to convince him to meet with me. Some agreed to try; others blew me off. Didn't matter. Nothing worked, so I had to find other ways to deal with his reticence.

— — — —

At first I planned to concentrate on three groups of prospective sources: Washington types, Navy shipmates, and men who had been with the admiral during his midshipman days.

But I realized early on that I needed to account for the years preceding his arrival in Annapolis. I couldn't ignore that part of his life even if I wanted to.

And I wanted to. As I later came to understand, I was shying away from giving his pre-Annapolis years the weight they deserved because reporting on them meant exposing myself to situations I hoped I had put behind me.

I'm talking about meeting new people, people who could tell me about Poindexter as a kid in Indiana, and having to steel myself for their stricken reactions when they first saw my face.

That experience was no less painful now than it had been back in the *Evening Capital* days, but because of where I worked and what I had been doing in the recent past, the occasions in which I encountered unsuspecting strangers were far less frequent. As a White House correspondent, I moved in something of a bubble. Most of the people I encountered each day, whether fellow journalists or government officials, knew me or had seen enough of me that the shock value of my face had largely worn off.

Now, though, I was preparing to meet with people who hadn't even known I existed a few weeks earlier. I had, of course, talked by phone with all of them, to arrange interviews. Several had to be coaxed. It helped open doors when I described my life before journalism, one that tracked pretty closely with Poindexter's.

I thought about it, but I never said, "By the way, my face is badly scarred. Hide the kids."

Even so, I lived with a sense of dread during the weeks before I hit the road in search of the young John Poindexter. By the time I kissed Kelley and Sam good-bye, though, I had come to accept the prospect that some bad shit awaited me.

Fuck it, I told myself, you just have to deal with it.

— — — —

Odon, Indiana, John Poindexter's hometown, population about thirteen hundred, is roughly one hundred miles southwest of Indianapolis, most of those miles through farm country. A world of winter wheat and small-town ambitions was how I portrayed it. Ellen Warren of *Knight-Ridder* did me one better. She called Odon "a one-stoplight rural cliché," a description worthy of Richard Ben Cramer.

The town was not, by any reckoning, a breeding ground for naval officers. The Poindexter family, in fact, had no military legacy. The men were neither soldiers nor sailors. Not even close. With a single exception, they were undertakers.

The exception was John's father, Marlan Poindexter, who became a banker, quite a successful one, rather than join the family funeral home business.

Young John didn't want to be a banker or an undertaker. The sea, to be sure, was not in his blood; he had never even seen the ocean. But as a teenager his imagination had been gripped by the seafaring tales of C. S. Forester and Jack London. I never would have guessed it, but he was a closet romantic, a boy who saw himself as growing into a heroic figure, a latter-day Horatio Hornblower.

Physically he stood six foot two, though he did not seem that tall. He had an average build, neither heavy nor slim. The eyeglasses enhanced his owlish countenance, which at times took on a vaguely East Asian cast. To Ellen Warren, his almost perfectly circular face resembled "a pan of warm milk."

That was kind compared to the way others portrayed him. Two members of the congressional committee that investigated Iran-Contra—Maine senators William Cohen and George Mitchell, a Republican and a Democrat, both highly regarded—published a book, *Men of Zeal*, in which Poindexter, North, and McFarlane were pictured as dangerous zealots.

To that point in the Iran-Contra saga there was little evidence to challenge that characterization. A zealot, as I understood it, was a person who was fanatical and relentless in pursuing a political or religious goal. Mitchell, Cohen, and others argued that Poindexter, McFarlane, and North fell into that category.

I wasn't so sure. Zealot didn't feel right to me, least of all as it applied to Poindexter. I pictured zealots as having a wild-eyed look. The admiral seemed too normal to me. He may have been guilty of any number of things, but I doubted zealotry was one of them.

Still, I couldn't dismiss the possibility that the senators were right, about McFarlane and North as well as Poindexter. I resolved to be sensitive to traces of zealotry as I went about my reporting.

— — — —

John's widowed mother, Ellen, and his boisterous, fun-loving, chain-smoking cousin Dickie Ray Poindexter helped me the most in Odon.

I met Dickie Ray first. He scooped me up as soon as I got there and proceeded to give me a whirlwind tour of the town and the rest of Daviess County. Lots of winter wheat, as I expected, and a thriving Amish community, which surprised me. The county had a dark side, too. Until the mid-1930s the Ku Klux Klan flourished there. Dickie Ray didn't mention that, and I saw no reason to bring it up.

Dickie Ray was proud of his cousin's achievements and anxious to tell me about them. Both he and John were Boy Scouts. Not surprisingly, John was the one inducted into the select Order of the Arrow, a Scout fraternity that stressed character, fortitude, and self-reliance.

The cousins were close but different, never more so than in their methods of tutoring younger Scouts.

"My idea was when you brought Tenderfoots in we'd take their pants off and paint their dicks with Mercurochrome," Dickie Ray explained. "John's attitude was to sit them down and teach them how to go through the Boy Scout manual and how a Scout is trustworthy, loyal, thrifty, brave, clean, and reverent."

How could you not love Dickie Ray? I didn't go to Odon to have fun, but I had fun with Dickie Ray, and I had to believe that growing up John did, too. As kids, Dickie Ray told me, he and John would race around the funeral home on the four-wheeled carriages used to transport caskets, driving them as if they were bumper cars.

Ellen Poindexter had resisted meeting with me, but she said John blessed our getting together. She was sweet, very smart, and enormously helpful. But even with John's okay, she was wary of me. How wary? Well . . .

I arrived at her home in the early evening. She greeted me at the door and invited me in, then led me to the living room. It was not well lighted, just a couple of lamps with low-wattage bulbs. A man and woman were already there, John's sister, Candace, and her husband. Mrs. Poindexter gestured to the chair in which she wanted me to sit. The others arranged themselves in a loose semicircle in front of me.

As we settled ourselves, Mrs. Poindexter said she hoped I didn't mind, but they were going to tape the interview. Not at all, I said, I'd like to do so as well.

I looked around the dimly lit room and saw that the Poindexter family's arsenal numbered three tape recorders. Seemed like overkill to me.

I felt mildly unsettled. As I asked my first question, I depressed the button on my machine. Click!

A split second later: Click! Click! Click!

The clicks switched on my occasionally overactive imagination. I felt a chill and for a moment, maybe a few moments, my mind started playing tricks. I was no longer in Mrs. Poindexter's poorly lit living room. I was on a gurney, staring at a blinding overhead light, awaiting the arrival of the warden and the chaplain and the doctor with the needle.

The weirdness disappeared as soon as we began conversing. I liked Mrs. Poindexter. I understood that her wariness sprang from her concern that she might say something that could damage John or, more likely since I was of the genus and species her son no doubt had warned her against, that I might twist something she said to create fresh problems for him.

She needn't have worried about saying the wrong thing. She provided a wonderful narrative of her son's life as a child and young man, speaking of him with great affection, along with an unmistakable trace of awe, as if she knew she had given birth to someone special.

"John was never a little boy," she told me. "He was born an old man."

I spent another few days in Odon, talking to Poindexter's friends, mostly schoolmates, and teachers.

What most surprised me was that no one, at least no one I could find, had a bad word to say about him. And no one seemed to resent the fact that he was smarter than they were. They may have called him Brain, but he was a popular kid and they elected him king of Odon's annual fall festival.

I concluded that evidence of zealotry was in short supply in Odon.

— — — —

M y time in Odon had been productive in more ways than one. I gained a sense of John Poindexter in his early years, the purpose of my trip to Indiana. But I also learned something about myself.

None of those I went to see freaked out on first meeting me, as I had dreaded. Some, I assumed, had been forewarned of my appearance by Poindexter. Certainly his family fell into this category.

There were others who didn't know what I looked like until we met but didn't react to my face, either. I thought of them as grown-ups, men and women who knew better than to display shock or any other inappropriate reaction on meeting a person who had been maimed in some way.

But there was also me. I had spun a complex web of defense mechanisms over the previous two decades. The process began at Stanford in 1968 when I rode my bike to school singing "Wichita Lineman" to help me avoid focusing on the staring faces in passing cars.

Since then I had added several strands to the web, though I was rarely aware when I did so. But in Indiana I realized I had added something new to my repertoire.

This is how it worked.

Heading to an interview I was usually on edge, wondering how I would be received. As I neared my destination, though, it was as if a phone booth had materialized on the side of the road. I didn't turn into Superman, but suddenly I was no longer a graying fifty-year-old reporter with a scarred face that frightened children and caused adults to bite their tongues.

Instead, people opened their doors to a good-looking twenty-six-year-old Marine lieutenant who nobody fucked with. (I was twenty-six when I became intimate with the VC land mine.)

There was something else that finally sunk in while I was in Odon. Kelley knew what I looked like and she loved me. In fact, she married me and we had a child. And the child seemed to love me, too.

Going back even further, Janie had pulled me through the worst time of my life and never seemed to notice that I no longer looked like the man she married. And we had three kids who had only made us proud.

So maybe the time had come for me to start thinking of myself as lucky and not as a victim.

Thirty-five

"LINDA IS COOL"

I never quite gave up on getting Admiral Poindexter to talk to me, but by the time I was three years into work on the book I pretty much knew it wasn't going to happen.

My fretting was easing toward depression when I remembered something. Those I spoke to about the admiral usually said something like "Have you talked to Linda? You should talk to Linda."

Yeah, right. Linda was Mrs. Poindexter. I explained to whomever I was conversing with that there was no way she was going to speak to me if her husband wouldn't. The person on the other end of the line invariably agreed, but nearly always added something like "Too bad. Linda is cool."

Mrs. Poindexter had recently been ordained an Episcopal priest, so how cool could she be? Nice, maybe, and no doubt a good person. But cool? Still, other than fretting, I had nothing on my plate that morning so I decided to write her a letter.

"Dear Mrs. Poindexter," I began, "I hate to think of Naval Academy guys as male chauvinist pigs, but perhaps we are."

I told her that I had taken Admiral Poindexter's refusal to meet with me as speaking for her, too.

"But maybe not," I wrote. I then told her how people had said I should talk to her and my knee-jerk chauvinist assumption that there was no chance she would agree to do so. If I was wrong, I wrote, I truly would love to get together with you. Here's my phone number.

I mailed the letter later that morning. I figured that was the end of it and resumed fretting.

Two days later, I was sitting at my desk, no doubt in mid fret, when the phone rang.

"Hello, Bob Timberg," I answered.

"Bob, this is Linda Poindexter. I think we should talk."

— — — —

I interviewed Mrs. Poindexter seven or eight times during the next few months, always over lunch, and always at the same restaurant, Fred & Harry's, a family-style seafood restaurant on Colesville Road in Silver Spring, about ten miles from her home in Rockville.

I always called her Mrs. Poindexter. I asked her once how people addressed a female priest, and she said as Mother. That made sense since a male priest was called Father, but I never felt comfortable with Mother so I stayed with Mrs. Poindexter.

Religion aside, she was most assuredly a mother. She had five sons, all very smart guys, one a Marine, two Annapolis graduates.

I liked her from the moment I met her. It was as if we had been friends since childhood. Ellen Poindexter's wariness was in no way evident in her daughter-in-law's demeanor. Over the course of our two-hour lunches, she revealed herself as smart, funny, and saucy. And her friends were right: She was cool.

The picture of John Poindexter that emerged from our interviews was totally at odds with his public persona, as well as from the way I initially viewed him.

In 1968, I was surprised to learn from Mrs. Poindexter, she and her husband voted for the liberal Hubert Humphrey, unlike most of their friends who backed Richard Nixon. By then Linda had taken to wearing a peace symbol around her neck.

Her emerging liberal sentiments, which her husband seemed to share to a degree, extended beyond opposition to the Vietnam War to civil rights, the other great issue of the Sixties and early Seventies. In the aftermath of the riots in Washington that followed the April 1968 assassination of Martin Luther King, she brought food to embattled inner-city churches.

She also became a worker bee in anticipation of the Poor People's March that began a month later—volunteering at the headquarters of the sponsoring organization, the Southern Christian Leadership Conference, compiling lists, addressing envelopes, helping marchers get settled when they arrived in DC.

Mother's Day fell in the midst of the pre-march preparations. Linda wanted to be with her family, and she knew they wanted her home that day. But she also knew she was needed downtown.

"It's your day," John said. "Do what you want to do. I'll watch the kids."

Thanks, she said, driving off.

"John would always say, 'Do what you want to do, go where you want to go, my career can take care of itself,'" she later explained. "It was sort of like John lived his life the way he wanted to and I would live mine the way I wanted to and we'd negotiate out the rest."

I found that hard to believe. Then she told me another story that astounded me. This happened in 1985. John Poindexter was then Ronald Reagan's deputy national security adviser. At the time, the president was resisting intense pressure from many sides to impose economic sanctions on South Africa because of its apartheid policies.

Linda was studying for the ministry but had not yet been ordained. She told John that she was going to join some friends that afternoon and picket the South African embassy, where protestors were being routinely arrested. She didn't ask his permission, but she hinted that she would drop the idea if it would embarrass him.

Go ahead, he said. She did, was arrested, handcuffed, put in a paddy wagon, and booked. She was released a few hours later.

No news organization wrote the story. Reporters may not have checked the police blotter too closely that day. Then again, one or two may have seen her name on it but laughed off the thought that she might be related to the Poindexter guy who worked in the White House. I mean, the wife of the deputy national security adviser publicly flaunting her unhappiness with the president's policy? Come on, what was the chance of that?

I remember thinking during the time I was interviewing her that any man who could keep Linda Poindexter happy and in love with him for some four decades had to be more than a pan of warm milk.

— — — —

In 1991 my Naval Academy classmate Tom Lynch became superintendent of the Naval Academy. By then Tom was a rear admiral and one of the most highly decorated members of the Class of 1964. Years earlier he captained the 1963 Navy football team that featured Heisman Trophy winner and NFL Hall of Fame quarterback Roger Staubach.

That fall Tom invited classmates and other friends living in the DC area to the Academy for a brunch preceding that Saturday afternoon's football game at Navy-Marine Corps Memorial Stadium in Annapolis.

For about a half hour, Tom's guests circulated in spacious Alumni Hall, greeting friends, chatting about old times, and handicapping Navy's football season.

At one point I directed Kelley's gaze to John and Linda Poindexter, who were chatting with a few people half a room away.

"Let's go say hello," I said, taking Kelley's hand.

We excused ourselves from the group we had been socializing with and headed in the Poindexters' direction. Before we reached them, though, there was an announcement that the meal was about to begin and that we all should find seats.

There must have been twenty tables with eight chairs each. Some groups had already formed and claimed tables that could accommodate their entire party. But Kelley and I were on our own, and tables were filling up rapidly. Most, in fact, were filled when Kelley spotted a table with two empty chairs, grabbed my hand, and pulled me toward it.

I was relieved as we hastily settled into adjoining seats. I had been concerned that Kelley and I might wind up sitting at different tables. Then I looked to my right, at the couple who occupied the seats next to me.

"Hi, Bob," said Linda Poindexter.

"Hi, Bob," said John Poindexter.

At least one of the people at the table was a classmate of mine and I knew several of the others. I don't think the Poindexters knew any of them.

Mostly we concentrated on our meal, but we also made small talk, chatting about Navy football, which had fallen on hard times, our pride in Tom Lynch, and the activities of other classmates.

About halfway through the meal, Poindexter—out of nowhere and for reasons I'll never understand—had this to say:

"Bob, is the reason it's taking you so long to write your book because I won't talk to you?"

He said it in a devilish tone, and he said it loud enough for everyone at the table to hear. I couldn't believe it. He was actually teasing me!

I'm sure those at the table were wondering if this was some inside joke between Poindexter and me or if something serious was going on. They all knew I was writing a book about the Iran-Contra scandal in which Admiral Poindexter was a principal figure.

I felt the eyes of everyone at the table on me as I formed my reply.

"To tell you the truth, Admiral, you've made my job easier by not talking to me," I said. "This way I can make up anything I want about you."

Everyone laughed, including the Poindexters. Then we all got up and watched Navy lose to Ball State, a team that wouldn't have been allowed on the same field as the squad that Roger Staubach and Tom Lynch led thirty years earlier.

That evening I sent Poindexter a note saying I assume he realized I was joking at the brunch and I still wanted to talk to him.

The following Tuesday I was in my basement office in Bethesda when the phone rang.

"Hello, Bob Timberg."

"Bob, this is John Poindexter. I guess it's time for you and me to talk."

And so we did. We met at his home in Rockville practically every Monday for the next year, while sipping coffee so bitter I kept waiting for it to eat through the bottom of the cup and bore a hole in my leg. Kizmie, his handsome golden retriever, kept us company.

I learned a lot about the admiral, his White House colleagues, President Reagan, and numerous foreign policy episodes. I also found myself liking him more than I ever thought I would, and I sensed that the feeling was mutual.

There was one exchange I still think about from time to time that was revealing of his sentiments toward the press.

We had just begun the day's interview when he brought up a story in that morning's *Washington Post*. He was furious about it. I can't remember what the story was about, but he felt it was inaccurate or overblown, one or the other.

He proceeded to criticize the story in harsh terms. At first his words were aimed at the two newsmen who shared the byline on the story. Then he expanded his criticism to encompass all reporters.

"But I don't mean you, Bob," he hastened to add. "I know you're not like them."

To which I replied, "Admiral, I am like them. I'm not just like them. I am them."

For perhaps half a minute silence claimed the room. Then we resumed the interview, as if nothing had happened.

Thirty-six

BUD

I n February 1987, when it seemed damn near everyone in Washington was blaming him for Iran-Contra, Bud McFarlane gulped down some wine he had spiked with three dozen Valium, climbed into bed, kissed his wife goodnight, and drifted off to sleep.

To his surprise, he woke up in a hospital bed instead of a satin-lined mahogany box.

Those who knew him best called it a failed attempt at *seppuku*, ritual suicide as practiced by disgraced samurai, an effort by Bud to pay with his life for the missteps of Iran-Contra.

That fit. During his years in the White House, he maintained a cool, unflappable, even impassive posture. But much of it was show. He was by far the most complex and, along with Jim Webb, the deepest thinker within the Gang of Five.

By the time he and I started a lengthy series of interviews in 1988, he was more than a year beyond that dreadful night. He had since righted himself and opened an international consulting firm on Eighteenth Street, Northwest, in downtown Washington.

He called it McFarlane Associates, though that was something of a reach since in those early days he was a one-man band, scrambling for clients and trying to figure out what to charge them for the kind of advice he had previously proffered gratis to a president, several cabinet secretaries, and numerous other senior government officials.

We almost always met at his office and usually talked for about two hours. He was in many ways a writer's dream, a source with enormous recall who could describe people and events with the rich detail and vivid color they deserved.

I hadn't expected that. During the time I covered the White House, there was no one who mounted the stage in the Briefing Room more capable of an anesthetizing the assembled press corps than Mc-Farlane. And it wasn't as if he was standing up there declining Latin nouns. He was talking about things that we reporters needed to know about—arms control, hijackings, terrorists, Gaddafi nuttiness, aggressive Soviet moves, and, most critically, the president's thinking on weighty global issues. By the three-minute mark, though, his stultifying baritone had taken its toll. You could see reporters nodding off, their heads dropping as if they'd been shot, then quickly snapping back up as they realized they couldn't afford to miss a word Ronald Reagan's national security adviser was saying. From the front where he was holding forth, it must have looked as if the old amusement park game Whac-A-Mole had taken on human form.

One-on-one was a different story. Across a desk he was engaging, occasionally funny, often passionate, at times emotional. Not once in all the time I was interviewing him was I even momentarily bored.

— — — —

Bud McFarlane was, to my mind, an unusual combination of combat-tested Marine and strategic thinker of surpassing skill. Those dual achievements should have been matters of great pride to him. I think for the most part they were. But too often in our conversations, he seemed distressed and almost painfully vulnerable. Iran-Contra certainly accounted for much of his anguish but, as I would learn, there were reasons that predated that affair by decades.

I never would have guessed it. Bud McFarlane, a retired Marine lieutenant colonel who had tasted armed combat and served as national security adviser to a very conservative Republican president, was the son of a populist Democratic congressman from North Central Texas who'd ridden the Roosevelt bandwagon into Congress in 1932.

Buddy, as he was then known, was the youngest of the five McFarlane kids. He was less than a year old in April 1938 when his mother collapsed and died in the family's Washington home. She was thirty-seven.

That same year his father lost his congressional seat even though FDR—aboard a ten-coach train on a cross-country whistle-stop tour—roared into Wichita Falls, the district's commercial center, to rally support for his political ally.

His father, William Doddridge McFarlane, was unprepared for child-rearing. He constantly scolded the children and occasionally beat them with a hairbrush, a tree switch, or a belt.

On the slimmest of pretexts he would drench Buddy with harsh words, telling him that his misdeeds—like leaving his new wool shirt at the park when he was eight—meant he "was going to end up like the dumb kids in your class, and you won't be admired, and you won't succeed in life, and you'll just be a failure."

What mattered, his father repeated throughout Buddy's childhood, was that he was born to lead.

"You are a McFarlane!" he would shout. "You are not an ordinary person."

When McFarlane left home for the Naval Academy in 1955, he carried with him emotional scars from those recurring rebukes. Three of them would eventually cripple his future: He was vulnerable to intimidation. He was too quick to accept blame. He did not challenge authority, at least not often.

His reluctance to do so drove Mike Deaver crazy. Deaver, one of President Reagan's closest aides, hoped for domestic political purposes to soften Reagan's rough, confrontational stance toward the Soviet Union. He viewed McFarlane as a potential ally because he was known to believe that warmer relations with the Soviets were possible.

"The real frustration I had with Bud was that Bud would come into my office and we'd have these long discussions about what ought to happen," Deaver told me. "And I could never get him to say it to Ronald Reagan. . . . I'd say, 'Bud, tell the president that. That's what you're paid for, for God's sake.'"

He also left with the need to redeem his father's oft-stated mantra that unless he achieved a position of great leadership he would be judged a failure.

The scars of his youth never healed, though they were barely noticeable until he reached the White House. By the time he departed the place, they had become disfiguring.

— — — —

McFarlane was part of the first contingent of U.S. troops to arrive in Vietnam as self-contained operational units rather than individual military advisers. The landing force consisted of two infantry battalions augmented by artillery and other supporting arms. It was an unopposed landing on a beach near the American airbase at Da Nang.

As the Marines splashed ashore, they were greeted by Vietnamese women with flowers and garlands. A banner stretched across the beach read *Welcome to the Gallant Marines*.

That was March 8, 1965, the beginning of a ground war in which the United States would find itself enmeshed for the next decade. The modest landing force of thirty-five hundred Marines that rolled onto the beach that day would eventually mushroom to half a million men. By the time it ended ten years later, the war had forever tarnished the way the survivors and the families of the dead viewed what Ronald Reagan called "a shining city on a hill."

McFarlane was a captain but he was given a major's billet, commander of Foxtrot Battery, an artillery unit attached to one of the infantry battalions.

He saw some action, but he had spent most of his thirteen-month overseas tour either aboard ship or at the Marine base on Okinawa, so his first foray in-country was limited to little more than a month.

He tried to extend his tour so he could stay with his troops but the Marines said no. They wanted him to take advantage of the George and Carol Olmsted Foundation scholarship he had been awarded at the Academy. The scholarship gave an officer with five years commissioned service two years off to study at a foreign college or university. His next duty station was thus the Graduate Institute of International Studies in Geneva, where he lived like a civilian and studied international relations.

Geneva redefined McFarlane. He arrived as a Marine officer fresh from combat, brighter than most but no less a Marine officer. He was still a Marine when he departed but now—under the tutelage of the respected international strategists who were his instructors—he thought more about changing the world than taking a hill.

At his request, the Marines shipped him back to Vietnam in September 1967 when his time in Geneva concluded. He hoped to again command an artillery battery, but he was assigned instead to the less glamorous though no less important role of regimental fire-support coordinator. The job involved planning artillery barrages, naval gunfire, close air support for the infantry, and the Arc-light strikes of Air Force B-52 bombers from Guam.

This time around he got a closer look at the war. What he saw shocked him. The greatest industrial power on earth seemed incapable of supplying boots to its troops. And lumber, piled up but barely touched at the command post at Dong Ha, never seemed to make it out to the field. The troops were reduced to breaking down ammunition boxes to reinforce their primitive bunkers. He had only been back a couple of weeks when a four-man fire team was lost after their ammo-box bunker caved in during a monsoon, burying them alive.

Challenging authority was not in his makeup, but in Vietnam he played against type. Furious at the supply problems he was witnessing almost daily, he became an advocate for the troops. One day he was introduced to a visiting three-star general. "Glad to meet you, General," he said. "By the way, the troops need boots."

His recognition that a fighting force needed adequate logistical support to survive was reflected years later in his efforts to keep supplies moving to the Contras.

— — — —

The war also got more personal for McFarlane on his second tour in-country. A month or so after he arrived, he ran into Jack Phillips, an old friend and Annapolis classmate.

"He was commanding a company in combat, the ultimate challenge for a Marine officer," McFarlane told me. "He was fit, strong, knowledgeable, a paragon of what our institutions from the Academy to the U.S. Marine Corps are supposed to produce. Two days later, literally, he took an RPG [rocket-propelled grenade] round in the chest and was destroyed."

The death of a fellow soldier in combat, especially a friend, is an imprinting experience. It changes the way you view the world, inserts a filter smeared with blood into your field of vision. Really, it changes everything, and not just for the next few days.

The death of Jack Phillips spurred McFarlane to spend more time out in the field, away from the protected headquarters compound. He visited with platoon leaders and platoon sergeants, giving them refresher courses on how to call in artillery support when they were under fire.

I will never forget one interview. We were seated on couches across from one another in the living room of the Georgetown house he and his wife, Jonny, had just moved into. It was late afternoon and the natural light was fading.

We were talking about an episode that began with McFarlane huddled in a foxhole conferring with a young lieutenant. Suddenly mortar fire began tearing up the landscape in front of them.

The lieutenant, alerted to the attack minutes before it began, pointed to a small rise to the rear and advised McFarlane to take cover behind it.

Observing the action from his relatively safe position, McFarlane marveled at the lieutenant's cool professionalism as he stood in the fox-hole, calling in artillery, shouting commands, encouraging the troops. Then a mortar round tore up the ground around them.

The explosion missed McFarlane, but not the lieutenant. His radio operator shouted, "Corpsman! Corpsman! The lieutenant's hit."

McFarlane left his position, crawled back to the foxhole. The lieutenant was lying on his stomach. McFarlane turned him over. Shrapnel had torn away half his face and part of his neck.

The lieutenant was trying to talk but he could only produce watery gurgles. McFarlane realized he was drowning in his own blood. He cradled the lieutenant in his arms, whispered what he hoped were soothing words.

Finally, as McFarlane related it to me, the lieutenant forced some words through the puddle of blood in his throat.

"God bless Mother and . . . Mother and Daddy . . . and Ruth . . . Oh, God." Hard to decipher the rest. Then he died. A moment later a sniper's bullet tore into his head.

"Were you still holding him?" I asked.

"Yes," McFarlane replied.

"In your arms?"

"Yes."

I think we were both in tears by then. Actually, I'm probably mis-remembering. Marines don't cry.

Thirty-seven

CALL OLLIE

O llie North was the only member of the Gang of Five with whom I was unable to conduct a lengthy series of interviews. Like John Poindexter, Ollie had legal issues that made him wary of writers, even a fellow Marine, Vietnam veteran, and Naval Academy graduate.

He also was writing a book, an autobiography, so he probably saw no reason to steal his own thunder by telling me things he planned to reveal himself.

We did meet twice, but the interviews were short and, for me, unsatisfying.

Of course scores of articles already had been written about him, which certainly gave me a head start on my reporting. That was a two-edged sword, though, since it meant working a seam from which much of the gold had already been extracted.

To further confuse the issue, I was just beginning work on *Nightingale* when a biography of North landed in bookstores.

Guts and Glory: The Rise and Fall of Oliver North, the handiwork of *Boston Globe* reporter Ben Bradlee Jr., was well researched, well written, and reasonably comprehensive considering how quickly it had been put together.

I reacted to Bradlee's fine book by briefly going into a limited, modified funk. I've always hated following another reporter's story. I had a crass and inelegant phrase for it. I called it "shoveling someone else's shit." In this case, though, I didn't have much choice.

Screw it, I told myself. I'll just do it better.

— — — —

I wanted to explain Oliver North—who he was, what he was, and how he got that way. Ben Bradlee's book would be a resource, a valuable one, but I had no desire to duplicate it.

North at least was evenhanded in blowing off writers: He hadn't spoken to Bradlee, the son of the legendary *Washington Post* editor, or anyone else as far as I could tell.

For a time I worried that no matter how successful I was in fleshing out North, my description of him and his activities would suffer in the same way I had once feared my work on John Poindexter would— from the absence of the subject's voice.

This led to a bout of hand-wringing, followed by a moment of truth. I was a reporter, I told myself, not a stenographer. And Ollie wasn't the first person to try to kill a story I was after by refusing to talk to me. There was more than one way to learn about a man without speaking to him directly, and at this point in my career I knew most of them. Vigorous reporting was one. But there were others.

There was also a need to be cautious. Sometimes people lie. They also get things wrong.

My first stop was Ollie's hometown in upstate New York. After that I moved on to other places where I might unearth more pieces of the puzzle that was Oliver North. My preliminary research pointed me to sources in Brunswick, Georgia; Oklahoma City; Albany; Grand Rapids; Indianapolis; Pittsburgh; Cincinnati; Buffalo; New York City; San Diego; and Rancho Santa Fe, California. I went to see all of them.

Then there was the Washington area, which was swarming with men and women who knew Ollie and either loved him or despised him (truly, there was negligible middle ground).

They were in the White House, Congress, the Pentagon, the Marine Corps, and at Annapolis. And maybe twenty other places easily reachable by Metro or at most a few hours' drive.

Baltimore was not on my list, but I remembered something—actually someone—from my newspaper days who helped me to understand the seductive charm of Oliver North.

— — — —

In the mid-1970s, when I was covering Baltimore City Hall for the *Evening Sun*, there was an irrepressible municipal employee named Buddy Palughi. He was last seen in these pages being serenaded with the theme from *The Godfather* at an East Baltimore banquet hall while Richard Cramer and I hovered nearby furiously taking notes. Buddy was a demiboss in the public works department and a reporter's dream, invariably up to something aromatic and always good for a killer quote. I called him once to tell him a crony of his had just been indicted. His response? "Oh shit! I'm next."

He was wrong. He wasn't next, though it often seemed as if an indictment bearing his name was no more than a city block away.

Just as well. I'm not sure how Baltimore would have fared if Buddy had not been around to jam his finger into the many dikes that sprung leaks during the sixteen years that William Donald Schaefer presided over the city. Palughi was the mayor's none-too-secret weapon, his man Friday, the person he turned to when he wanted something done right away, with little discussion, and even less red tape. All it took were two words:

"Call Buddy."

Like Schaefer, Ronald Reagan resorted to a two-word summons when he needed to muster his designated, if unofficial, fixer:

"Call Ollie."

— — — —

North's willingness to take on any chore no matter how messy or formidable fit my sense of him. But I was surprised to learn that growing up he was not especially tough or aggressive.

In high school, for example, he chose track over football, generally the game of choice for young men looking to test their manhood.

Kids in Philmont used to jump off the railroad bridge into the churning waters of Agawamuck Creek, but Ollie was never the first to jump.

"Sometimes we had to throw him off," laughed his friend Dale Rowe.

North belonged to a small clique of boys that his old girlfriend, Lynore White Carnes, thought of as a little different. I asked her to elaborate. She searched for a word, settled on one, but held back. She hadn't seen him in years, but she was still protective of him. Finally, under my prodding, she whispered it.

"Nerds."

"I think that's how people looked at them," she said. "They weren't your glamour boys. They were the sort of boys who grow up into interesting men."

Lynore had Ollie pegged. As a kid in Philmont, he was a nice guy going nowhere. A few years later, damn near everyone in the United States and several foreign countries were talking about him.

Oliver North had grown up to be one of the most interesting men in the world.

— — — —

Ollie shed his nerd persona during the two years he spent at Brockport State Teachers College. The vehicle was a Marine Corps program for recruiting college men called the Platoon Leaders Course.

Participants trained for six weeks over two summers at the sweltering Marine base in Quantico, Virginia, their overseers hard-bitten drill instructors with no love for officers, even those still in knickers. On graduation the survivors were commissioned second lieutenants with an obligation to serve three years in the Corps.

After one six-week session at Quantico, though, Ollie knew he wanted to be a career Marine officer and decided the Naval Academy was the preferred launching site. That fall, back at Brockport for his sophomore year, he began the application process for Annapolis. The following July he entered the Academy as a member of the Class of 1967.

I was then a senior in the Class of 1964, so we overlapped for a time. But I never knew him during his first year, which ended prematurely and disastrously for him.

It was Washington's Birthday weekend. He was in a car with four other plebes headed north toward upstate New York. A heavy snow had finally let up, but by then it was after midnight and all the passengers were drowsy if not already asleep.

Around 2:00 a.m. the driver, Bobby Wagner, nodded off and the car plowed head-on into an oncoming tractor-trailer. Wagner was killed instantly.

The four passengers all sustained serious injuries. North broke his nose, jaw, and leg. He also suffered damage to his head, knee, and back.

Another mid broke his back and was paralyzed from the waist down. A concussion deprived a fourth mid of his memory for three weeks. The fifth passenger received burns, a broken pelvis, and a broken leg.

The next day, lying on a gurney at a small hospital in Corning, a battered North told a visitor, "I'll beat this."

He did, but it took a superhuman effort.

— — — —

North spent the better part of the next six months in one hospital or another. He was shipped from the facility in Corning to Bethesda Naval Hospital when his condition stabilized, then on to a smaller hospital on the grounds of the Academy. After a time he was sent home to Philmont to complete his recuperation.

Home did not mean relaxation for Ollie. Back in Philmont he put together a brutal regimen to strengthen his damaged knee. His daily workout routine included jumping off the roof of a small shed.

Academy authorities quickly determined that his injuries precluded him from continuing with his original class. He was given a choice: an honorable discharge from the Navy and a return to civilian life or starting all over in the Class of 1968.

He decided he wanted to stay. Bad knee or not, he was determined to make it through the Academy and become a Marine officer. So he joined his new class as a freshman even though by then he had the better part of three years of college under his belt.

All those years and he's still a plebe, marveled a fellow midshipman.

Ollie's new class, the Class of 1968, would prove to be one of the most celebrated in Academy history. Its members included:

Mike Mullen, Chief of Naval Operations and chairman of the Joint Chiefs of Staff

Jay Johnston, Chief of Naval Operations

Michael Hagee, Commandant of the Marine Corps

Dennis Blair, Director of National Intelligence

Charles Bolden, astronaut, Administrator of the National Aeronautics and Space Administration

Jim Webb, United States senator, Secretary of the Navy, Assistant Secretary of Defense, best-selling author

— — — —

Janic and I visited the Academy sometime in 1968. Can't remember why. Ollie and Jim probably were still there. Or they may have just graduated.

What I do remember is The Board, which stood in the stately marble rotunda of Bancroft Hall. It looked innocent enough from a distance, a freestanding bulletin board with pictures of midshipmen tacked to it. I guessed the football team. I was wrong.

"All of a sudden Vietnam jumped out at us," said Kendell Pease, a classmate of North and Webb. "Maybe not the first three or four pictures, but suddenly there was someone you knew. The Board was always there. It was the shadow in the woods, the fog that crept over the Academy until it covered everybody."

The pictures were from *The Lucky Bag*, the Academy yearbook.

"It wasn't like it was somebody you hadn't seen in two or three years, who maybe had grown a mustache or something, or aged a bit," said Pease. "It was a picture of him that last time you saw him. And he was dead."

The Board went up when Ollie and Jim were plebes. By the time they graduated, The Board had become three boards and no one planning to go into the Marine Corps had to wonder what was in store for them.

The Board was a living thing, mirroring the course of the war, and it blossomed with new pictures during the Tet Offensive of 1968 as Ollie, Jim, and their classmates prepared to officially make their service selections.

"There's a half dozen guys I know whose girlfriends and families talked them out of going Marine Corps because of the way The Board filled up that week," recalled Mark Trainor, who hung tough and took the Marine option.

— — — —

In his sophomore year North's knee put him back in the hospital and he feared that the war would end before he ever saw action.

"Don't worry, Ollie," said a major who had done hard time in Vietnam. "You'll get to go. You may even get to go twice. This fucker is going to go on forever."

Ollie wasn't taking any chances. On graduation he passed up the thirty-day leave he had coming to him and headed straight to Quantico and the Basic School.

Years later, when Ollie had become a household name, a classmate, Rich Petrino, wrote an article in the *Los Angeles Times* in which he recalled coming upon North one night after lights-out, wandering the corridors of Bancroft Hall.

According to Petrino, Ollie said he was looking for his medical records so he could remove information about his knee injury that might keep him from getting a Marine Corps commission.

North denied it, but within the class there was a feeling that Ollie probably had been up to something along the lines of what he allegedly told Petrino.

When I heard about it, I thought it was another great Ollie story and was not surprised to learn that most classmates chalked it up to North's congenital determination.

But one of his classmates, a Marine named Jack Holly, told me it was a mistake to view the episode as just another amusing Ollie North tale.

For many first classmen, Holly said, a knee injury would be the million-dollar wound. They could take their prestigious Annapolis diploma, burnish it in grad school, slide into a junior executive slot in the private sector, and never spend a day in the service. Let alone in Vietnam.

"Think about it," Holly said. "Ollie's doing this so he can go to Vietnam!"

Thirty-eight

"DIBS ON THE BOOTS"

I met Oliver North a couple of times in the mid-1980s when I was covering the Reagan White House for the *Baltimore Sun* and he was a star on the National Security Council staff, first under Bud McFarlane, then John Poindexter.

Our encounters were not memorable—I can't even remember the occasions—but I came away with the sense that he was a talented, capable, levelheaded Marine officer.

I had no reason to question that impression over the next couple of years as Ollie's name came up in one context or another, usually as a minor player in some national security matter, invariably in a positive light.

Iran-Contra changed my sense of him. I still thought he was talented and capable, but levelheaded seemed a stretch, so much so that once, in print, I compared his judgment to a wedge of cheddar cheese.

By then I had done enough reporting to have reached some preliminary conclusions about him. A few would change as I learned more about him and his activities, but one impression that I formed back then has never been even slightly shaken.

I believed then and I believe now that when you have an Ollie North under your command, someone you can count on to be there when you need him and who will move heaven and earth to accomplish any mission you give him, you have an attendant responsibility to protect him, as much from himself as from anyone or anything else.

In other words, it's a two-way street. If you're going to use him—and Ollie North was most assuredly used by his superiors—you have to take care of him.

And you do that by providing him with something he had for most of his career in the Marine Corps but which was in scandalously short supply when he needed it most, at the White House.

Adult supervision.

— — — —

As I suspected, North's efforts to resupply the Contras in the face of fierce congressional opposition had its roots in Vietnam.

A firefight and related combat activities were not intellectual concepts to Ollie North, as they were to so many of his critics in Congress and the press.

One of North's Marines, Randy Herrod, in his book *Blue's Bastards*, described the aftermath of a two-hour mortar barrage the platoon endured on a piece of high ground overlooking the DMZ called Mutter's Ridge:

> There were guys with arms and legs torn away, feet missing, guts hanging out. And the corpsmen cleaned them up and stuffed them in bags, the way you'd gather spilled garbage—quickly, mechanically, without looking at what you were doing or risking a deep breath.

So for a little more than a year that was life as Ollie North knew it, armed combat in its many macabre combinations and permutations, an existence not unlike the one the Contras were then experiencing.

Ollie knew that and he believed—because the president had said as much—that the United States had an obligation to do all it could to help the guerrillas. Christ, hadn't Reagan said, "I'm a Contra, too?"

North's fellow platoon leader, Don Moore, tied up the loose ends for me. He insisted that North's experience in Vietnam gave him an acute appreciation of the material needs of combat troops whether they were Nicaraguan Contras or United States Marines.

"The supply situation was atrocious," said Moore. "We were stripping the bodies of our wounded and dead to get canteens, to get boots and ponchos. In a firefight, you'd hear, 'Corpsman! Corpsman!' then, 'Dibs on the canteen, dibs on the boots.' When you're talking about Ollie North and the Contras, you're talking about Ollie North and Mutter's Ridge. He knew what it was like not to have beans, boots, Band-Aids, and bullets."

— — — —

As I pursued this complex tale—a curious admixture of geopolitical issues and personal ones—I found that the Marines I talked to about North provided me with the best insights. Some liked him, others didn't, but they all seemed to feel he was getting screwed. At the same time, most wondered how the hell he had gotten himself mixed up in the biggest Washington scandal since Watergate.

For a long time, I struggled to get a fix on North. At times I admired him, at other times I decided he was a fool. Now and then he seemed dangerous to me.

"You can't pin him down," said Tom Hayes, his Academy classmate. "He's like mercury. Try to put your finger on him and he squirts somewhere else."

As I did more than once during this process, I relied on guidance from an old friend and Academy classmate Chuck Krulak, a Marine's Marine who would soon be named Commandant of the Marine Corps.

Chuck served with North in Vietnam and I knew he liked and admired him. One day I said to my friend, "Explain Ollie to me." Chuck paused for a few seconds as if collecting his thoughts, then said, "Scrape away all the veneer, he's a Marine infantry officer." He added, "He's not the smartest guy in the world."

Thirty-nine

THE KICK-ASS
TROUBADOUR

I interviewed Jim Webb for the first time a few weeks after the Iran-Contra revelations had turned Washington into Scandal Central. Again.

Webb was Secretary of the Navy at the time, and we met in his office at the Pentagon. I was working on the *Esquire* article, so I went to see him to ask about his relationship with Oliver North.

Webb was in his early forties, however, the combination of a boyish countenance, solid build, and full head of red hair unflecked by gray made him look easily ten years younger.

He had a deep voice and was more formal than I had expected. I addressed him as Mr. Secretary. That's what protocol demanded, but since I had graduated from the Academy four years ahead of him, it would not have been unusual for him to say, "Call me Jim." He didn't.

I later learned that classmates on duty at the Pentagon, greeting him in the corridors with a friendly "Hiya, Jim," were quietly informed by Webb aides that such familiarity, a breach of protocol, was not looked on warmly by the Secretary.

At the time it hadn't occurred to me that Webb might have a place in the Iran-Contra book I was struggling to formulate. After spending the better part of two hours with him on two separate occasions, I couldn't imagine the book without him.

— — — —

In the *Esquire* article, I described Webb as "the kickass troubadour for a generation of combat veterans for whom reconciliation will invariably be a concept proclaimed by others, always prematurely."

By then I had come to realize that Webb had thought through the impact of Vietnam to a far greater extent than I had. My reaction was largely emotional and colored by my wounds. Jim's was not without emotion, but he was able not only to see what was happening but to analyze it, explain it, and put his explanation into words whose power resonated with much of the Vietnam veterans community.

At one point I read to him a passage from his third book, *A Country Such as This*. In it, one of the major characters, a former POW named Red Lesczynski, reacts to televised footage of the humiliating American pullout from Vietnam:

> There was a weakness in his country, in its leaders or maybe its system, that had botched this thing badly, called on citizens to sacrifice and then rebuked their efforts, fading again and again in the clutch. He felt a pulse of fear and for a moment thought he would contact his son and warn him to leave the military, to flee from these cowards and madmen who would ask him to bleed and whisper that he should be ashamed of his scars.

I looked up from the book.

"That's about as close as I can come to how I felt," he said.

Webb, no less than Ollie North, saw the retreat from Vietnam not only in terms of lost comrades but as the betrayal of an ally. Still glued to the TV, Webb's Lesczynski says to his wife, "No, I'll never get used to it. It's the most deplorable thing this country has ever done."

— — — —

My research into Webb's military service put him in the same class of warrior as such extraordinary Marine junior officers as John Ripley, Fred Fagan, Ron Benigo, Mike Wunsch, Jim Messer, Paul Goodwin, John McKay, Chuck Krulak, and, of course, Oliver North. Like North, Webb had the medals documenting his heroism: the Navy Cross, the Silver Star, two Bronze Stars, and two Purple Hearts.

One of those Purple Hearts, for shrapnel wounds that forced his unhappy retirement from the Corps, probably deprived the Marines of an exceptional general. But that was a worthy trade-off. The nation lost a general but in exchange it got its kick-ass troubadour, a man who could look at what Vietnam had done to America and play it back to its citizens, complete with dissonant chords, atonal riffs, and screeching feedback. Jim Webb, with his intellect, eloquence, and literary skill, defined that job, made it his.

"The first duty is to remember," Webb said in a speech at Arlington Cemetery. "Those of us who have seen war's ugliness know that a battlefield does not honor its dead, it devours them without ceremony.

"Nor does a battlefield honor heroes. It mocks their sacrifice with continuing misery and terror. It is for those who survived to remember sacrifice and to honor our heroes."

— — — —

This is the first rule of military leadership: Take care of your men. I interviewed a number of Marines who had served under Jim Webb in Vietnam. Some I spoke with on the phone. I went to see several others. The overriding feeling I gained from those interviews was that Webb had never lost touch with them, that over the years he offered advice and guidance, providing help when needed, in short taking care of his men when they returned from Vietnam to a greater degree than any officer I ever knew.

Mac McGarvey was Webb's radioman during a two-month period when Webb's platoon had fifty-six men killed or wounded. One day someone tripped a booby trap and McGarvey's right arm was sheared off. "Knock it off, Sir, it's just an arm," he said as tears rolled down the face of his twenty-three-year-old lieutenant. Looking back, McGarvey said, "For a split second Jim was human, he was not a warrior."

Webb's guys were tough cookies. I went to see McGarvey in Dallas where he was working at the VA. He showed me his stump, the words "Cut along the dotted line" tattooed on it.

As for Webb, Mac said, "I would place my life or my family's life in his hands. Our relationship is a little deeper than blood."

The last time I checked in on McGarvey, he was working in Webb's senatorial office.

Then there was Dale Wilson. Like me, Dale was a short-timer when his luck ran out; with eleven days left in-country a booby trap remade his homecoming plans.

"I thought I'd been hit by napalm because there was smoke coming off me," he recalled. "The sun was in my eyes, so I tried to cover my eyes with my right hand, and my hand fell off in my face."

He passed out, but awoke when the morphine wore off a few hours later. "I realized I had lost more than I thought." He was talking about both legs and his right arm.

I pretty much knew what to expect when I visited Dale at his home in Statesville, North Carolina. Even knowing what I knew, though, I still worried about how I would react to his wounds. I was, in fact, shaken—I pray not visibly—when I first met him: It was early in the day and he had not yet donned his prostheses. But it took him less than a minute to put me at ease, and we were laughing our asses off ten minutes after I got there.

Dale proved to be much more than a survivor. He had put himself through college, had a wife, two kids, and had designed the house we were sitting in.

He told me about getting a call from Webb in 1977. He'd phoned to announce that he had retrieved from the Pentagon dustbin the Silver Star he had put Wilson in for eight years earlier.

Dale had no sooner caught his breath than Webb arrived with several members of the old platoon to join in the celebration of Dale Wilson Day in Statesville. He brought with him a three-star general from the Pentagon to pin on the medal and the Marine band from Camp Lejeune to serenade Dale and his family.

— — — —

When I asked Webb why he started writing, he cited a poem by W. H. Auden about another poet. "In Memory of W. B. Yeats" contains the line, "Mad Ireland hurt you into poetry." Webb's Ireland was Georgetown University's law school, which he entered in 1972 after he was medically retired by the Marine Corps.

The members of his law school class assembled for the first time at an orientation lecture in late July. Webb wore pressed khakis, a button-down shirt, and polished shoes.

To his surprise, many of his new classmates were dressed like the troops he had recently bade farewell to—jungle utilities, bush hats, combat boots, and Sam Browne belts.

Webb felt overdressed and a little foolish, but he was pleased to see so many Vietnam vets in the class. He felt even more foolish when he learned they were all Sunny's Surplus commandos, outfitted not by Uncle Sam but by the local Army-Navy store. It turned out that he was the only Vietnam veteran in a class of 125.

There were other surprises. A woman in his class told him he was the first person she had ever met who had gone to Vietnam. Not only that, she did not even know anyone who had been drafted.

Webb readily admitted to initial discomfort as he entered the unfamiliar world of civilians. He explained to me his state of mind back then: "I'm a first-year law student still trying to figure out what civilians eat for dinner."

Webb did not enter Georgetown looking for trouble. An older

friend, a lawyer whose judgment he respected, told him to open his mind to the thoughts and ideas of the people he would meet there.

He did. Vietnam was a frequent topic of discussion, and he was usually one against many in defending the war against what he saw as a pampered, unbloodied elite. More than anything else, the absence of veterans was confusing to him.

"When I was in the military, it never occurred to me that this was not an experience shared by all," he said.

The paucity of veterans and the sizable antiwar clique at George-town is not what turned the school into Webb's Ireland. A professor of criminal law named Heathcote Wales handled that chore all by himself.

Webb would not discuss with me his encounter with Wales, one of the few times he simply shut down. But I sensed that something I needed to know about had occurred, so I talked to others, Wales among them, and pieced the story together.

Wales, a member of the school's sizable antiwar faction, was aware of Webb's service as a Marine in Vietnam. He also routinely used students' names in exam questions. On one test the first question was about search and seizure. It involved a sergeant Wales had named Webb who attempts to smuggle pieces of jade back to the States in the coffins of two Marines from his platoon who had been killed in action.

Webb would later say to a friend that he felt as if he'd been shot when he read the question.

"All those broken bodies and nights in the rain, for what?" said Webb, according to the friend who spoke to me.

It took Webb a full fifteen minutes before he could even start the exam. When it ended, he confronted Wales.

"I just want you to know it wasn't funny," Webb said. "I went over to Vietnam with sixty-seven lieutenants, twenty-two died, and it wasn't funny."

I interviewed Wales by phone. He confirmed including the question about the fictional Sergeant Webb on the exam, but said he had no intention of offending Webb.

About this time Webb began to write.

— — — —

Like many Americans, perhaps most, Webb harbored doubts about whether the Vietnam War was worth the toll it ultimately took in American lives. And though he did not harbor antiwar views, even privately, he viewed opposition to the conflict as a legitimate philosophical position.

What he could neither understand nor tolerate was the sight of so many of his fellow Georgetown students actively cheering on the VC, the NVA, and the National Liberation Front. Waving Vietcong flags, they chanted "Ho-Ho-Ho Chi Minh, the NLF are gonna win." Didn't they know, Webb wondered, who they would have to kill in order to win?

To Webb's mind, many of the protestors—especially draft-age males—were acting out of suppressed guilt. It was far easier to impute to themselves courage and integrity if they could demonize the troops as fighting an illegal and immoral war as they went about shooting civilians, torching hooches, and smoking dope.

That was about as far as he would go on the subject of the protestors. I interviewed him almost every other week for the better part of two years. In those conversations, which usually lasted about two hours, he told me many things—about his youth, his family, his time at the Academy and in Vietnam as a Marine infantry officer. Rarely, though, would he talk at any length about his views on the men and women who comprised the antiwar movement.

I was frustrated by his reluctance to do so, then I remembered Watergate and found the answer to the problem. The key phrase that kept Woodward and Bernstein on the trail of Nixon and his toadies was "follow the money." For me, with Webb, the dictum was "read the books."

I had, of course, read all Webb's books, but I read them again more closely, searching for clues to his views on opponents of the war. I found what I was looking for in the novel *A Country Such as This*, in this passage about the 1967 march on the Pentagon:

> The students, the people of books and pep clubs and prom committees, who had from their childhood feared the simple power and brutality of the blue collar kids, the rednecks, the bowling alley kings, the hot-rodding, ducktailed greasers who once mocked their studies and their lack of manliness, who might attack them over the tiniest issue of honor, now found their scourges trapped as a result of those same aggressive instincts. The boys whose sense of danger and action lured them into the Army instead of college wore their uniforms like straitjackets, becoming quiet, enduring objects, repositories for the insults of those they could have squashed in a microsecond if the odds were fair.
>
> So the students unloaded on the soldiers, cursing them, daring them, under the accepted guise of hating Army, Pentagon and War. The insults issued, and the soldiers did not move. Tomatoes and bottles smacked into them, and the soldiers did not move. Girls undid their blouses, dangling firm inviting breasts over tightly gripped rifles, and the soldiers did not move. Students spat on them, grew more hateful, megaphones telling them they were dupes, fools, fuckheads, that their war was sinful, immoral, *genocidal*, and the soldiers did not move.

I wondered if Webb's remorseless judgment left room for amnesty for any members of the antiwar movement. It turned out that Webb, like me, had ungrudging respect for men like David Harris who were willing to go to jail for their beliefs. As Webb later wrote, "Thoreau went to prison, not to Canada."

— — — —

A pril 30, 1975, the day the war ended. Webb, like his fictional POW Lesczynski, was repulsed by what he saw on TV: tanks of the victorious enemy rumbling through the streets of Saigon. South Vietnamese who had been loyal to the Americans wailing at the gates of the embassy, begging for entrance into the compound and a chance at salvation. Helicopters tumbling from the decks of carriers.

Webb switched off the TV, grabbed his books, and headed to Georgetown. Final exams were approaching and he had to study. When he got to the school, he saw clumps of students outside the law library—animated, joyous, their beliefs and virtue redeemed.

One of Webb's few friends at Georgetown was a Quaker who had spent two years in Vietnam as a Peace Corps volunteer. Webb spotted him in the crowd.

"Are you really happy about this?" Webb asked.

"Yes, I am," replied his friend.

"You make me want to puke," said Webb.

Forty

LOST

A round the time Webb told me this story—and I had to prod him to get him to reveal the exchange with his erstwhile Quaker friend—he said something that troubled me.

"I'm not sure I'm as angry as you want me to be."

The remark surprised me and caused me to reappraise my role in writing the book. For one thing, it made me realize I had a greater stake in the story than I had been willing to admit even to myself.

Webb's comment also made me wonder if I was losing my edge as a reporter, becoming too personally involved in the story I was covering. The last thing I needed was for my book to be dismissed as still another diatribe by a Vietnam veteran who had lost faith in God and country and every other damn thing in which he once believed.

So no, I couldn't go on a tirade even though my description of the disillusioned Vietnam vet in the paragraph above was not too far off the mark. But I didn't have to dance around issues, either. I was writing a book, not a newspaper article, so I had much more freedom to take a point of view.

As for Webb not being angry enough for me, that was never a problem.

— — — —

That's not to say I wasn't having problems. About a year and a half after I started work on *Nightingale*, I entered what I came to think of as my Ed McBain Phase. During this time I read a staggering number of McBain's fifty or so 87th Precinct police procedurals, usually when I was supposedly working on the book. His cops —Steve Carella, Meyer Meyer, Eileen Burke, Cotton Hawes, Fat Ollie Weeks, even the clueless homicide dicks Monaghan and Monroe, became my friends. All too often I called on them to keep me company during the day when I should have been working on my so-called book (yes, lack of progress had caused me to resurrect that phrase).

Crime novels, thrillers, and spy stories kept me going at a time when I had, to put it gently, lost my way. Less gently, it's fair to say I realized I didn't know where I was going or how to get there. McBain, James Ellroy, James Lee Burke, Elmore Leonard, Stephen Hunter, T. Jefferson Parker, Raymond Chandler, John D. MacDonald, Ross Mac-Donald, P. D. James, Mickey Spillane, Sue Grafton, Michael Connelly, my favorite espionage writer John le Carré, and who knows how many others? I was even feeling warmly toward the bad guys: Carla, the Soviet spymaster, the notorious Deaf Man, the mole Bill Haydon (though I still haven't forgiven him for cuckolding George Smiley, my all-time favorite character). They all dropped by my basement office at one time or another. I don't know if Kelley knew or even suspected their visitations since she was usually at work when they stopped in.

I was probably two years into the process when I hit my low point. By then even pep talks from fictional friends were no help.

I had started writing, mostly as an act of self-preservation. I had done so much research and interviewed so many people that my head was swimming and I had to get something down on paper, or what passes for paper in the digital age.

And so I did. I would write a chapter when I felt my research on an episode had matured sufficiently for me to do so. It wouldn't be a finished chapter by any means, more of a draft. But it was something concrete, not just a bunch of dislocated ideas, quotes, facts, and factoids swirling around in my head.

Believe it or not, this method worked for me; at least I thought it did. I soon had quite a few chapters in the can. But the bigger picture had become a mystery. I knew I had written some good chapters, but how they fit together and what thematic purpose they served was eluding me. More to the point, I was beginning to think I didn't know what the hell I was doing.

Flip Brophy, my agent, played many roles during this time, not least that of hand-holder. Every month or so, sometimes more frequently, she'd call to check on my progress and my state of mind. I would always thank her for her interest but assure her that I was fine and work was going well.

One day, though, I lapsed into honesty. "Flip," I blurted out, "I'm fucking lost! I don't know where the hell I'm going."

Flip doesn't get rattled. She heard me out, which meant listening to me say much the same thing in a variety of ways over the next several minutes.

When I finished unpacking my woes, she said, "I have a thought."

She told me to send her everything I had written. She would then pass it on to a very highly regarded editor friend and ask him, as a favor to her, to look it over and suggest a way or ways to impose order on what I had come to think of as an irredeemable mess.

So I did. I sent her everything. And she dutifully shipped it to her editor friend, a man I happened to know and like and whose opinion I valued.

So my draft chapters went from me to Flip to her friend. Then we waited. This guy was a busy editor and I figured it would be at least a couple of weeks before we heard from him.

It took the weekend. Flip called me that Monday and said her friend had read everything.

"So what did he say?" I asked.

"Bob," she began, then her voice trailed off.

"Flip, what did he say?"

I waited. One second, two seconds, three . . .

"He said, 'I don't know what Bob's doing. I have no idea where he's going with all this.'"

— — — —

You'd think that someone who had pretty much put his life back together against reasonably daunting odds could absorb a punch in the gut from Flip's editor friend.

And you'd be right. True, I almost went down, but I kept my feet even as I stumbled drunkenly around the ring. I took a standing eight count (in real time this translated to several weeks), long enough to clear my head. Then I moved back to the center of the ring.

When I got there, I experienced a rare moment of clarity. Maybe no one else knows what I'm doing, I told myself, but I do.

I'm writing a book about a generation of well-meaning but ill-starred warriors and a nation deeply scarred by a war that some of its young men fought and some didn't.

That was the story. Time to stop pissing and moaning and just do it. Finish the reporting and write the damn thing.

Forty-one

FULL CIRCLE

I went back to the book with a fresh sense of purpose, resuming my efforts to run down men and women who might be able to help me illuminate and explain the Gang of Five.

And, in fact, the more I made progress on the book, the more I realized that something important had changed: Despite my earlier trepidations, I was now able to plug back into my previous life as a midshipman and Marine officer without fear of being crippled by the experience.

My worries had been twofold. First, I suspected my Academy classmates and fellow Marines, in an abundance of kindness and sympathy, would spin a cocoon around me as protection from the pain they knew awaited me if I set foot in the real world.

But I understood, thanks to my well-honed survivor's instinct, that what I needed was not to hide from the world but to take it on.

There was as well my wariness of meeting acquaintances who knew me before I got my new face. For years, I avoided all but my closest friends. Were I again to spot my classmate Sandy Coward strolling past Rookie's butcher shop in Annapolis, I felt confident I would greet him and reintroduce myself rather than watch him go on his way.

The reasons for this brighter outlook were various and cumulative.

I had a job that I liked and was good at. I had friends who took me as I was. I had four kids who never disappointed me and were always fun to be with.

I also had Kelley, who took the rough edges off my life. She taught me about Washington, she kept me from acting intemperately when someone pissed me off, and she always looked fabulous, at home and when we went out. I think people who saw us together figured I had something on her.

Mostly, Kelley made me feel attractive, even desirable. I'll never know how she did that.

As I neared the end of my years of work on *Nightingale*, I realized I had come full circle. I had fought a war, become a casualty of that war, and was now chronicling the impact of my generation's uneven response to that misbegotten conflict.

It also was becoming increasingly clear to me that Vietnam, with the many shades of meaning that name had taken on, would continue to haunt the nation well into the twenty-first century.

— — — —

A round this time I volunteered to help a neighbor, Steve Vance, coach my son Sam's Little League baseball team. For someone who had a deep-seated fear of how younger kids would react to his scars, this was a major step forward.

Sam and his teammates were in the ten-year-old range, not an age at which boys are known for their sensitivity. But I coached for three years and I can't recall any kid ever saying or doing anything that made me uncomfortable. Never even caught one of them staring.

I'm sure they were curious about what had happened to me, but my guess is that Sam or Steve filled them in if they asked. It helped that they were very good kids who had been raised right.

Coaching was truly a happy experience. It helped that we had a lights-out pitcher, Sam's best friend George Williams, and a slugging shortstop, Sam.

Now that I think about it, none of the friends of my three older kids seemed to notice that my face had seen better days, either. I figure Scott, Craig, and Amanda ran some heavy-duty interference for me.

The truth is, by the late Nineties next to no one seemed to react to my scars, at least not in my presence. I think I know why. I stopped thinking of my face as a fright mask. I mean I knew what I looked like—morning encounters with the mirror had been a routine, if unwelcome, part of my life for many years. But I didn't spend much time thinking about being disfigured. And I didn't act like I was. I had come a long way since that well-meaning corpsman at the San Diego Naval Hospital convinced me I'd be happier wearing a brown paper bag over my head.

— — — —

Nothing was easy in the years I spent working on *Nightingale*. And I continued to lose my way now and again. But I never doubted I was doing something that mattered, to me certainly and—I hoped— to that portion of my generation that I had come to think of as Those Who Went.

I began this project believing it was at least possible that Ollie, Bud, and John were being railroaded. If so, I considered it my mission to derail that train because I suspected a factor, or factors, far more insidious than what they supposedly had done were at play.

This was a leap of faith, to the extent that I had any faith left after Vietnam. Naval Academy guys are hardly angels. Some are dicks, some are bullies, some are assholes, more than a few of them are jerks. But most Academy guys are none of those things, and whatever their other failings, they don't lie, cheat, steal, or do the kind of shit Ollie, Bud, and John were accused of doing—at least not in the context in which their actions were being portrayed.

I had no doubt that they had made mistakes, but none so serious as to warrant the avalanche of criticism that descended on them as details of the Iran-Contra affair became known.

It took me a few years and much study, but I finally sorted out how

I felt about Iran-Contra. On the big stuff, I pretty much gave Ollie, Bud, and John a pass. They were not zealots, they were not madmen, they certainly were not criminals. And they acted with the best of intentions.

There's little question that they screwed up a number of times in trying to do what they thought of as the right thing. And I'm fully aware that the road to Hell is paved with good intentions. At a certain point, though, I realized that the comparison to Watergate—a standard criticism during this period—didn't hold up when looked at in light of the motives of the two sets of participants.

McFarlane, North, and Poindexter wanted to bring about the release of six Americans held hostage by terrorists in Lebanon. That was the Iran half of the Iran-Contra equation.

For McFarlane, with his broader global perspective, there was an added dimension. Iran was a nation of enduring strategic importance to the United States. The two nations had been alienated from each other since 1979, when the American embassy in Tehran was seized by Iranian students. To Bud, the prospect that the secret negotiations on arms and hostages could lead to a diplomatic opening was irresistible.

North, McFarlane, and Poindexter also were facilitating the shipment of supplies and other forms of support to anti-Communist guerrillas in Nicaragua, the Contras, men the president called "the moral equivalent of our Founding Fathers."

Richard Nixon's Watergate crew—the ratfuckers, as some were known in college and later—had a less lofty motive. They were out to sabotage a presidential election.

As much as I grew to like him, I came to believe that the brilliant John Poindexter might have headed off the anguish and turmoil of Iran-Contra had his dislike of the press not blinded him to the obvious—made him half-stupid, as my grandmother would have said.

He had a model to guide him in handling the public unveiling of the activities that made up Iran-Contra: In 1971 Henry Kissinger secretly traveled to Communist China, the nation that the United States believed so strongly had predatory designs on the whole of Southeast

Asia that we went to war. We were, in fact, still fighting in Vietnam when Kissinger was cozying up to the Chinese.

But when Kissinger's trip became public knowledge he was not condemned, let alone investigated or indicted. Instead, he was hailed as a hero and genius. Why? Because the administration had a press strategy all prepared. Thus it was able to tell the story in its own way, in its own time.

No doubt the press-savvy Kissinger also had a public relations plan for dealing with any fallout if the trip was revealed prematurely.

Not so Poindexter. He had so little regard for reporters that I doubt the idea of putting together a press strategy ever crossed his mind.

Unless, of course, you consider *deny, deny, deny* a strategy.

President Reagan, their boss and a man they greatly admired, had brought all five men central to this book as well as their fellow soldiers back into the mainstream of American society. Few spoke of "baby killers" anymore and men and women in the Armed Forces once again wore their uniforms with pride. So even those soldiers who could not imagine ever buying into Ronald Reagan's politics understood that they owed a hell of a lot to the old actor and the song he played for them.

— — — —

As I neared the finish line on *Nightingale*, I was back at the *Sun*, working as a reporter during the day and writing the last part of the book at night and on weekends.

This was pretty much as I had planned it, except that I went back to work in the fall of 1993 rather than 1990, the original target date for my return to daily journalism. I'm tempted to say, what's a few years among friends? But I'll resist doing so since I'd like to keep those friends. Too many of them were left shorthanded or otherwise inconvenienced by my extended absence and string of what proved to be bogus return dates.

Now, as I moved toward finishing the book, I realized that I had become the victim of an obsession I hadn't been able to shake but hadn't been able to do anything about, either.

It began on Sunday, October 23, 1983, a day the Marine Corps will never be able to delete from its memory bank and three years before anyone had heard of the Iran-Contra affair.

I awoke that morning as the first reports were coming in about a terrorist truck bombing of the Marine barracks at Beirut's international airport.

I dressed hurriedly. The action may have been thousands of miles away, but I knew in times of crisis all roads lead to the White House.

As the number of dead mounted, I felt the unspeakable horror one feels when tragedy befalls people you know or with whom you feel a deep kinship. To a Marine, every other Marine is a brother.

The final casualty count was 241 American servicemen dead—220 Marines, 18 sailors, and 3 Army soldiers. A similar bombing of the nearby French barracks killed 58 paratroopers. For the Marines it was the largest single-day death toll since they landed on the beach at Iwo Jima nearly forty years earlier.

Almost from the moment I heard about the bombing I was asking myself hard questions. What kind of security existed at the barracks? Were there sufficient sentries? What kinds of weapons were they carrying?

My most pressing question was—and these were close to the exact words that flew through my brain: What the fuck were that many Marines doing in a single building in what was essentially a combat zone? Practically the first thing they teach Marines at the Basic School in Quantico is don't bunch up! That's to limit the damage that can be done by one machine gun, one grenade, one mortar shell—or one truck bomb.

The tragedy of the Beirut bombing has haunted me ever since that dreadful Sunday, but most poignantly in the years immediately following the event. And that emotion bled into my work on *Nightingale*.

One day I was interviewing a retired Marine officer who knew

Webb and North well. We were in his office just south of Quantico. Beirut came up in our conversation. He had been in the area shortly before the bombing, and he said the security at the barracks seemed light to him, maybe too light.

On his wall was a framed photograph of the building minutes after the blast, much of it rubble, rubble under which we both knew lay scores of dead or dying Marines.

He walked slowly over to the picture. Unbidden, I followed. Together, in silence, we stared at it. Then we put our arms around each other and, for a few moments, quietly sobbed.

I kept pushing myself to find out more about the bombing, consuming large chunks of time as I did so. Only vaguely did I think about how the tale of the bombing would fit into *Nightingale*. I just knew it would if I ever nailed down precisely what happened.

Then, one day, I knew it wouldn't. At the length and the depth it deserved, it would blot out everything else. It didn't belong in *Nightingale* except in summary form as one of many incidents that shed light on the main characters.

I knew I had to let it go. The barracks bombing deserved a book of its own; *Nightingale* wasn't it. Maybe someday I'd write it. Or someone else would write it. No way could a tragedy of that magnitude be forgotten.

— — — —

I was now entering the homestretch. Turning away from Beirut was painful but necessary. Pretty much everything else fell into place once I had done that. It also cleared the way for Jim Webb and John McCain to come back into focus. Both had prospered because of Ronald Reagan.

Reagan championed Vietnam veterans so vigorously that it soon became unheard of to spit on them or routinely disrespect them. Before long, people were thanking them for their service.

In this new world, Webb became known for more than his books. Reagan made him an Assistant Secretary of Defense, then Secretary of the Navy. In 2006 he was elected as a Democrat to the United States Senate.

Within that new world, the tale of McCain's heroism during his five and a half years as a prisoner of war took root. In 1982 he was elected to Congress from Arizona's First Congressional District.

Four years later, he was elected to the Senate, becoming one of its most respected voices on foreign policy issues and military matters.

That's where he was in 1994 when I finally finished work on *Nightingale.*

In 2008 he was the Republican candidate for president. He lost to Barack Obama, and it hurt, but he had come a long way from the days when he looked like a "bug-eyed" refugee from a Nazi concentration camp.

My editor at Simon & Schuster, Dominick Anfuso, was enthusiastic about the manuscript when I finally shipped it off to him. He edited with a light touch.

We had one disagreement that had the potential to get out of hand, but that was headed off by Dominick's boss, Carolyn Reidy, the president and publisher of Simon & Schuster.

Dominick told me that *Nightingale* needed a subtitle, a line that gives a potential buyer some idea of what the book is about if the title itself is not self-explanatory.

My guess is they were looking for something like *The Nightingale's Song: The Inside Story of . . .* something.

I hated the idea of a subtitle and told Dominick so. He offered up a few candidates, but I vetoed all of them. I wanted the title unadorned. To my mind, a title should intrigue the reader, pique the reader's interest, and stoke the desire to know more, not reveal what's in the book before he or she even opens it.

Dominick said no one would even open the book if we didn't tell them a little of what was in it.

Stalemate.

Finally, after a day or two, Dominick called to say that Carolyn had an idea that might break the impasse. She suggested putting a passage from the book on the cover, along with small illustrations at top and bottom that would hint at what was inside. We settled on the Capitol Building and a midshipman's cap.

Here's the passage:

> They are secret sharers, men whose experiences at Annapolis and during the Vietnam War and its aftermath illuminate a generation, or a portion of a generation—those who went. Each in his own way stands as a flesh-and-blood repository of that generation's anguish and sense of betrayal. Whatever they later became—hero, hotdog, hustler, or zealot—they were for a time among the best and the brightest this nation had to offer. And in their formative years—at Annapolis and during the Vietnam era—they shared a seemingly unassailable certainty. They believed in America.

Forty-two

HIGHS AND LOWS

The *Nightingale's Song* received strong positive reviews. It was selected a *New York Times* Notable Book of the Year in 1995, and by *Time* magazine as one of that year's five best nonfiction books.

Amid a healthy sprinkling of kudos, two meant the most to me. The first came from the journalist I've tried to model myself after and who a few years back honored me with his friendship, the incomparable David Halberstam.

> The Nightingale's Song . . . *has an almost hypnotic authority all its own and belongs on the same shelf as the classics of the Vietnam War,* Neil Sheehan's A Bright Shining Lie, *Philip Caputo's* A Rumor of War, *and Harold G. Moore and Joseph Galloway's* We Were Soldiers Once . . . and Young.

Then there was this from an old friend.

"God, in His wisdom, makes only a handful of great reporters," Richard Ben Cramer wrote. "The Nightingale's Song *will show the whole country: Robert Timberg is one of those."*

I was able to report and write *Nightingale* because the *Sun*, a kinder, gentler *Sun* than I ever could have imagined, granted me a one-year leave of absence that I managed to string out for five years before returning to work.

My final position at the *Sun* was deputy chief of the Washington bureau, under Paul West. This was an editing job, which meant, in the loopy theology of reporters, that I had crossed over to the dark side.

I always thought editing was easy until I had to do it, and it took a while before I got the hang of it. It helped immensely that I was working with Paul, Fred Monyak—our capable, steady news editor—and a talented staff of correspondents.

In 2004 Simon & Schuster published another book of mine, *State of Grace: A Memoir of Twilight Time*, about the Lynvets, the extraordinary sandlot football team that I played with for two years between my graduation from high school and my entrance into the Naval Academy.

In it I chronicled the lives of young men coming of age in the late Fifties, as the shadow of Vietnam gathered over the nation. Reviewing the book for *Sports Illustrated*, Charles Hirshberg described it as "a beautiful, intimate, nearly cliché-free memoir that would have pleased both Lombardi and Camus." *SI* named it one of the best sports books of 2004.

In 2005, out of the blue, I was offered a job as editor-in-chief of *Proceedings*, a publication dating back to 1873 and the flagship magazine of the U.S. Naval Institute. I wasn't looking to leave the *Sun*, but this seemed like a new adventure, and I was ready for one.

Within a matter of weeks I came to love the job. I had a great staff and my efforts received highly positive feedback.

The job rejuvenated me professionally. Suddenly I was overflowing with ideas and innovative ways to implement them. We did a number of special issues—Women in the Military, Military Medicine, Modern Day Piracy.

Sadly, a job that began with such promise ended horribly. In November 2008 I was fired. I tried to stop the firing of a valued colleague and we were both sacked. I was sixty-eight at the time, so if I hadn't had the good sense to roll over a land mine when I was twenty-six—

thus qualifying for a Marine Corps pension—you'd probably see me bagging groceries at the local supermarket.

I'm not aware of any serious protest to my firing from the Naval Institute's editorial board, all active-duty or retired members of the armed forces. I had worked productively with the board for my entire tenure and enjoyed warm relations with all of them, or so I thought. What did this silence from honorable men and women, all of whom had splendid military careers, tell me? I guess there's no avoiding the conclusion that I was wrong and they were right.

— — — —

Time to tidy up.

My mother and my father have both passed on. Throughout the ordeal of my recuperation they played above the rim. I knew they were worried about me, but they never got weepy and always expressed confidence that I would put my life back together.

My mother was very conscious of physical appearance, her own and that of my sisters and me. In high school I injured my nose playing football. It wasn't serious, but it required minor surgery. The result was a nose with a slight ski slope appearance instead of the straight one I had before.

Before I was wounded, my mother would tell friends that I had a beautiful nose "until he started playing football." After I was wounded, she'd say the same thing, as if my slightly reshaped proboscis was the only facial feature that had seen better days.

My father was also circumspect about my disfigurement. He rarely if ever mentioned it to me. My sisters Pat and Rosemarie said he almost never spoke to them of my injuries, either. Instead, he would frequently tell them how proud he was of my refusal to surrender to misfortune. But Pat, reluctantly and only when I demanded she fill me in more fully on my dad's response to my wounds, remembered that from time to time he would lament, "He used to be such a good-looking boy."

Pat Furgurson, who hired me into the *Sun*'s Washington bureau, proved to be one of the nicest men I've ever known, both as a boss and as a friend. In addition to his work as a newsman, he is the highly re-garded author of four books on the Civil War, which share space on his shelf with his earlier biographies of William Westmoreland and Jesse Helms, the powerful right-wing senator.

In addition to his Pulitzer Prize for reporting from the Middle East, Richard Ben Cramer wrote *What It Takes*, a 1,049-page tome on the 1988 race for the White House that may have no peer as a descrip-tion and explication of presidential politics in the twentieth century. This is the book he came to see me about all those years ago when he called Flip Brophy to tell her she had a new client.

Richard also wrote a best-selling and much acclaimed biography of New York Yankee slugger Joe DiMaggio.

Most of Richard's friends, me included, were shocked when he died of lung cancer in 2013. He received an amazing send-off, reflect-ing his enormous circle of friends and the high regard in which they held him.

Martin O'Malley, the governor of Maryland, eulogized him at a memorial service at Washington College on the state's Eastern Shore, where Richard and his wife, Joan, had lived for years.

A couple of weeks later, Vice President Joe Biden did the same at Columbia University, where Richard had earned a graduate degree in journalism. Biden was one of the candidates featured in *What It Takes* and he and Richard had been friends ever since.

The journalism world lost another giant and I lost a friend and role model in 2007 when David Halberstam was killed in a car crash south of San Francisco. He was on his way to an interview for his latest book, on the 1958 NFL championship game between the New York Giants and the Baltimore Colts, perhaps the greatest football game ever played.

Jack Germond, a truly great political reporter who graced the pages of the *Baltimore Sun* and *Evening Sun* for years, passed away in 2013. He was my friend and one of the sweetest men I ever knew. Jack is celebrated for his many dynamite stories, but in journalism circles he is also well remembered for his kindness to young reporters and for the

Germond Rule. The latter decrees that when reporters go to dinner together the check is split equally, whether your meal was a three-pound lobster, as Jack's often was, or a bowl of soup.

The Yoons, who fed me so well in Cambridge, had to cut their Nieman experience short and return to Bangkok two months early: problems with the paper that apparently only Suthichai, as the owner, could correct.

Today Suthichai in the best-known journalist in Thailand, an author, a television personality, and the owner of a television station. During a visit to Washington several years ago he took me to dinner and confessed, as if admitting to a sin that could only be whispered among friends, that he had become wealthy beyond his wildest dreams. It did not fit with his sense of himself.

Try as I might I couldn't console him.

Tragically, the immensely talented Mike Kelly, my partner in crime in reporting on the Iran-Contra scandal for the *Sun*, was killed in the early days of the Iraq War, which he was covering for the *Atlantic*. Everyone who knew him misses him terribly and mourns his loss to this day.

Tragedy also struck my Stanford friends Carol and Lory Marlantes, whom I had always thought of as the Golden Couple.

They moved to New York after Stanford. Lory rose in the business world as if he had been fired from a platinum slingshot. By the turn of the century, he was president and chief executive of the Rockefeller Group International. Two years later, at age fifty-nine, he died after a long battle with cancer.

During the intervening years, Carol again worked for Bill Moyers, this time while raising two daughters and earning a law degree at NYU in her spare time. The daughters now carry on the Marlantes tradition of over-the-top excellence. Both are magna cum laude graduates of Harvard. Catherine is with a major New York City law firm. Liz is an ABC News Washington correspondent. And Carol is still beautiful.

Tragedy also struck John and Linda Poindexter. Their astronaut son, fifty-one-year-old Captain Alan Poindexter, who commanded the next-to-last mission of the Space Shuttle *Discovery*, was killed in a Jet Ski accident off the coast of Florida in July 2012.

With chilly operating rooms no longer part of our relationship, Lynn Ketchum and I are now friends. He practiced plastic and reconstructive surgery in Kansas City until early 2014, when he retired after fifty years in medicine. These days he also writes, and not just for medical journals. In 2011 he published a book, *From Dawn to Dust*, which laid out in biting prose his reservations about organized religion, dating back to his youth.

As part of my research for this book, I flew to Kansas City to interview Lynn about the work he had done on me years before. We discussed serious things but we also had some fun. We went to the Negro Leagues Baseball Museum, which is fabulous. And I finally made it to Arthur Bryant's BBQ, which more than lived up to its reputation.

David Denby, the graduate assistant in my film class at Stanford—the one who told me "show, don't tell," guidance for which I will be forever grateful—has a dream job. He is a film critic for the *New Yorker*.

Jim Webb was elected to the U.S. Senate from Virginia as a Democrat in 2006. He stepped down after one productive six-year term. He was mentioned as a possible running mate for Barack Obama in 2008 until he announced that he was not interested in the vice presidency.

I haven't seen, read, or heard an explanation for his decision to relinquish his Senate seat. The way I see it, some politicians are made to be executives and others to be legislators; Webb is one of the former.

I addressed him as Mr. Secretary throughout my work on *Nightingale*. We are now Jim and Bob.

THE FOOTLOCKER

*There is no greater sorrow than to recall in misery
the time when we were happy.*

—DANTE, THE INFERNO

I knew it would come to this. Sooner or later I'd have to open the goddamn thing. It's one of the reasons I didn't want to write this book in the first place.

It had followed me around for more than four decades, a sturdy, seemingly unthreatening black footlocker stenciled in yellow with my name, rank, and USMC service number. I took it to Vietnam. Somehow it stayed with me despite my abrupt and ungainly departure from that land of horseflies as big as the Ritz.

The date chalked on it, 12/20/66, suggests it was shipped back to the States in anticipation of my presumably safe return a month or so later.

I have lived in ten different places since I was evacuated from Yokohama to the naval hospital in San Diego. The footlocker has been with me in all those locations.

And here it was before me again, in the basement of my house on the outskirts of Annapolis, where I moved after my second marriage to the always classy and impossibly wise Kelley Andrews fell apart for reasons that had far more to do with my failings than anything else.

Indeed, there was much to be regretted, but especially on this day as I prepared to stare directly into my own distressing, often appalling past.

I have over the years felt a temptation to look inside the footlocker, circling it, fingering the clasps, nudging it with my toe. Invariably I left it alone. I knew what was in it—letters from Janie, probably some other items I didn't need to see. So it sat for decades, like a boil waiting to be lanced.

Until now.

The lock and hinges are rusty, but curiously there is only a slight creaking when I snap the clasps and lift the lid. A surprise, there is no odor. I expected one. A tray about four inches deep sits atop the main compartment.

The first thing to catch my eye and the last thing I expect to find is my wallet, the one I was carrying when the land mine put me down for a nine count. But there it is, a black Lord Buxton Convertible, no evidence of aging, its shape and condition almost indistinguishable from the one in my pocket today.

There are a few letters scattered on the tray. One is to Janie from Tom Dempsey, the Bravo Company commander, explaining that a Marine patrol had stumbled on the wallet a couple of weeks after I had been wounded.

Like the wallet itself, everything in it seems to be in the shape it was in when it went missing. Much of its contents are predictable: ID card, Geneva Conventions Identification Card, government driver's license (this for the Ontos, the First Antitank Battalion's weapon of choice).

There is some currency, three military payment certificates (two for five cents each, the third for ten cents), and a fifty-piastre note, which could have been worth a nickel or a million bucks but since it was issued by the Republic of Vietnam, which as we all know ceased to exist in 1975, it's the Southeast Asian equivalent of Confederate money.

Other items in the wallet strike long-forgotten chords. There are three calling cards—snowy white, regulation dimensions, font and point size as prescribed by *The Marine Officer's Guide*—all perfectly acceptable were I still a lieutenant of Marines. There is a baggage claim check with "Danang" scrawled on it. No idea what it's for and I suspect it's a little late to submit a claim.

The most inexplicable item is a photo, the only one in the wallet. It shows Bob Welsh, a Naval Academy friend, and me as Third Class midshipmen, in uniform, sitting at a table with drinks in front of us, apparently at some officers club.

I can't imagine why I was carrying the photo around with me. Bob and I were friends, but not close friends except for the few weeks we traveled around Europe together in the summer of 1963 after our First Class Cruise in the Med, and I haven't seen or spoken to him since well before graduation.

Resting innocently in the tray are four telegrams in their trademark buff Western Union envelopes. All date to 1967 and are addressed to Janie from General Wallace M. Greene, the Marine commandant, reporting my wounding and subsequent travels from Station Hospital Da Nang to Kishine Barracks to the San Diego Naval Hospital.

There is my Short Timer's Calendar, with all but fourteen boxes filled in. I must have neglected to black out Day 14 the night before when I learned I was taking another lieutenant's turn as pay officer and would not be going to Okinawa on a second R&R to bargain-hunt for pearls and a stereo.

Also in the tray is a hand-lettered document, constructed from a flattened-out Manila folder, titled "R&R Scoreboard," delivered to me in the dark of night by one or more of Bravo Company's intrepid enlisted Marines on the eve of my first—and as it turned out only— R&R, a five-day jaunt to Hawaii to meet Janie. Days are listed down the left side, as in "1st Day," "2nd Day," and so on down to the "5th Day." Across the top are categories of achievements or lack thereof, e.g., "Swings," which according to a key at the bottom of the document meant "passes made," "Hits," meaning "girls made," etc. Below is a complex scoring system that I was spared having to work through since, as I told my disappointed troops, I would be spending R&R with my wife.

Missing from the footlocker is another creative gift, also pegged to my R&R in Hawaii, a handmade swing, fashioned from a piece of wood and some rope.

There was no need for the troops to explain this item as it was the central prop in one of the more inventive Hong Kong fuck books that I assume just about everyone in the company headquarters group, officer and enlisted, had read.

Many of these books were sophomoric, but the one with the swing was as good as it gets. As recounted by the anonymous but imaginative author, the swing hangs trapezelike above a swimming pool. The man sits on the swing, the woman sits on the man, and the motion of the swing does all the work. As they reach their big moment both the man and the woman go flying backward off the swing and into the pool.

I regret the absence of the swing in the footlocker and idly wonder what had become of it. Did one of my Marines filch it, perhaps to surprise his girlfriend when he got back home?

I do find my thank-you note to the troops. In it I lament their failure to include an instructional booklet for the swing and tell them, "If I return with my leg or anything else in a splint, it will be because I muddled along without proper directions."

Another R&R-related item is nestled in my wallet, an appointment card for Janie to see Dr. Philip Conboy, an eye specialist on Royal Hawaiian Drive in Honolulu. I know immediately what this is about. No sooner had Janie arrived in Honolulu than she came down with a sore throat, laryngitis, and conjunctivitis, the last a malady in which a discharge from the eyes forms a crust that causes the lids to stick together.

Conjunctivitis is very contagious. Janie was so distressed that she broke out crying at dinner in one of Honolulu's most elegant restaurants, causing the burly Asian maître d' to rush to our table and nail me with a dark, threatening glare. Even so, we had a wonderful time in Hawaii.

The war, though, had gone on without me. When I returned to Da Nang, I learned that Lieutenant Colonel Bob Harris, a tough-as-nails

Marine who succeeded MuMu as battalion commander, had been killed in my absence.

— — — —

There is one more item on the tray worth mentioning, a picture of my late mother from a dinner program of the Ziegfeld Club, an organization of long-ago beauties dedicated to keeping alive the name of the fabled impresario Florenz Ziegfeld.

My mother's picture is from an oil painting by Neysa McMein, a well-known artist of the day, showing her at thirteen or fourteen—heart-shaped face, intelligent green eyes, flowing blond locks—that graced the cover of *McCall's Magazine* in the 1920s. She wasn't the easiest of mothers, but her life was no picnic, either, and it breaks my heart to look at her barely into her teens, unaware of the troubles that would soon shatter her sweet innocence.

— — — —

I lift the tray and set it aside. The compartment below is pretty much as I envisioned it, boxes of letters marked "Janie," "Family," or "Friends." Like nearly everything else in the footlocker, the boxes show no sign of age. The letters themselves don't, either. They could have been written yesterday.

But they weren't. They are from another place and time, filled with love and hope and anticipation of a lifetime of happiness. There are scores of them, mostly from Janie, but also from my parents, my sisters, other relatives, and friends. The effect is akin to hearing a favorite song from long ago, one that transports you back to days when your whole life lay ahead of you and everything seemed possible.

Rereading the letters today makes me wonder if in any way I had justified all that love during the intervening four decades since they were written. I think the honest answer is no. In betraying Janie, I displayed a shallowness that I will forever regret. We were both casualties of war. She saved me. I nearly destroyed her—hardly a fair trade-off.

I expected to release a monster when I finally opened the footlocker. I was wrong. I set loose something far worse, far more vicious, my own Marley's ghost, a past that refuses to grow whiskers and stay in the grave. Hello, it says, you were twenty-six the last time you checked the contents of this footlocker. Remember what you looked like then? Too bad you zigged when you should have zagged.

— — — —

My life since that long-ago day has been anything but perfect, or all that happy, but it has been a life that in an odd, idiosyncratic way has met my need to fulfill my destiny and not let a land mine win.

I fathered and helped raise four wonderful children, two of whom, Scott and Craig, followed me into journalism and now have delightful, if mischievous, children of their own. Amanda is a top executive with an educational nonprofit in London, where she lives with her husband, Matt Horine. Sam, who inherited Kelley's nuanced palate and unflappable demeanor, is managing director of a new wine-importing firm— Meridian Prime—based in New York.

I am less proud of my record as a husband, though Kelley has, as always, landed on her feet, living with her two rambunctious dogs in Wilmington, Delaware, not far from her sister, Dee. Janie, meanwhile, has retired from a long career as a teacher and school counselor and now resides a short drive from me, with her kind, devoted second husband, Lee Spence, a lawyer whose true calling appears to be preparing succulent smoked meats with his Big Green Egg. We are all friends now, and they quietly ensure that I don't spend a holiday alone.

I recently read a story by Alice Munro about a man who suffers a grievous personal loss. She describes him "as pretending that he had as ordinary and good a reason as anybody else to put one foot in front of the other."

That pretty much describes me these days. One foot in front of the other, the Wichita Lineman, a little older but still on the line.

SEMPER FI

Author's Note

In *Blue-Eyed Boy* I'm unsparing of able-bodied men of my generation who employed various forms of subterfuge to avoid military service during the Vietnam War. At the same time I want to salute my colleagues in the press corps who either served in uniform during the Vietnam era or covered the conflict as war correspondents.

I also recognize that many men had legitimate medical and emotional reasons that kept them from serving.

My closest friend among White House reporters was Walter Robinson of the *Boston Globe*. Oddly enough Robby and I had been friends for months before I learned that he had been an Army intelligence officer in Vietnam.

Robby mentioned his Vietnam service only in passing. I don't recall any of my other colleagues in the Washington press corps volunteering to me that they had been in Vietnam, either. But we all pretty much knew who we were even if we didn't talk much about those days.

David Rogers, like Robby a *Boston Globe* reporter, was widely considered one of the two or three best congressional correspondents in Washington. He had been an Army medic. Mike Shanahan of *Newhouse Newspapers* was awarded a Bronze Star and a Combat Infantryman's Badge as an Army lieutenant. Another Army man, the late Jack Smith, earned a Bronze Star and Purple Heart in the bloody battle of the Ia Drang Valley before becoming a correspondent for ABC News. Editorial cartoonist Eric Smith was an Army interrogator. Don Graham, a child of affluence who later became president and publisher of the *Washington Post*, enlisted in the Army and served with the First Cavalry Division in Vietnam.

Then there were the Marines: the late Woody West, executive editor of the *Washington Times*; Henry Allen, a Pulitzer Prize–winning feature writer at the *Washington Post*; Carlton Sherwood, a Pulitzer Prize winner at the Gannett News Service.

Many newsmen whose careers did not involve Washington reporting served in Vietnam. Three friends come immediately to mind— *Evening Sun* colleagues Bill Hawkins and Wayne Hardin, along with Joe Nawrozki of both the Baltimore *News-American* and the *Evening Sun*.

Of course there were scores of journalists, including a number of women, who went to Vietnam and elsewhere in Indochina to cover the wars there. For them I have only admiration. Several saw more combat than me. Some were wounded; a few were killed.

Originally I planned to list all the Vietnam War correspondents in this Author's Note. When I almost missed Homer Bigart, who covered World War Two and the Korean War in addition to Vietnam, I realized I was on a fool's errand; I was sure to forget someone no matter how many colleagues I conferred with.

Instead I symbolically honor them all by saluting my *Baltimore Sun* breathren for their fine work as war correspondents. This distinguished group includes John Carroll, Peter Kumpa, Arnold "Skip" Isaacs, Ben Orrick, Michael Parks, Bob Erlandson, Matt Seiden, Ralph Kennan, John Woodruff, and my old boss, fellow Marine, and close friend Pat Furgurson.

All the above were correspondents for the *Sun*. The *Evening Sun* sent Carl Schoettler, a gifted reporter whose elegant writing style was the envy of the newsroom.

Should I fail to mention her, no one could protect me from the *Sun*'s crusty onetime maritime reporter—the indomitable Helen Delich

Bentley, who later became head of the Federal Maritime Commission and a five-term Baltimore congresswoman. She truly covered the waterfront, even the Saigon waterfront, which she chronicled in a series on its wartime shipping problems. A crowd of five hundred joined her in celebrating her ninetieth birthday in November 2013.

I'm sure I've left some fine journalists off one or more of these lists, which I regret and apologize for.

Robert Timberg
Annapolis, Maryland
April 2014

Acknowledgments

A lot of people contributed to this book. Two were indispensable.

My son Craig bullied me into writing it. If not for him, it would not exist. He also edited, nurtured, and encouraged me all the way through. He was with me at the beginning when I might well have thrown up my hands and said the hell with it and at the end when we finally put it to bed.

The other essential person was my first wife, Jane Timberg. Many of the experiences I describe in this book occurred more than five decades ago and it was only through Janie's help that I was able to re-create them in some detail. She allowed me to interview her more than ten times. We talked about the terrible days, of which there were many, and the small victories, of which there were never enough, but enough to keep us moving forward for a long time. I know the interviews were painful for her, and I thank her for her willingness to endure them—with a smile no less.

Kelley Andrews, my second wife—and sadly my second ex-wife—was another blessing. A fine editor, she read and critiqued much of the book, often finding holes in the narrative and identifying sections that were dull, overwritten, or more than the reader needed to know.

Several friends, colleagues, and other family members read and commented on drafts of the book or specific chapters, among them

Ernest B. (Pat) Furgurson, Art Pine, Jim Webb, Don Graham, Nick Gardiner, Susan Seliger, Mark Bowden, Ginger Doyel, Teri Witcraft, Lynn Ketchum, Charity Winters, Hal Burdett, my daughter Amanda Timberg, and Craig's brothers, Scott and Sam Timberg, the latter who demonstrated that having a killer slap shot and the ability to hit a base-ball a mile doesn't foreclose editing skills.

Throughout my life my sisters Pat Timberg and Rosemarie Shaw have encouraged me in all my various undertakings. They did so again this time as well as sharing with me often painful memories.

Lynn Ketchum, surgeon extraordinaire, first reconstructed my face, then—decades later—took time to explain to me how he did it. Lynn and his wife, Carly, were wonderful hosts when I visited them in Kansas City.

Ellen Tuttle at the Nieman Foundation at Harvard researched information and material that I could not have done without. I picture her working her way through dusty stacks to unearth documents I needed but doubted could be found. Ellen found them.

Two institutions were crucial to my work. The Nimitz Library at the U.S. Naval Academy is a true resource for writers, and not just those looking into military matters. I found my first newspaper, the *Annapolis Evening Capital*, on microfilm there and spent hours in the reading room refreshing my memory of the times I was writing about and stories of mine dating back decades. My thanks to the Library's directors—first Richard Werking, later James Rettig—and members of the Library's knowledgeable staff for their gracious assistance.

The *Baltimore Sun* Library was equally valuable. My thanks to Sam Davis, Assistant Managing Editor/News, for arranging access for me. The *Sun*'s superb librarian Paul McCardell is a treasure and a much-tapped resource for reporters, editors, and the occasional vaga-bond book writer like me.

Flip Brophy, my one and only agent, once again made good things happen for me. Most important was bringing the distinguished Scott Moyers into the game as my editor.

Scott, publisher of Penguin Press, provided extraordinary professional guidance throughout the writing process. Most notably, he recognized a major flaw in my first draft and showed me how to rectify it. He also displayed great patience and forbearance as I blew through deadline after deadline.

A special thanks to Akif Saifi, Scott's assistant, whose diligence and attention to detail kept the process moving forward.

The computer savvy of my old *Evening Sun* colleague Mike Himowitz pulled me through this book-writing adventure as he has previous ones. He has never failed to respond on the many occasions when I frantically fired off an SOS to him. Several times he drove the thirty-five miles from his home in Baltimore to mine in Annapolis on missions of mercy. Mike is a know-it-all who actually knows it all when it comes to computers, and a lot of other things, too. He is also one of the kindest and most generous men I know.

The encouragement of friends was priceless. In addition to those mentioned above, thanks to Jim Caiella, Mac Greeley, Mark Hyman, Jessica Berry, Fred Peck, Joanne Schilling, Cassie Furgurson, Paul West, Dave Danelo, Eric Smith, Joyce Smithey, Tom Wall, Bob and Barbara Bushman, Cy Avara, Frank DeFilippo, Debbie and Dave Winters, Alice Germond, and the late, great Jack Germond.

And I can't forget my brother-in-law, Pat's husband, the inimitable George (aka Krazy George) Henderson, always fun as well as supportive even when he was fighting, and beating, cancer. Krazy, I should note, is a professional cheerleader who invented The Wave. You could look it up.

Index

Acheson, Dean, 194
Agnew, Spiro T., 176
Alvarez, Everett, 219
Amtrac (Amphibian Tractor), 8
Andrews, Kelley, 183–85, 227, 232, 236–37,
   271, 290
   The Nightingale's Song and, 208–9
   RT's marriage to, 187, 285
   RT's meeting of, 183
   work of, 207, 208
Anfuso, Dominick, 277–78
Arendt, Hannah, 197
Aristocort, 61
Atlantic, 283
Auden, W. H., 261

Baez, Joan, 92
Balboa (San Diego Naval Hospital), 57–58, 62,
   66, 67, 69–72, 97, 138, 159, 272, 287
Baltimore Evening Sun, 107, 133, 173, 180, 282
   RT at, 148–49, 152–56, 157–59, 170–72,
   173–74, 180, 184–87, 195–96
   RT's leaving of, 186–87
   Washington bureau of, 184–86
Baltimore News-American, 133
Baltimore Sun, 107, 108, 133, 148, 150, 170,
   172, 173, 175, 178, 180, 184, 185, 200, 282
   RT at, 186–87, 188, 192–93, 207, 254, 274,
   279–80, 281, 283
   RT's leaving of, 280
Barnes, Fred, 184
basketball court, 18–21
Baskir, Lawrence M., 213
Beatles, 36, 169
Beirut, bombing of Marine barracks in, 275–76
Benigo, Ron, 14, 16, 31–32, 117, 259
Berkeley, Calif., 82–83

Bernstein, Carl, 263
Best and the Brightest, The (Halberstam),
   146, 177
Biden, Joe, 282
Blair, Dennis, 251
Blue's Bastards (Herrod), 255
Bolden, Charles, 251
books:
   crime novels, thrillers, and spy stories, 267
   Marines and, 21–22, 288
Boston Globe, 246
Boston Herald, 182
Bradlee, Ben, 182
Bradlee, Ben, Jr., 246–47
Bravo Company, 7, 22
Breitrose, Henry, 97
Broder, David, 182
Brophy, Flip, 200–201, 211, 268–69, 282
Burdett, Hal, 111
Bush, George H. W., 194

Calley, William, 129–30, 214
Calvert, James, 118–21
Campbell, Glen, 84
Camp Pendleton, 62
Carnes, Lynore White, 249
Carpenter, Carlton, 60
Carroll, John, 178, 180
Carter, Jimmy, 170, 214
Chabrol, Claude, 94
CHAMPUS, 141
Chance and Circumstance (Baskir and
   Strauss), 213
Charity Hospital, 60
Child, Julia, 181, 182
China, 273–74
Chomsky, Noam, 183

Churchill, Winston, 204
civil rights movement, 32–33
Clark Air Base, 44–46, 48
Clarke, Torie, 205
Cohen, William, 228
Conant, James, 174
Conboy, Philip, 288
Contras, 190–91, 244, 255–56, 273
    see also Iran-Contra
Copulos, Milt, 215
Corddry, Charles, 184
counterculture, 196–97
Country Such as This, A (Webb), 258, 264
Coward, Asbury, III, 124
Coward, Sandy, 124–26, 270
Cramer, Joan, 282
Cramer, Richard Ben, 148–51, 152–55,
    157, 162, 180, 192, 199–200, 208,
    227, 248
    death of, 282
    The Nightingale's Song and, 199–201, 297
    What It Takes, 282
Craner, Bob, 220
Cronkite, Walter, 91
cummings, e. e., ix

Da Nang, 5–11, 18, 288
    field hospital at, 25–27, 42–44, 48, 49,
    53, 166, 287
Dante Alighieri, 285
Dawber, Betty, 37
Day, Bud, 220, 222, 223
*Death and Life of Great American Cities,
    The* (Jacobs), 77
Deaver, Mike, 241–42
DeFilippo, Frank, 200
Democratic National Convention,
    170–72, 176
Dempsey, Tom, 286
Denby, David, 97, 284
Denton, Jeremiah, 222, 223
Denver Post, 102, 106
Des Moines Register, 177, 179
Diggs, Sidney, 116
DiMaggio, Joe, 282
Discovery, 284
Donovan, Bob, 80
Dypski, Cornell, 150–51, 162
Dypski, Ray, 162

Edsall, Tom, 172
Eichmann, Adolf, 197–98
Esquire, 201–3, 204, 257, 258
Evans, Phil, 108, 109, 110–11, 129, 140
Evening Capital, 107–9
    RT at, 109, 110–15, 116–21, 122–23,
    127–30, 132–34, 136–37, 139,
    158, 159
    RT's leaving of, 140
Evening Sun, see Baltimore Evening Sun

Fagan, Fred, 259
Faith of My Fathers (McCain and Salter),
    220–21
Fearey, Diane, 36, 37
Feldon, Barbara, 209
Fields of Fire (Webb), 201–2, 210
First Antitank Battalion, 9–10, 15–23, 24,
    32, 35
Fitzgerald, F. Scott, 215
Fletcher, 47, 52–53
Ford, Glenn, 27
Forester, C. S., 228
Forman, Stanley, 182
Franklin, Jon, 180
From Dawn to Dust (Ketchum), 284
Furgurson, Ernest B. (Pat), 170–72, 176,
    184, 185, 186, 281–82

Galbraith, John Kenneth, 181
Gartner, Michael, 177, 179
Germond, Jack, 282–83
Get Smart, 209
Giralamo, Ronald, 40, 53, 54–55, 64
Godard, Jean-Luc, 94
Goodwin, Paul, 259
Graham, Billy, 119–21
Grease, 162–63
Greene, Wallace M., Jr., 38, 287
Gregory, Bill, 110–11, 133
*Guts and Glory: The Rise and Fall of Oliver
    North* (Bradlee), 246–47
Guys and Dolls, 135–36

Hagee, Michael, 251
Halberstam, David, 146, 177, 183–84, 279
    death of, 282
Halle, Louis, 194
Halsey, William "Bull," Jr., 222
Harris, Bob, 288–89
Harris, David, 92–93, 264
Haughey, Dave, 195
Hawkins, Bill, 185–86
Hayakawa, S. I., 83
Hayes, Tom, 256
Heggen, Thomas, 15–16
Heisler, Phil, 173
Helms, Jesse, 282
Hemingway, Ernest, 106, 204
Herrod, Randy, 255
Hill, Fred, 173–75, 180
Hirshberg, Charles, 280
Hirshey, David, 201–3
Hodges, William L. "Bip," 149–51, 162
Hoffman, Abbie, 83
Holly, Jack, 253
Holocaust, 197–98
Hopkins, Al, 111
Horine, Matt, 290
Horner, Matina, 183
Hosler, Karen, 180

hospitals, 142–43
  staph infections at, 145
Hubbell, John, 218–19
Humphrey, Hubert, 234
Humboldt Times, 96, 99

Imhoff, Ernie, 107–8
Inferno, The (Dante), 285
"In Memory of W. B. Yeats" (Auden), 261
Iran, 189–90, 273
Iran-Contra, 188–93, 194–98, 210, 212, 215,
  228, 272–73, 283
  in RT's book, *see Nightingale's Song, The*
  service academies and, 195, 196, 199,
    200, 203
  Vietnam War and, 203
  see also specific people
Iraq, 189
Iraq War, 283
Irving, John, 182
Iwo Jima, 275

Jacobs, Jane, 77
James, Billy, 176
Javits, Jacob, 183
Jay, Peter, 175
John, Elton, 169
Johnson, Lyndon, 33, 91, 95, 220
Johnston, Jay, 251
Jones, Dave (editor), 106, 107, 109
Jones, David (Stanford friend), 94
Jong, Erica, 213

Kansas City Star, 02, 106
Kansas City Times, 106
Kelly, Jerry, 175
Kelly, Michael, 192–93, 195–96, 215
  death of, 283
Kennan, George, 194
Ketchum, Cindy Jeansonne, 61
Ketchum, Lynn, 57–62, 166, 284
  From Dawn to Dust, 284
  marriage of, 61
  medical career of, 59–61, 75, 284
  Navy discharge of, 75
  Navy joined by, 62
  parasitic infection suffered by, 58–59
  RT discharged from hospital by, 75–76, 81
  RT's surgeries performed by, 57–58, 63–67,
    69, 73–75, 136, 140–47
  sports and, 59
Khomeini, Ayatollah Ruhollah, 190
King, Martin Luther, Jr., 32–33, 235
Kishine Barracks (Army General Hospital
  in Yokohama), 39–40, 46, 47–56, 64,
    166, 287
Kissinger, Henry, 194, 273–74
Klaaste, Aggrey, 182
Knight-Ridder, 227
Korean War, 8

Krulak, Chuck, 69, 256, 259
Krulak, Victor, 69
Kurosawa, Akira, 98

Laboon, Jake, 203
Laguna Beach, Calif., 6, 13, 33–35, 36,
  66, 70, 75, 82, 84, 138
Larsen, Jon, 175
Leary, Timothy, 13
Le Carré, John, 32, 267
Lehman, Tenney, 177, 180
Lerille, Red, 59
Levine, Dick, 139, 160
Lewis, Mike, 112, 115
Lindsay, Lovie G., 112–15
Lippmann House, 181, 182
Little League, 271
London, Jack, 228
Los Angeles Times, 80, 102, 106, 252
Loyola College, 165
Lucky Bag, The, 252
Lynch, Tom, 236–37

MacArthur, Douglas, 8, 204
Maccoby, Nathan, 88
Marine Corps Wife, The, 34–35
Marine Officer's Guide, The, 34, 286
Marlantes, Carol, 94–95, 283
Marlantes, Catherine, 283
Marlantes, Karl, 94
Marlantes, Liz, 283
Marlantes, Lory, 94, 283
Maryland General Assembly, 170, 176
Matterhorn (Marlantes), 94
McBain, Ed, 267
McCain, Jack, 220, 222, 224
McCain, Joe, 205
McCain, John, 3, 205–6, 217–24, 276–77
  confession forced from, 222, 223–24
  early release refused by, 219–22
  Faith of My Fathers, 220–21
  military heritage of, 222–23
  The Nightingale's Song and, 206, 208,
    210–11, 217–24, 276–77
  RT's interviews of, 217–19, 222–24
  RT's meeting of, 205
  Vietnam War service of, 3, 206, 210–11,
    218–24, 277
McCain, John "Slew," 222, 224
McCall's Magazine, 289
McFarlane, Jonny, 244
McFarlane, Robert "Bud," 188, 189, 191–93,
  194–98, 215, 228, 239–45, 254, 272–73
  childhood of, 241, 243
  in Geneva, 243
  The Nightingale's Song and, 203, 204, 206,
    208, 210, 239–45, 272–73
  Phillips and, 244
  suicide attempt of, 239
  Vietnam War service of, 242–45

McFarlane, William Doddridge, 241
McFarlane Associates, 239
McGarvey, Mac, 259–60
McKay, John, 259
McMein, Neysa, 289
McNamara, Robert, 91
McPhee, John, 183
Meese, Ed, 191, 192, 195
Mencken, H. L., 107
Men of Zeal (Cohen and Mitchell), 228
Meridian Prime, 290
Merrill, Philip, 111
Messer, Jim, 259
Miedusiewski, American Joe, 150–51
Mifune, Toshiro, 98
Miller, Arthur, 182
Milwaukee Journal, 174
Mineta, Norman, 183
Missouri, 222
Mister Roberts (Heggen), 15–16
MIT, 183
Mitchell, George, 228
Monyak, Fred, 280
Moore, Acel, 182
Moore, Don, 255–56
Moore, Walter ("MuMu"), 68–69, 289
Moyers, Bill, 95, 283
Moynihan, Daniel Patrick, 76
Mullen, Mike, 251
Munro, Alice, 290
My Lai Massacre, 129–30

Nation, 182
Naval Academy, *see* United States Naval
    Academy
Nelson, Jack, 80
Neustadt, Richard, 183
New Right, 185
New Yorker, 182–83, 284
New York Times, 99, 108, 177, 220, 279
Nicaraguan Contras, 190–91, 244, 255–56, 273
    see also Iran-Contra
Nieman, Agnes Wahl, 174
Nieman, Lucius, 174
Nieman Fellowship, 172, 173, 175, 181–83, 186
    RT's winning of, 173–80, 181
Nieman Foundation, 181
nightingales, 209
Nightingale's Song, The (Timberg), 199–201,
    204–6, 207–11, 212–16, 266–69, 270–78
    McCain and, 206, 208, 210–11, 217–24,
        276–77
    McFarlane and, 203, 204, 206, 208, 210,
        239–45, 272–73
    North and, 204, 208, 210, 246–53, 254–56,
        272–73
    passage from book on cover of, 278
    Poindexter and, 204, 206, 208, 210, 225–32,
        233–38, 246, 247, 272, 274
    reviews of, 279–80

Vietnam veterans and, 210, 212–16
Webb and, 204, 206, 208, 210, 257–65, 266,
    276–77, 284
Nixon, Richard, 234, 263, 273
North, Oliver, 188, 189, 191–93, 194–98, 201,
    213, 215, 228, 246–53, 254–56, 272–73
    car accident and knee injury of, 250–51, 253
    childhood of, 248–49
    at Naval Academy, 246, 249–53
    The Nightingale's Song and, 204, 208, 210,
        246–53, 254–56, 272–73
    Vietnam War service of, 253, 255–56, 259
    Webb and, 201–3, 205–6, 257

Obama, Barack, 217, 277, 284
Ochsner, Alton, 60–61
Ochsner Clinic, 60–61
Odon, Ind., 227–32
O'Malley, Martin, 282
Ontos, 9, 10, 15, 17, 286

Palin, Sarah, 217
Palo Alto, Calif., 82–84, 85
Palughi, Buddy, 155–56, 248
Patti, Lou, 155–56
Pease, Kendell, 251–52
Petrino, Rich, 252–53
Philadelphia Inquirer, 177, 178, 182, 200
Phillips, Jack, 244
Piper, Hal, 173–75, 180
PM, 96–97
Poindexter, Alan, 283–84
Poindexter, Dickie Ray, 229
Poindexter, Ellen, 229–30
Poindexter, John, 188, 189, 191–93, 194–98,
    215, 225–32, 233–38, 254, 272, 274, 283
    childhood of, 229, 230–31
    family of, 227–28
    intelligence of, 225
    The Nightingale's Song and, 204, 206, 208,
        210, 225–32, 233–38, 246, 247, 272, 274
Poindexter, Linda, 233–37, 283
Poindexter, Marlan, 228
P.O.W. (Hubbell), 218–19
Proceedings, 280–81
Pulitzer, Joseph, 107
Pulitzer Prize, 177, 180, 182, 186, 282
Puller, Lewis "Chesty," 4

Rafsanjani, Hashemi, 189
Reagan, Mike, 31
Reagan, Nancy, 215
Reagan, Ronald, 188–92, 195, 197, 204,
    213, 235, 238, 240–42, 248, 254,
    255, 274, 276–77
    The Nightingale's Song and, 209, 210
Record, 179
Reidy, Carolyn, 277–78
Reese, PeeWee, 185
Resistance, The, 92

Ripley, John, 259
Roberts, Gene, 177–80
Robinson, David, 61
Robinson, Jackie, 185
Rochester, Lenny, 138, 152
Roosevelt, Franklin D., 241
Rowe, Dale, 249
Rubin, Jerry, 83

Sadler, Barry, 36
Saint Louis Post-Dispatch, 106–7
Salter, Mark, 220
San Diego Naval Hospital (Balboa), 57–58, 62, 66, 67, 69–72, 97, 138, 159, 272, 287
San Francisco, Calif., 82, 85
San Francisco State College, 83
Santoni, George, 162
Schaefer, William Donald, 153–55, 156, 248
Scowcroft, Brent, 194
Seabees, 19–20
Secord, Richard, 196
Seven Days in May (Knebel and Bailey), 193
Simon & Schuster, 211, 212, 277, 280
Smith, Eric, 90–91
Snoops, Hilda Mae, 153
Southern Christian Leadership Conference, 235
Speakes, Larry, 189
Spence, Lee, 290
Sports Illustrated, 280
Stacy Tower (Walter), 21–22
Stanford, Leland, 85
Stanford University, 92
    arson at, 83
    RT at, 78, 82–89, 91, 93–95, 96–98
State of Grace: A Memoir of Twilight Time (Timberg), 280
Staubach, Roger, 236, 237
Stegner, Wallace, 78, 79
Sterling, J. Wallace, 83
Stewart, Ken, 96–97, 99
Stockdale, Jim, 222, 223
Strauss, William A., 213
Stucker, Jan, 178–79, 182
Stuyvesant High School, 137–38
Sullivan, Scott, 107
Sylvia Samurai, 98

Thanksgiving, 163–64
Thomson, James, 177–79
Thoreau, Henry David, 264
Timberg, Amanda (daughter), 162–63, 166, 168–70, 187, 208, 272, 290
Timberg, Craig (son), 134, 168–70, 187, 208, 272, 290
    birth of, 131–32
Timberg, Janie (first wife), 6, 12–13, 14, 29–41, 46, 57, 79, 117, 132, 135–39, 157–60, 185, 232, 251, 287, 288, 290
    Carol Marlantes and, 95
    conjunctivitis contracted by, 288

Craig's birth and, 131–32
    Ketchum and, 58, 63, 65
    move to Palo Alto, 82–84, 93
    nightmare of, 36
    personality of, 29, 31
    Pink Bathrobe Year of, 165–67
    pregnancies of, 75–76, 95, 123, 131
    on road trip, 100–101, 102–4, 108, 109
    RT's affair and, 160, 166, 289
    RT's correspondence with, 35–36, 37, 44–45, 48–49, 50, 77, 286, 289
    RT's journalism career and, 77, 79–80, 84, 87, 98, 109, 117, 122–23, 132–34, 152, 157–59
    RT's marriage to, 12, 32
    RT's meeting of, 12, 29–30
    RT's scars and, 56, 70, 72, 74, 167
    RT's separation from, 160, 161, 163, 165–67, 168–70
    RT's staph infection and, 145
    RT's surgeries and, 63, 65, 66, 74, 140–41
    RT's wounding and, 37–40, 43, 44–45, 48, 50–54, 56, 138, 287
    Scott's birth and, 88
    in *Sylvia Samurai,* 98
    as teacher, 33–34, 36, 38, 67, 70, 82, 84, 93, 95, 123, 138, 165, 290
Timberg, Kelley (second wife), *see* Andrews, Kelley
Timberg, Robert:
    affair of, 160, 161, 166, 289
    childhood of, 11–12
    discharged from hospital, 75–76, 81
    dragonfly story of, 78
    father of, 11–12, 39–40, 86, 281
    film made by, 98
    footlocker of, 285–90
    in high school, 12, 86, 137–38
    job applications and interviews of, 98–100, 102, 106–9
    journalism chosen as career of, 77–81
    as Little League coach, 271
    Marine career of, 4, 6–10, 12–14, 32, 34–35, 46, 80, 88, 89, 137
    Marine pay problem and, 67–69
    Marine retirement of, 73
    medals of, 73
    mother of, 11–12, 40, 41, 281, 289
    move to Palo Alto, 82–84
    Murray Avenue apartment of, 161, 168–69
    at Naval Academy, 3, 12, 14, 29–31, 118, 120, 124, 137, 250
    Nieman Fellowship won by, 173–80
    promotion of, 68, 69
    psychiatrists and, 72, 159–60
    road trip of, 100–101, 102–9
    scars of, 2, 3, 4, 56, 64, 69, 70, 71–72, 73 74, 76, 79, 84, 88–89, 95, 99, 114, 115, 117, 126–28, 136, 138, 146, 156, 167, 227, 231–32, 271–72

Timberg, Robert: (*cont.*)
  sisters of, 40–41, 98, 281
  in Stanford's journalism program, 78, 82–89, 91, 93–95, 96–98
  staph infection acquired by, 145–46
  surgical operations of, 4, 27, 44, 54–55, 57–58, 63–67, 69, 73–75, 136, 140–47
  treatment and convalescence after wounding, 42–46, 47–56
  Vietnam War service of, 1, 5–12, 14, 15–23, 35, 138
  wounded in Vietnam, 2, 3–4, 23, 24–28, 37–41, 43–46, 58, 61, 117, 126–28, 137, 138, 231, 281
Timberg, Sam (son), 187, 207–8, 227, 271, 290
Timberg, Scott (son), 117, 123, 132, 134, 168–70, 187, 208, 272, 290
  birth of, 88, 94, 131, 138–39
  on road trip, 101, 102, 103, 104, 108
  in *Sylvia Samurai*, 98
Time, 76–77, 279
Trainor, Mark, 252
Trewhitt, Henry, 184
Tribe, Laurence, 183
Truffaut, François, 94

United States Naval Academy, 3, 14, 128, 202, 206, 233, 236, 272
  The Board at, 251–52
  Iran-Contra and, 195, 196
  North at, 246, 249–53
  religious services at, 118–21
  RT at, 3, 12, 14, 29–31, 118, 120, 124, 137, 250
  RT's reporting on, 118–21, 128
University of Kansas Medical Center, 61, 140–47
Updike, John, 182
urbanology, 76–77

Vance, Steve, 271
Van Loan, Jack, 221
Vietnam Day Committee (VDC), 83
Vietnam veterans, 90, 197, 213–14
  Iran-Contra and, 196–98
  The Nightingale's Song and, 210, 212–16
  Webb and, 258, 261, 262
Vietnam War, 32, 33, 34, 89, 90–93, 191, 271, 274
  avoidance of duty in, 213–14
  casualty count from, 213
  end of, 265
  Iran-Contra and, 203
  Karl Marlantes' service in, 94
  McCain's service in, 3, 206, 210–11, 218–24, 277
  McFarlane's service in, 242–45

My Lai Massacre in, 129–30
North's service in, 253, 255–56, 259
opposition to, 32, 33, 36, 82–83, 91–93, 94, 196, 234, 263–64
RT's service in, 1, 5–12, 14, 15–23, 35, 138
RT's wounding in, 2, 3–4, 23, 24–28, 37–41, 43–46, 58, 61, 117, 126–28, 137, 138, 231
Webb's service in, 259–63
Vocational Rehabilitation program, 76
Voting Rights Act, 33

Wagner, Bobby, 250
Wales, Heathcote, 262–63
Walt, Lewis, 27
Walter Lippmann House, 181, 182
Walter, Robert H. K., 21–22
Walters, Barbara, 203
Warren, Ellen, 227, 228
Washington Post, 107, 108, 133, 182, 201, 238
Washington Star, 133
Washington Week in Review, 184
Watergate, 263, 273
Webb, James, 201–4, 214, 239, 251, 257–65, 266, 276–77, 284
  A Country Such as This, 258, 264
  Fields of Fire, 201–2, 210
  McGarvey and, 260
  The Nightingale's Song and, 204, 206, 208, 210, 257–65, 266, 276–77, 284
  North and, 201–3, 205–6, 257
  Vietnam War protesters and, 263–64
  Vietnam War service of, 259–63
  Wales and, 262–63
  Wilson and, 260–61
Webb, Jimmy, 84
Welsh, Bob, 287
West, Paul, 192, 280
West Point, 118, 196
Westmoreland, William, 282
What It Takes (Cramer), 282
"Wichita Lineman," 84–85, 231, 290
Williams, George, 271
Wilshin, Dave, 31–32
Wilson, Dale, 260–61
Wilson, Norman, 171, 172
Woodward, Bob, 263
Work and Family Conference, 208–9
World War II, 222
Wunsch, Mike, 259

Yokohama, Army General Hospital in (Kishine Barracks), 39–40, 46, 47–56, 64, 166, 287
Yoon, Nantawan, 182, 283
Yoon, Suthichai, 182, 283

Ziegfeld, Florenz, 289